T0210115

LILLIAN "SISSY CRONE" FRAZER

UNCOVERING
ROOTS

THE RHEAS OF AUGUSTA, BATH AND
ROCKBRIDGE COUNTIES, VIRGINIA

authorHOUSE®

AuthorHouse™
1663 Liberty Drive
Bloomington, IN 47403
www.authorhouse.com
Phone: 1 (800) 839-8640

Published by AuthorHouse 01/23/2020

ISBN: 978-1-7283-4439-3 (sc)
ISBN: 978-1-7283-4438-6 (e)

Library of Congress Control Number: 2020901163

Print information available on the last page.

*Any people depicted in stock imagery provided by Getty Images are models,
and such images are being used for illustrative purposes only.
Certain stock imagery © Getty Images.*

This book is printed on acid-free paper.

*Because of the dynamic nature of the Internet, any web addresses or links contained in
this book may have changed since publication and may no longer be valid. The views
expressed in this work are solely those of the author and do not necessarily reflect the
views of the publisher, and the publisher hereby disclaims any responsibility for them.*

INTRODUCTION

The purpose of this writing is to discover the Rhea ancestors in what was Augusta County, Virginia during colonial days and trace the heritage to the family of Palmer Rhea, Sr. In doing so, other Rhea family members, such as uncles, aunts and cousins were discovered, and those have been listed briefly.

This writing originated with the research of my own family. While doing so, Palmer Rhea, Jr. graciously, without complaint, accompanied me to courthouses, cemeteries, and numerous other locations as well as endured the countless hours I buried myself in our home office organizing and writing. Realizing the richness of family, I toyed with the thought briefly before stating, "When we finish researching my family, we will search for your roots?" Little did I know the Rhea family involved voluminous family members nor was I prepared for the tremendous effort required to document Palmer's heritage and the magnitude of names I would encounter.

I do not credit myself as an historian nor a researcher by profession or education; however, during these last ten years of various family searches, I have become an amateur one. Joy of local history and the quest to solve puzzles and the patience and thirst for accuracy and verification serve as great tools.

Discovering family satisfies a curiosity. One learns of the challenges faced by ancestors, struggles endured, accomplishments shared, the good and sometimes the bad. For some, ancestors played a part in who we become, whether encouraging or pushing us to become someone different. We are partially a result of accumulations of our experiences and surroundings, and many ancestors play vital parts in these experiences. In this writing, it is evident the Rhea family actively participated in important roles in the development of our colonial life. Not only has the generations of the Rhea family been affected but so have numerous other families trailing them.

On frequent occasions over the past few years, Palmer, Jr. and I jumped into his truck and ventured to courthouses, church cemeteries, and farmland once owned by Rhea family members. Many of these were small communities, places of age and endurance, separated by mountains. Their beginnings were in the mountains with their majestic trees and soft peaks, and at times shrouded in clouds and fog. The distance was centuries in time. We attempted to capture a spirit of a time gone by as we snapped pictures, stood solemnly over gravesites with faded headstones, viewed farmland, and visited countryside churches in which families had worshipped. Some of this land appeared to be in an isolated world, beautiful and intriguing, with little change in the past two-hundred-plus years while other land reflected modernization and growth.

We ordered books on the Rhea family, searched ancestor sites and old newspapers, checked court records, viewed cemetery records and county historical society records, talked to family members, documenting family and history and at times sat sprawled over the green grass and thick spread of trees as we thought of ghostly ancestors. It took years of research, documenting, and writing to absorb the wealth of Rhea family names. All was pulled together for this writing. When completed, I felt a connection to the family, strangely feeling as if I had known them. I had developed an admiration and respect for them and their lives.

Certainly, there are descendants not included and some information was passed from family and unable to be documented. Throughout this writing, great care and enormous effort were given for accuracy and a curious nature was displayed for knowledge on the family. As much as I desired to hear faded echoes of voices guiding and leading me to family history, instead, much of our findings I contribute to researchers who have already documented many of the Rhea family, enabling me to collect numerous information on the various family members. Additionally, we spent years of personally researching everything we could locate and talking with many who amiably were willing to share information with us.

The Rheas of what was Augusta County, Virginia, which later became Bath County and other counties, included in this writing descended from Robert, Archibald, and William Rhea who first settled in Augusta County in the mid-1700s and those of Margaret Rhea, thought to be a cousin to the brothers. An elder Archibald Rhea lived in Augusta County during these years and circumstances lead to him most likely being the father of the three Rhea brothers and an uncle to Margaret, although this has not been proven. Several researchers, sources, circumstances, and records indicate these three Rhea brothers and Margaret are thought to be grandchildren of Matthew Campbell Rhea of Scotland and Ireland. And, so, my story begins with him.

MATTHEW CAMPBELL RHEA
OF SCOTLAND AND IRELAND

FIRST GENERATION

According to family legend, Matthew Campbell of Scotland took an oath to the Protestant faith, and in 1685, assisted his cousin Archibald Campbell, the 9th Earl of Argyll, in raising an army for the cause of the Duke of Monmouth (James Scott, the illegitimate son of England's King Charles II and Lucy Walter). During the Monmouth Rebellion in the uprising, Archibald Campbell, the Earl of Argyll, was captured and beheaded. Matthew Campbell was supposedly captured and sentenced to life in prison but escaped and fled to Ireland and changed his name to Reah (one of the variations of the name and later changed to Rhea).

That the three Rhea brothers of Augusta County are grandchildren of Matthew Campbell "The Rebel" Rhea of Scotland, who is thought to be the son of Walter Campbell, has not been proven nor disproven to my knowledge nor has this Matthew Campbell Rhea yet been proven to be the son of Walter Campbell. These stories are passed from researchers of the Rhea families and descendants of Matthew Campbell Rhea, including the historical writings of memoirs of U.S. Congressman John Angus Rhea (1753 – 1832) of Sullivan County, Tennessee. When no documented records are available, it is information shared by descendants that is often relied upon.

U.S. Congressman John Rhea's father was Rev. Joseph Rhea and his grandfather was Matthew Campbell Rhea II, son of Matthew Campbell Rhea of Scotland and Ireland. Rhea County in Tennessee and Rheatown, an unincorporated community in Greene County, Tennessee, were named in U.S. Congressman John Rhea's honor. John Rhea's memoirs, historians, and other sources located believed due to circumstances and obtainable records this Matthew Campbell Rhea of Scotland is the founder and the root of the Rheas in Virginia, Tennessee, Pennsylvania and other areas unless additional information becomes available to state otherwise. You may come to your own conclusion.

One such source quoted by Richard C. Fremon as written by Edward F. Foley in his book, *The Descendants of Matthew "The Rebel" Rhea of Scotland and Ireland* is as follows:

> *About Matthew, there was a Campbell of that name of about the right vintage who lived in Kintyre, second son of Walter Campbell, Captain of Skipness and Provost of Campbelltown. In 1930, a lady whose name now escapes me (later identified as Mary Latham Norton) wrote an article in the Clan Campbell (USA) journal to the effect that she had visited Scotland and ascertained that the Matthew of Skipness was indeed the one who found himself on the losing side of the Monmouth Rebellion, escaped to Ireland, changed his name, had some adventures, and married Janet Baxter. I am inclined to believe this story and that Matthew and Janet had sons William, Archibald, and Matthew Jr. in that order. I don't know what happened to William. He may have come to America. I believe pro tem that Matthew Sr's son Archibald was the immigrant who arrived in Augusta Co., Va with his three sons about 1743.[1]*

If this lineage is true, the ancestor and grandfather of the Rhea brothers of Augusta County was previously of the Campbell Clan of Scotland. Matthew Campbell Rhea's life was historically eventful in both Scotland and Ireland, and his legacy lives on in America where many of his descendants played major roles in our frontier development. By these accounts, Matthew Campbell Rhea of Scotland and Ireland would be a direct ancestor to Palmer Rhea, Sr.

---

[1] Foley, Edward F., *The Descendants of Matthew "The Rebel" Rhea of Scotland and Ireland*, Heritage Books, 2008, p. 1.

MATTHEW CAMPBELL RHEA: (A.1.) (Born abt. 1665 in Scotland, died in County Donegal, Ireland, death date unknown)

Occupation: merchant, shipmaster
Married 1687: Janet (Jenot) Baxter
Children of Matthew Campbell Rhea and Janet Baxter:

> **WILLIAM RHEA (See B.2.)** (A.1. Matthew). **See chapter on William Rhea**.

> **ARCHIBALD RHEA (See B.3)** (A.1. Matthew). **See chapter on Archibald Rhea. Thought to be the direct ancestor to Palmer Rhea, Sr.**

> **MATTHEW CAMPBELL RHEA II (See B.4.)** (A.1. Matthew). **See chapter on Matthew Campbell Rhea II.**

Matthew Campbell Rhea married Janet Baxter, daughter of Sir Francis Kinlock, in 1687 in Londonderry at the Derry Cathedral at Templemore Parish.[2] It has been documented Matthew and Janet Baxter had three sons. Matthew Campbell Rhea II has been researched thoroughly and documented as a son. The connections with William and Archibald have had less documented research. Association and similarity of names have led those researching the Rhea family to conclude these were very probable the other two sons of Matthew and Janet. As others have, I have included them in my writing as though it has been proven unless additional information becomes available.

The family name of Rhea, pronounced as "Ray" has been spelled and recorded as Rhea, Reah, Reagh, Reaugh, Reaoh, Rea and Reach. By 1800, the preferred and more consistent spelling of the name became Rhea. The Rhea family are many. This makes identification more difficult. Family names have been repeated throughout generations, but the name "Matthew" has been used infrequently, which I thought unusual.

---

[2] Foley, Edward F., *The Descendants of Matthew "The Rebel" Rhea of Scotland and Ireland*, Heritage Books, 2008, p. 2.

Various Rhea family members have been mentioned in historical society writings. These Scotch-Irish immigrants were true and brave frontier men and women who played major roles in the development of our colonial America, stretching from Virginia, Tennessee, Kentucky and multiple other states. Their paths crossed with men such as George Washington, Daniel Boone, John Sevier, and so many others. The family has fought for their home and country from those early days of 1750s and perhaps earlier. It is families such as these who endured the hardships of frontier development and had the courage to face fear with duty and honor that allows us to be here today.

History books, movies, and documentaries tell of famous and well-known individuals who have carved a niche in our great country. Some stories have been embellished for enjoyment and some passed down so many times the true story may have been lost. Along with those well-known characters are others whose names may have not been remembered or alluded our memories, but these men were side by side, fighting, exploring and building with those well-known characters. The Rhea ancestors were among those.

In the hours spent in researching, accumulating and documenting the Rhea family, we painstakingly strived for accuracy. Thanks to many historians and historical societies much was located on Rhea families in general. Every effort was made to ascertain that the information in this writing is accurate, although with multiple family names there is the possibility mistakes may have been made.

During our quest for answers, we stood overlooking a valley with quiet green hillsides knowing a Rhea family once lived there. We viewed the same thick spread of trees, and aged and strong rugged mountain tops. I was absorbed and dazzled by the mountain views. We walked the peaceful rural church cemeteries where family members once worshipped inside the church walls and now laid to rest nearby. It's as if we could almost hear the faded echoes of voices. This awarded me with a feeling of a personal connection to those family members.

Questions scrambled through my mind. I fantasized what life was like for these families. One church cemetery had nearly half of the burial sites of the Rhea family, knowing many other burial sites were once their friends or neighbors. Looking beyond the cemetery were lush trees and green countryside where the sun streamed through the trees. Soon autumn would touch those trees with brilliant colors of reds and golds. Generations of the Rhea family had lived here in this county. They had celebrated, mourned, anguished, thrived, loved, and died in this surrounding countryside.

It is believed these three Rheas recorded as living in Augusta County: Robert, Archibald, and William were brothers. It is unknown when they first arrived in America, and their arrival in Virginia is unknown. They first appeared documented in the counties together, bought land in Borden Grant near each other in what was Augusta County, and together joined the Augusta County Militia in September 1758 during the French and Indian War.[3] Whether they were brothers or closely related, the historians followed in this writing, historical society writings and county records indicated these three men were brothers, so for this writing they are referred to as brothers.

[3] The Bath *County History Society, The Bicentennial History of Bath County, Virginia 1701-1991,* Heritage House Publishing, pp.325-331.

AUGUSTA COUNTY IN 1750S

Much of the territory mentioned in these early days was in Augusta County at the time, but in current day those territories are parts of Botetourt, Rockbridge and Bath Counties and even parts of other states. To better understand the territory in which the family lived, it is important to understand the land that made Augusta County.

I read several books and writings on Augusta County of the 1750s for a better understanding of the land and life in those days. Among the writings were the *Annals of Augusta County, Virginia, with Reminiscences Illustrative of the Vicissitudes of Its Pioneer Settlers* by Waddell, Joseph Addison.

The boundaries of Augusta are not the same today as in the days of the mid-1700s. Orange County, Virginia was created in 1734, covering areas which extended from the Mississippi River and Great Lakes. By 1738, Augusta County was created from parts of Orange County and was a huge territory. It is stated:

> *The County of Augusta originally extended from the Blue Ridge to the Mississippi river, east and west, and from the great lakes on the north to the northern boundary of the present State of Tennessee on the south.*[4]

Although the county was huge in land, it was sparsely populated. It was not until 1745 that the government of the county became organized. Prior to 1745, court records and proceedings were held in

---

[4] Waddell, Joseph Addison, *Annals of Augusta County, Virginia, with Reminiscences Illustrative of the Vicissitudes of Its Pioneer Settlers*, 1823-1914, p. iii.

Orange County. In years to follow, parts of Augusta would be carved out to form other counties and states. By the year 1790, the borders of Augusta County were finalized. The county is currently located on the western edge of Virginia in the Shenandoah Valley.

Botetourt, Rockbridge, Bath, and Fincastle (1772-1776) Counties did not exist as counties during the year of 1738. Botetourt County was founded in 1770 from parts of Augusta County. It is currently in the Roanoke Region of Virginia and bordered by the Blue Ridge and Appalachian Mountains. During the formation days of this county, its territory was a vast area and later was carved out to make the state of Kentucky.

Fincastle County was created in 1772 from portions of Botetourt County.[5] In 1776, Fincastle County was abolished and divided into Montgomery County, Washington County, and Kentucky County (which later became the Commonwealth of Kentucky). The town of Fincastle remains today.

Rockbridge County was formed in 1777 from parts of Augusta and Botetourt Counties. Current day Lexington and Buena Vista are in Rockbridge County.

Bath County was created in 1790 from Augusta, Botetourt, and Greenbrier (now part of West Virginia) Counties. It is currently located on the central western border of Virginia, on the state line of West Virginia.

The first records located on the Rheas in Augusta County are during the days the Scotch-Irish were escaping the British government. The Scotch-Irish (Scots-Irish) trail back to Ulster, Ireland. Ulster today is a province in the north of Ireland consisting of nine counties (six are in Northern Ireland, which is a self-governing territory within the United Kingdom and three are in the Republic of Ireland). The primary language spoken is English.[6]

During the 1600s, colonists from Scotland and ones from north of

---

[5] Pendleton, William C., *History of Tazewell County and Southwest Virginia: 1748-1920*, 1920, pp. 255-57. W. C. Hill Printing Company.

[6] Douglas, Deane C., *Ulster, Wikipedia*, "*The Ulster Countryside*", 1983, Century Books, ISBN 0-903152-17-7.

England were placed into Ulster, Ireland by a planned process of James I of England and James VI of Scotland. The colonists were placed on land confiscated from members of the Gaelic nobility of Ireland, whose land was taken as they fled the area for their safety. The Scotch people who emigrated to Ulster, Ireland maintained their customs and religious faith, and they prospered.

In Ulster during this time, it was common to refer to Presbyterians as "Scotch," Roman Catholics as "Irish," and English church members as "Protestants." The Scotch-Irish settlement in Ulster for the most part were peoples of the Lowland Scotch Presbyterians.[7]

Ulster in the 1600s and into early 1700s flourished, and this began upsetting rivals in England. The rivals obtained legislation to damage industries in Ulster, putting many out of work. The British confiscated their lands as well as industrial persecution and religious persecution. Marriages performed by their clergy were considered invalid. They were not allowed to hold a high office and excluded from the militia. The list went on and by 1719, the people of Ulster began to flock to America to escape the persecutions and for a new life.

These families heard of the religious liberty promised to newcomers in Pennsylvania, so in large numbers they emigrated and landed in Pennsylvania and received land grants in the western mountain region of Pennsylvania. Many were farmers and tradesmen. These newcomers served as buffers between the colony and the Indian frontier. Once in the Alleghany region, families spread and moved on toward the southwest along mountain country, and by 1730s moved through the Shenandoah Valley and into the Carolinas. And, so, it was for the Rhea family.

The Valley of Virginia was unknown to the white man for more than a hundred years after the landing at Jamestown. No one during this time ventured to overcome the high and endless mountains and what they considered as "the race of brutal and cruel savages." After return of the Knights of the Golden Horseshoe Expedition, who traveled across

---

[7] Ford, Henry James, *Library Ireland*, "*The Scotch-Irish in America*," 1915 and Fiske, John, "*Old Virginia and Her Neighbors*", 1897.

the Blue Ridge Mountains exploring the land, word was brought back of the rich fields and streams. This section of the country abounded with wild animals. Buffalo roamed the hills and valleys as well as bear, wolf, deer, fox and other wild animals.

Shenandoah in Indian language, according to ancient legend, is thought to be translated "Daughter of the Stars."[8] The Legend is as follows:

> *After the Great Spirit had made the world, the morning stars came together on the shores of a quiet silver lake bordered with blue mountains, the most beautiful place they could see.*
>
> *Hovering above the quiet waters and lighting the mountain tops with their robes of fire, the stars sang their songs of joy and pledged to gather here every thousand years.*
>
> *One time, when the stars were singing, there came a mighty crashing!! A great rock in the mountain wall torn asunder, and through the deep opening the lake waters began to pour out and rush to the sea.*
>
> *As time passed, the stars looked over the earth for another place to meet. They finally agreed upon a lovely valley through which a winding river ran.*
>
> *Suddenly, the stars realized that this valley had been the bed of their beautiful lake, and the blue mountains around it were the same ones upon which they had cast their robes of light in ages past.*
>
> *The stars were so joyous they placed the brightest jewels from their crowns in the river where they still lie and sparkle. And ever since that day, the river and its valley have been called... Shenandoah, Daughter of the Stars.*

The Shenandoah Valley was considered the frontier during this period. It rendered an atmosphere of excitement and fear and hope for a new life. The dress in those days are often those seen in Daniel Boone movies and frontier shows as this is the same time period, and Daniel Boone and his men explored and hunted in the area during their

---

[8] Peyton, Lewis, *History of Augusta County, Virginia*, Samuel M. Yost & Son, MDCCCLXXXII.

travels. Biographies of Daniel Boone state Daniel Boone came from Pennsylvania on an excursion to Augusta County, along with his cousin Henry Miller, in 1748-1749. His cousin, Henry Miller, would later return to the county and build the first iron furnace on Mosey Creek.[9]

Men wore hunting shirts, which were loose frocks or tunic style with loose sleeves and the shirts were fastened around the waist with a belt. Along his side in leathern cases were a knife and tomahawk. The pants were of the same material. The men often wore moccasins. The women dressed plainly. Women's duties were to take care of the household and their children. The men would build the homes and hunt for food. Fur from the animals could be sold. The men became familiar with every mountain and peak and stream. Mountains stir curiosity to climb and explore and to see what is beyond the ring of mountains. Some men became guides. These pioneers had a great impact on Augusta County.

The Valley, a timeless and mystical place, was a natural migration route to follow to avoid crossing the rugged mountains. There were no roads; immigrants arriving in the area traveled on foot or horseback following buffalo and Indian trails. They carried their worldly goods by hand or packed on horses and mules. To cross water, often they crossed on a fallen tree that made a bridge, and at times they had to swim the rivers and streams. If they had not already been accustomed to hardships and frontier life, they certainly would have to become so quickly to endure this difficult life. These men and women had to be self-reliant, high-spirited, determined, and courageous.

Homes were crude, built of wood and chimneys of stone or dried brick. Furniture was built from available timbers in the forest and beds were stuffed with geese feathers when possible. Men, women, and children all helped. Many of the immigrants brought along pewter plates, wooden bowls and some even brought glass, silver, and the Bible. These items were usually brought in by horseback or mule or even carried. Basic needs of the families in these frontiers were mostly necessities, not fashion and luxuries. Each home had gardens for both

---

[9] *Waddell, Joseph Addison, Annals of Augusta County, Virginia, with Reminiscences Illustrative of the Vicissitudes of Its Pioneer Settlers,* 1823-1914, p.40.

vegetables and flowers. Water was their primary drink. But these frontiers also had their wine and beer. The settlements were set near springs of clear drinking water.

Around the settlement of cabins, a stockade would be built to serve as protection from the Indians. Inside the stockade was a common square of land. At each corner of the stockade, blockhouses were built without the use of any nails at an angle two-stories high, allowing rifles to be discharged at the enemy. When an alarm was called out of enemies approaching, the women and children ran to the compounds inside the stockade. The first two public buildings erected would be the church, which was also the meeting house and the schoolhouse. The Presbyterian clergymen were the school instructors.[10]

Young couples married early in life, and families were large, and the population increased rapidly. When a newcomer arrived or a young couple married, all united to build a dwelling. When land needed to be cleared, all united to assist. Many died early in life from lack of medical treatment and medicine.

Young boys as early as ten or twelve years old were taught to shoot and were supplied a firearm to help protect the family, as well as to hunt. They were taught to race and wrestle. They were also taught to throw a tomahawk and acquired skills of those of Indian tribes. Young girls were taught to weave and quilt and cook. Music and dancing were important parts of learning. Family and community gatherings and cookouts were entertainment. Cockfights and horse races also prevailed and were popular among some men.

As night crept in and shadows slipped all around into darkness, it brought the howl of wolves. The county had so many wolves a law was established for payment to those who killed the wolves. Among the laws of Virginia, were the wolf levies as follows:

Be it therefore enacted, by the Lieutenant-Governor, Council, and Burgesses, of this present General Assembly, and it is hereby enacted: by

---

[10] Peyton, Lewis, *History of Augusta County, Virginia,* Samuel M. Yost & Son, MDCCCLXXXII, No., 41-42.

the authority of the same, That the justices of the said county shall levy, for all certificates to be produced to them since first day of November, 1744, unto the first day of May, 1746, six shillings, for every old Wolf, and two shillings and six pence, for every young Wolf; and after the said first day of May, 1746, there shall be a reward of ten shillings, for every old Wolf, and five shillings, for every young Wolf killed in the said county; to be levied in current money upon the tithable persons within the said county, for all certificates obtained and produced, as aforesaid, annually, at the court held for laying the county levy, and to be paid to the persons respectively entitled thereto, within six months after such levy laid, for and during the remainder of the term of four years, aforesaid: And if the justices of the said county shall refuse or neglect to levy such reward, every justice of the peace, so refusing or neglecting, shall respectively forfeit and pay the sum of five pounds;. . . [11]

Augusta County received its name in honor of Princess Augusta, mother of George II of England. The settlers were organized into colonial militia under British Crown. Male landowners were required to enlist to protect the settlers and records for tax purposes. Court proceedings during these days were much different than today. A few examples are as follows:

Feb. 19, 1751 – Catharine Cole being presented for having a bastard child, and refusing to pay her fine or give security for the same, according to law, it is ordered that she receive on her bare back, at the public whipping-post, twenty lashes, well laid on, in lieu of said fine, and that the lashing be done immediately.

May 28, 1751 – James Frame was presented for a breach of the Sabbath, in unnecessarily traveling ten miles.

May 21, 1756 – On motion of Thomas Lewis, Gent., setting forth that his negro, Hampton, frequently absconds from his service, and that he

---

[11] *Laws of Virginia, The Statutes at Large: Being a Collection of all the laws of Virginia, from the First Session of the Legislature*, in the Year 1619 pp. 373-374.

has several times attempted to ravish Ann West and other white women, and praying, to prevent the like mischief, he may be dismembered; it is ordered that the said Lewis employ such skillful person, as he may think proper, to castrate the said slave. [12]

---

[12] Peyton, Lewis, *History of Augusta County, Virginia*, Samuel M. Yost & Son, MDCCCLXXXII, No. 57.

WILLIAM RHEA

SECOND GENERATION

SON OF MATTHEW CAMPBELL RHEA
OF SCOTLAND AND IRELAND

WILLIAM RHEA (B.2.) (A.1. Matthew) William was born about 1687 in Ireland and died about 1777 in Augusta County, Virginia. He married Elizabeth (last name unknown) and had two children. According to U.S. Congressman Rhea's memoirs, William came to America, settling in Chester County, Pennsylvania. He died in Augusta County, Virginia. (Noted in Highlander Vol. 1, 1930 article by Mary Latham Norton.) (Descendant information also noted in Edward F. Foley's *Matthew "The Rebel" Rhea*.) Little information was found on this William Rhea. William Rhea, by these accounts, would not be a direct ancestor to Palmer Rhea, Sr. but would be a distant great uncle.

Parents: Matthew Campbell Rhea and Janet Baxter
Married: Elizabeth (last name unknown)

Known children of William Rhea (A.1. Matthew) **and Elizabeth:**

MARY RHEA BROWN (B.2. William, A.1. Matthew). Born about 1710. Mary married John Brown of Wilmington, Delaware. Congressman John Rhea in his memoirs referred to John Brown's property as "a grand possession."

ELIZABETH RHEA MCCORKLE (B.2. William, A.1. Matthew). Born about 1720. Elizabeth married James McCorkle, "a pastor of high standing in the Presbyterian Church" as stated by Congressman John Rhea. In 1775, James McCorkle was a member of the Fincastle County Committee of Safety.[13] William Preston, a prominent colonial Virginia figure whose final home was the historical Smithfield Plantation was Chairman of this committee. Fincastle County was formed in 1772 and prior to then was part of Botetourt County. Botetourt County was formed in 1770 and prior to then was part of Augusta County.

An excerpt of *William Preston and the Revolutionary Settlement* by Richard Osborn regarding The Fincastle County Committee of Safety (Fincastle County, Virginia existed 1772-1776) of which Elizabeth's husband, James McCorkle, was a member is as follows:

Preston clearly placed his allegiance with the revolutionary movement when he joined with other freeholders from Fincastle County on January 20, 1775 to organize their local county committee in response to requests by the Continental Congress that such committees be established. Within a few short weeks these committees, later known as Committees of Safety, took over the role of government on the county and state level as English officials fled from America. Recognizing his key leadership status, the freeholders elected Preston along with thirteen of his co-military officers from the recent conflict against the Shawnees and the Reverend Charles Cummings as their Fifteen member committee.[14] Fincastle, thus,

---

[13] Armstrong, Zella and French, Janie Preston Collup, *Notable Southern Families, Volume 2.*

[14] Osborn, Richard, *William Preston and the Revolutionary Settlement*, Cummings was a Presbyterian clergyman. Proceedings of the Fincastle County Committee, 20 January 1775, Richard Barksdale Harwell, ed. The Committees of Safety of Westmoreland and Fincastle. Proceedings of the County Committees, 1774-1776 (Richmond: Virginia State Library, 1956), 61, hereafter referred to as Fincastle Committee Proceedings. The originals can be found in Original Records, Montgomery County, VSL. The other officers elected to the committee included Colonel William Christian as chairman, Captain Stephen Trigg, Major Arthur Campbell, Major

became the first western county to elect such a committee, placing itself squarely on the side of the growing patriotic movement.

. . . And he (William Preston) also echoed the anti-English theme so natural to the Scotch-Irish:

Many of them are Descended from those brave men who so nobly defended their Religion & Liberty in Ireland in a late inglorious & Despotick Reign, & were so instrumental in Supporting the Revolution in that Kingdom. Those Transactions almost every Descendant from the Protestant Irish is well acquainted with either by History or Tradition. Therefore they cannot bear the Thought of degenerating from their Worthy Forefathers, whose Memory, & ought to be held very dear to them."[15]

Among James and Elizabeth Rhea McCorkle's known children were:

James McCorkle, (Elizabeth, B.2. William, A.1. Matthew).

William McCorkle, (Elizabeth, B.2. William, A.1. Matthew). William lived in Pennsylvania and was the editor of a newspaper.

William Inglis, Captain James McGavock, Captain William Campbell, and Captain Evan Shelby. For further biographical details, see Mary Kegley, "Who the 15 Signers Were," Journal of the Roanoke Valley Historical Society: 9:33-7.

[15] Osborn, Richard, "William Preston and the Revolutionary Settlement", Journal of Backcountry Studies, 1990 University of Maryland dissertation, directed by Professor Emory Evans, republished in JBS., pp.1-2.

ARCHIBALD RHEA OF AUGUSTA COUNTY

SECOND GENERATION

SON OF MATTHEW CAMPBELL RHEA OF SCOTLAND AND IRELAND

ARCHIBALD RHEA (B.3.) (A.1. Matthew), (Born abt. 1688) **THOUGHT TO BE THE DIRECT ANCESTOR TO PALMER RHEA, SR.** Archibald was born about 1688 in Ireland. Records indicate he died in Walker's Creek, Augusta County, Virginia (conflicting dates of his death). He married Ann (last name unknown). Archibald came to America, first to Pennsylvania and later settled in Augusta County, Virginia. He is thought to be the father of the three Rhea brothers of Augusta County. This has not been proven nor has it been disproven, but research has led to this being the most probable lineage. By these accounts, this Archibald Rhea would be a direct ancestor to Palmer Rhea, Sr.

Parents: Matthew Campbell Rhea and Janet Baxter
Married: Ann (last name unknown)

> **Children of Ann and Archibald Rhea:** These are the Rhea brothers of Augusta County, Virginia **(See separate chapters pertaining to each son):**
>
> **WILLIAM RHEA, SR. (See C.5.)** (B.3. Archibald, A.1. Matthew), **(Direct ancestor to Palmer Rhea, Sr.)**

ROBERT RHEA (See C.6.) (B.3. Archibald, A.1. Matthew)

ARCHIBALD RHEA (See C.7.) (B.3. Archibald, A.1. Matthew)

The earliest reference of Rhea in the Augusta, Bath, and Rockbridge Counties located was documented in 1746 in the Draper Manuscripts. The Draper Manuscripts are a 491-volume collection of genealogical and historical notes, records, newspaper articles, and other material on the frontier history collected by Lyman Copeland Draper. This Archibald Rhea is thought to be the son of Matthew Campbell Rhea of Scotland and likely the father of Robert, Archibald and William Rhea, the three brothers of Augusta County and uncle to Margaret Rhea Looney Rentfro of Augusta County. Date of immigration unknown.

A document in the Draper Manuscripts indicated in 1746 an Archibald Roaugh (one of the various spellings of the Rhea family name), a member of Captain Joseph Culton's Company of Augusta County, Virginia, was exempted from mustering. One of the primary purposes of the Virginia Militia in Augusta County during the mid-1700s was to combat Native Americans with whom clashes were constantly occurring. During the mid-1700s, from 1754 through fall of 1764, the Indian Wars in Augusta County took many lives. All Captains were to excuse *"all such old or infirm persons . . . unfit for mustering."* This indicated Archibald Rhea was of elder age or physically unable to perform in 1746. He would have been about fifty-six years old.

Joseph Culton, Captain of the militia, came to Virginia from Ireland about 1740. He purchased land at Bordon's Grant in Augusta County, which later becomes part of Rockbridge County. Culton's land was between Walker's and Hay's Creeks, adjacent to the New Providence Church.[16] This is the same area the Rhea brothers and the elder Archibald Rhea settled in the mid-1700s as did many of the Scotch-Irish.

In 1806, according to Chalkley, Vol. II, 269, William Patton gave a deposition referring to an Indian massacre that occurred about 1763

---

[16] Chalkey, Lyman, *Chalkey's Chronicles.*

wherein sixteen or seventeen people were killed. Archibald Rhea was one of ten names Patton mentioned. It was unclear whether Archibald Rhea was killed or if he was assisting in the burial of those dead, although it seems he was one of those killed. Other sources state Archibald may have died earlier.

Archibald Rhea was thought to have been killed in the Second Massacre at Kerr's Creek. Below refers to the massacre:

In May, 1763, the warriors were to attack 14 British garrisons along the frontier. Of those 14, all but four were captured. One of the four was Detroit, Pontiac's personal goal. That summer, war raged up and down the frontier. Once again, the Shawnee Chief Cornstalk was assigned the area he knew well, the eastern Alleghanies, the Cowpasture and Jackson rivers, Botetourt, Kerrs Creek, Augusta. Small forts dotted the frontier from the French and Indian War. A confident Cornstalk knew he could take them all.

The following is a deposition taken by William Patton that describes the 2nd Kerr's Creek Massacre:

Vol 2: Page 269. - 1806 November 7 Page 145—Wm. Patton, aged 64, deposes, in Rockbridge, 7th November, 1806, he has lived in Rockbridge 56 years since last May. After the Revolution there was a rapid increase of immigration from the North. James Wardlaw and deponent's father were intimate. James had a son Hugh and a son Robert. There were Indian troubles for about 10 years. Fifty years ago, there was a fort at McClung; the last incursion was 43 years ago, when 16 or 17 people were killed. Deponent helped bury them and they were attacked at the burial. These were very early settlers, viz: James, Alexr. Saml. Walker, James Moore, Saml. Coalter, Jno. Wallace, Archd. Rhea, James Rutherford, James Buchanan, Andrew and Charles Hays.[17]

---

[17] *Old Augusta*, "The Kerr's Creek Massacres (1759-1763)", www.werelate.org/wiki/TheKerr's_Creek_Massacres.

Another account of the second Kerr's Creek Massacre:

> *William Gilmore and another man turned toward the mountains to scout for Indians. Concealed nearby, the Indians shot the two men, and swooped upon the nearly 100 men, women and children milling around. Two or three younger men advanced toward the enemy and lost their lives immediately. In one account, when the Shawnees sprang from cover, Mrs. Dale grabbed a stud colt that had never been ridden and swung onto its back. Managing to balance her baby and cling to the horse, she fled the pursuing Indians. Out running them, she dropped her baby in a rye field and hid herself in the brush, obviously sending the horse on. Later, she returned and found the baby unharmed in the rye.*
>
> *She said the terror-stricken people ran in every direction, trying to hide. The Indians chased first one, then another, killing everyone in their path. Another account says even the cattle were shot, bristling with arrows. Mrs. Dale recounts that some people threw up their hands, entreating for mercy. The Shawnees killed most, spared some. Any man resisting was shot immediately. Some whites fled for the spring pond, hiding both in the water and in the weeds along the banks. The warriors found them, killed them and tossed the bodies in the pond.[18]*

William, Robert and Archibald Rhea, thought to be the elder Archibald Rhea's sons, were all recorded living in Augusta County. Their information is included in further chapters.

---

[18] *Old Augusta*, "The Kerr's Creek Massacres (1759-1763)", www.werelate.org/wiki/TheKerr's_Creek_Massacres.

MATTHEW CAMPBELL RHEA II

SECOND GENERATION

SON OF MATTHEW CAMPBELL RHEA
OF SCOTLAND AND IRELAND

MATTHEW CAMPBELL RHEA II (B.4) (A.1. Matthew) Matthew was born abt. 1689 in Ireland and died in Ireland. He married Elizabeth McClain (born abt. 1690) and later Matthew married Mary Lockhart. Memoirs of Congressman John Rhea, a grandson of Matthew II, stated the following:

> *Matthew Rhea, the youngest son of the 'Rebel' by his first wife, settled on the family farm named Kennecally, near St. Johnson. He had a son William. The son William got in a quarrel. The quarrel was between him and Matthew Cochran who lived near him. As a result of this quarrel, Matthew Rhea was wounded and died; his son William took possession of the farm Kennecally.*[19]

Matthew Campbell Rhea II did not come to America. Among his children, I only discovered Margaret Rhea Looney Renfro who lived in Augusta County, Virginia, although others may have. (See Chapter on Margaret Rhea Looney Renfro.) Matthew Campbell Rhea II had several notable children, grandchildren, and great grandchildren who made a lasting mark in our colonial development. More information is

---

[19] Foley, Edward, *The Descendants of Matthew "The Rebel" Rhea of Scotland and Ireland*, Heritage Books, 2008, p.4.

included on some of these remarkable descendants of Matthew. This line of Rheas has been researched by U. S. Congressman John Rhea in his memoirs and by descendants of Rev. Joseph Rhea as well as historians. Much has been written about this Rhea family lineage.

By these accounts, Matthew Campbell Rhea II would not be a direct ancestor to Palmer Rhea, Sr., but he was a distant great uncle number of times removed.

Thought to be children of Elizabeth McClain and Matthew Campbell Rhea are listed below. However, Elizabeth, according to a researcher (Mrs. Gordon Fletcher), was previously married, so some children may be from her previous marriage and may be stepchildren to Matthew Campbell Rhea II:

Parents: Matthew Campbell Rhea and Janet Baxter
Married: (1) Elizabeth McClain Rhea and (2) Mary Lockhart

Children of Matthew Campbell Rhea II and Elizabeth McClain:

ELIZABETH MCCLAIN RHEA (B.4. Matthew. A.1. Matthew)

ABRAHAM RHEA (B.4. Matthew. A.1. Matthew)

JAMES RHEA (B.4. Matthew. A.1. Matthew)

MARGERY RHEA (B.4. Matthew. A.1. Matthew)

JOSEPH RHEA (B.4.Matthew. A.1. Matthew) (Additional information shown below on Joseph Rhea.)

AGNES RHEA (B.4. Matthew. A.1. Matthew) Agnes was born abt. 1720 in Ireland and died in Ireland.

MARGARET RHEA LOONEY RENTFRO (See C.8.) (B.4. Matthew. A.1. Matthew) (Born abt. 1722) This is the Margaret Rhea of Augusta County, Virginia. She married Robert Looney and after Robert's death, she married Stephen Rentfro. (**SEE CHAPTER ON MARGARET RHEA LOONEY RENTFRO**)

Children of Matthew Campbell Rhea II and Mary Lockhart:

SAMUEL RHEA (REA) (B.4. Matthew. A.1. Matthew) (Additional information shown below on Samuel Rhea.)

ISAAC RHEA (B.4. Matthew. A.1. Matthew) (b. abt. 1727)

MATTHEW RHEA III (B.4. Matthew. A.1. Matthew) (b. abt. 1729)

WILLIAM RHEA (B.4. Matthew. A.1. Matthew) (Additional information shown below on William Rhea.)

ELIZABETH MCCLAIN RHEA (B.4. Matthew. A.1. Matthew) (born abt. 1710)

ABRAHAM RHEA (B.4. Matthew. A.1. Matthew) (born abt. 1711)

JAMES RHEA (B.4. Matthew. A.1. Matthew) (born abt. 1712)

MARGERY RHEA (B.4. Matthew. A.1. Matthew) (born abt. 1713)

JOSEPH RHEA (B.4. Matthew. A.1. Matthew) (1715-1777). (Son of Matthew Campbell Rhea II and Elizabeth McClain.) Joseph was born in County Donegal, Ireland. In 1752, he married Elizabeth McIlwaine (1732 – 1793). Joseph was a Presbyterian minister. In 1769, Joseph resigned his position as minister of a church in Fahan, Ireland, and he and his family sailed to America. After a long passage across the Atlantic Ocean, they landed in Philadelphia. For several weeks, they remained in Philadelphia staying with a relative, Matthew Byers. In Spring of 1770, they moved to the home of Elizabeth's half-brother, Joshua Anderson in Octorara, Pennsylvania. They soon rented a home where they lived for a couple of years. In 1771, Joseph accepted a call to Piney Creek Church in Taneytown, Maryland.

Reverend J. F. Minor Simpson writes in his book, Monocacy Valley Maryland Presbyterianism, that "There are few rural Presbyterian churches in the whole North American continent which have made their influence more widely felt than has the one at Piney Creek." Simpson goes on to explain his claim, stating that many sons of the congregation have founded other churches throughout the years and direct descendants of the church's first minister, Revered Joseph Rhea, helped to found the University of Tennessee and brought Presbyterianism to the same state....

. . . Only a few months after the land was transferred, in April 1771, Piney Creek presented a call to Reverend Joseph Rhea to be the first installed minister of the church, according to Scharf. Reverend Rhea was born in Ireland in 1715 and received a Master of Arts degree from Glasgow University, graduating with honors, Simpson wrote in his book. Simpson explained that Rhea and his family arrived in America in 1769, Rhea joined the Presbytery in 1770, and he was soon offered several different churches in the area. Piney Creek commissioners, Patrick Watson and Matthew Galt, relayed the call to Rhea. As recorded in the "Book of Congregational Affairs," they offered a salary of 110-112 pounds and stated that the church would provide living expenses for him and his family for the first year. At the time, Rhea was wanted by at least four different churches in the area, and disputes between Tom's Creek Church and Piney Creek prevented the gain of a minister for either church.

Reverend Rhea was installed in 1771 and guided his church members at Piney Creek until 1776. Rhea was interested in the settlers of Virginia and what is now Tennessee. According to Scharf, Piney Creek was unable to pay Rhea's salary as well, and it was in arrears. Whether more frustrated by the back salary, interested in the welfare of the settlers and Cherokee Indians to whom he eventually ministered, or desiring to be a part of the Revolutionary War effort as a chaplain, it is unclear as to the exact reason that Reverend Rhea submitted his resignation in April of 1776. . . [20]

Rev. Joseph Rhea died at the age of 62 and is buried in Piney Creek Reformed Presbyterian Church Cemetery, 4472 Harney Road, Taneytown, Maryland. Piney Creek Presbyterian Church, established in 1763, is the oldest church in Carroll County, Maryland. The original church no longer stands. It was torn down in 1818. The current church was built in 1818, remodeled in 1869, and the tower added in 1915 with remodeling. The church is about two miles outside Taneytown. A Social Hall was erected in 1946. This church was originally established by Scotch-Irish who came out of Philadelphia.

Joseph had planned to move to Tennessee but died before he had the opportunity. One year after Joseph's death, his family set out for Holston County along with fellow church members, arriving at their new home in 1779. Joseph's wife, Elizabeth McIlwaine Rhea, is buried at Weaver Cemetery, Weaver Union Church, 132 Peoples Road in Bristol, Tennessee. Another monument to Joseph Rhea was erected at Weaver Cemetery in Bristol at his wife's grave. (Joseph Rhea is father of U.S. Congressman John Rhea.)

Known children of Joseph Rhea and Elizabeth McIlwaine:

John Angus Rhea (Joseph, B.4. Matthew. A.1. Matthew) (1753-1832) John is buried at Blountville Cemetery, Blountville, Sullivan County, Tennessee.

Matthew Rhea (Joseph, B.4. Matthew. A.1. Matthew) (1755-1816) Matthew is buried at Weaver Cemetery, Weaver Union Church, 132 Peoples Road, Bristol, Sullivan County, Tennessee.

---

[20] Grant, Amanda Woodruff, Emmitsburg Area Historical Society,1996, *Piney Creek Church – 250 Years of Continuous Worship.*

Margaret Rhea Preston (Joseph, B.4. Matthew. A.1. Matthew) (1757-1822) Margaret married Robert Preston (1750-1833). She is buried at Walnut Grove Cemetery, 3012 Lee Highway (Rts. 11 &19), Bristol City, Virginia.

William Rhea (Joseph, B.4. Matthew. A.1. Matthew)

Joseph C. Rhea (Joseph, B.4. Matthew. A.1. Matthew) (1762-1825) Joseph is buried at Weaver Cemetery, Weaver Union Church, 132 Peoples Road, Bristol, Sullivan County, Tennessee.

Elizabeth Rhea Rhea (Joseph, B.4. Matthew. A.1. Matthew) (1767-1821) Elizabeth married Major Robert Rhea (1776-1841), son of William Rhea (B.4. Matthew. A.1. Matthew) and Elizabeth Lockhart. Elizabeth is buried at Weaver Cemetery, Weaver Union Church, 132 Peoples Road, Bristol, Sullivan County, Tennessee.

Samuel Rhea (Joseph, B.4. Matthew. A.1. Matthew) (1769-1848) Samuel is buried at Blountville Cemetery, Blountville, Sullivan County, Tennessee.

James Rhea (Joseph, B.4. Matthew. A.1. Matthew)

SAMUEL RHEA (REA) (B.4. Matthew. A.1. Matthew) (Son of Matthew Campbell Rhea II and Mary Lockhart.) (b. abt. 1725-1811) Samuel was born in Ireland. In 1754 or 1755, he emigrated to Pennsylvania, first to Chester County. After a short time, he moved to Lancaster County and then to Conococheague Valley, which became a part of Franklin County, then Cumberland County. He married Eleanor Snodgrass, daughter to Rev. James Snodgrass, one of the early Presbyterian ministers of the settlement on the eastern bank of the Susquehanna. Samuel became a prosperous farmer and was a man of means and education. His property was known as the

"Rea Mansion." Samuel changed the spelling of his name to "Rea." He was the father of the U.S. Congressman John Rea.

Samuel's second marriage was to Rosanna English and third marriage to Martha Greer (Grier) Wallace. Samuel Rea is buried at Rocky Spring Presbyterian Church Cemetery, Franklin County, Pennsylvania in the same grave as his first wife. The historical church building was built in 1794 and is a one-and-one-half -story brick Georgian style building with wooden pews and straight-backed seating. The church required members to sign a financial agreement for pew holders requiring an annual fee for occupancy of the pew. The ends of the pews are carved with names of previous occupants and identified military ranks of those who served in the Revolutionary War. *Pew No. 49 still bears the Rhea name.*[21] This church is in the National Register of Historic Places.[22]

Known children of Samuel Rea:

Ann Rhea (Rea) (Samuel, B.4. Matthew. A.1. Matthew)

John Rhea (Rea) (Samuel, B.4. Matthew. A.1. Matthew) (More information listed below on John Rea.)

William Rhea (Rea) (Samuel, B.4. Matthew. A.1. Matthew)

Sarah Rhea (Rea) (Samuel, B.4. Matthew. A.1. Matthew)

Samuel Rhea (Rea) (Samuel, B.4. Matthew. A.1. Matthew)

Hannah Rhea (Rea) (Samuel, B.4. Matthew. A.1. Matthew)

James Rhea (Rea) (Samuel, B.4. Matthew. A.1. Matthew)

---

[21] Foley, Edward, *The Descendants of Matthew "The Rebel" Rhea of Scotland and Ireland*, Heritage Books, 2008, p.32.

[22] *National Park Service (2009-03-13). "National Register Information System". National Register of Historic Places.*

WILLIAM RHEA (B.4. Matthew. A.1. Matthew) (Son of Matthew Campbell Rhea II and Mary Lockhart.) (Born abt. 1735 in Ireland) William married Elizabeth Lockhart. They first settled on the family farm Kennecally in Ireland. Later William moved to Lancaster, Pennsylvania and then moved to Washington County, Virginia.

Known children of William Rhea and Elizabeth Lockhart:

Matthew Rhea (William, B.4. Matthew. A.1. Matthew)

Jennie Rhea (William, B.4. Matthew. A.1. Matthew)

Joseph Rhea (William, B.4. Matthew. A.1. Matthew)

William Rhea (William, B.4. Matthew. A.1. Matthew)

Sarah Rhea (William, B.4. Matthew. A.1. Matthew)

Elizabeth Rhea (William, B.4. Matthew. A.1. Matthew)

Robert "Major" Rhea (William, B.4. Matthew. A.1. Matthew) Robert is buried at Weaver Cemetery, 132 Peoples Road, Bristol, Sullivan County, Tennessee.

JOHN REA – FOURTH GENERATION
Grandson of Matthew Campbell Rhea II of Augusta County and son of Samuel Rea (Rhea)

JOHN REA (Son of Samuel Rea/Rhea) – Fourth Generation (Samuel, B.4. Matthew, A.1. Matthew) (Jan. 27, 1755 – Feb. 26, 1829) John Rea was born in Chester County, Pennsylvania at "Rea's Mansion" near Chambersburg. He was the son of Samuel Rea. John was raised in the Conococheague Valley during the outbreaks of Indian attacks.

During the Revolutionary War, he enlisted and was in Capt. William Hendrick's company. He served in the 5th Battalion with Colonial Smith commanding. On May 10, 1780, John was made Captain of the 2nd Company, 1st Battalion, Cumberland County Militia with Col. James Johnston commanding. He rose to the rank of Brigadier-General. In the War of 1812, he was Major-General of the 7th Division of Pennsylvania Militia.

John married Elizabeth Culbertson in November 1806. He was commissioned the first coroner of Franklin County, Pennsylvania on October 20, 1784. He was a member of Assembly from Franklin County and in 1803 was elected to Congress, serving until 1811. On May 11, 1813, he was elected to Congress again. In 1823, he was elected to the State Senate, resigning in 1824. John is buried at Rocky Spring Churchyard, Chambersburg, Franklin County, Pennsylvania.

John Rea and Elizabeth Culbertson had nine sons and two daughters. His son John became a physician.

John Rea is mentioned in the "Rocky Spring Presbyterian Church and the Revolutionary period" as follows:

From the records, which give rather imperfect lists, it is beyond question that this congregation alone furnished one general, four colonels, twelve captains, and a like number of other officers. Among these none were more prominent than Captain John Rhea, for after serving as captain for various companies of the Revolution, he was commissioned Brigadier-General in 1812 and Major-General in 1814, and was a state senator and the great-grandfather of Samuel Rhea, who is president of the Pennsylvania Railroad . . . [23]

John Rea died suddenly in 1829. A record of his death:

Died on the morning of the 6th instant, General John Rea, after a very short illness, aged 74 years. He came to Chambersburg with some of his neighbors on Wednesday and while preparing to return him in the evening, he suddenly became unwell and so rapid was his disease that in less than a day and a half, he breathed his last. He was sensible during

---

[23] "Rocky Spring Presbyterian Church and the Revolutionary period," The Franklin County Chapter of the Daughters of the American Revolution.

his illness and with perfect composure and resignation he spoke of the near approach of death. He was repeatedly chosen a member of the State Legislature and for eight years in succession he was elected to Congress. [24]

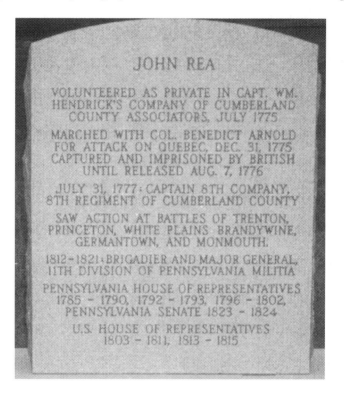

SAMUEL REA
SIXTH GENERATION
Descendant of Matthew Campbell Rhea II of Augusta County, Grandson of U.S. Rep. John Rea of Pennsylvania and son of James D. Rea

SAMUEL REA (James, John, Samuel, B.4. Matthew, A.1. Matthew) (September 21, 1855 – March 24, 1929) Samuel was son to James D. Rea and Ruth Blair Moore. He was born in Hollidaysburg, Pennsylvania. Samuel was an engineer and became the ninth president

---

[24] "The Rea Family of Franklin County, PA" Source: Republican Compiler, Gettysburg, PA, February 18, 1829.

of the Pennsylvania Railroad in 1913. His grandfather was John Rea who served as a U.S. Representative during terms of Thomas Jefferson and James Madison.

Samuel was known as a great engineering executive and corporate organizer, one who was "confident, well-groomed, with upright posture and ready to deal with crises." A description of Samuel Rea as printed in *The New York Times* on March 29, 1929:

Mr. Rea's appearance was that of a man of great strength and power. He was more than six feet in height, and his strong, rugged face was surmounted by a shock of iron-gray hair. He would deal with tremendous problems and immense figures almost as with trifles, and while his associates often were struggling with a problem he would snap out his decision and the problem would be ended.

Samuel married Mary Black (1856-1933). They lived in Allegheny, Pennsylvania. There is a statue in New York City's Pennsylvania Station of Samuel Rea, placed after his death in his honor. The sculptor was Adolph A. Winman. The statue was dedicated in 1930 and stands ten-feet tall, bronze and pedestal three feet. It is located at the entrance of New York's Pennsylvania Station, Two Penn Plaza, Seventh Avenue at 32nd Street. It stands at the top of the Seventh-Avenue stairs to Penn Station. Samuel published a book: *The Railways Terminating in London: With a Description of the Terminating Stations.*

Honorary degrees were awarded to Samuel from The University of Pennsylvania, Princeton University and Lafayette College. In 1926, he received the Franklin Medal and in 1926, he was elected an Honorary Member of the Institution of Civil Engineers.

Samuel Rea died at the age of 73 on March 24, 1929. He is buried at Church of the Redeemer Cemetery, Bryn Mawr, Montgomery County, Pennsylvania. He has two known children: George Black Rea and Ruth Rea.

Samuel Rea
Photo from United States Library of Congress,
Alman & Co., photographer, 1905

The following is included on a plaque:
SAMUEL REA
VICE PRES. 1899-1912 PRESIDENT 1913-1925
PENNSYLVANIA RAILROAD COMPANY

UNDER WHOSE ABLE SUPERVISION THE PENNSYLVANIA STATION AND THE EXTENSION OF THE RAILROAD SERVING IT, INTO NEW YORK CITY, WAS DESIGNED AND CONSTRUCTED. THE ORIGINAL STATION WAS OPENED TO THE PUBLIC IN SEPTEMBER 1910 AND WAS REDEVELOPED, PROVIDING FOR MADISON SQUARE GARDEN CENTER ABOVE STREET LEVEL, DURING THE YEARS 1963-1968

BORDEN TRACT

HOME OF THE AUGUSTA COUNTY
RHEA BROTHERS

Borden Tract was located South of Beverley Manor (approximately 118,000-acre tract granted to William Beverley in 1736 by the Crown) in what was then Augusta County. Records show all three Rhea brothers settled In Borden Tract in the mid-1750s. These tracts of land were sold primarily to the Scotch-Irish immigrants.

Borden Tract was a grant of land received by Benjamin Borden, a New Jersey Quaker, on November 8, 1739. Borden was promised 1,000 acres from the Governor of Virginia, William Gooch, for every settler he located to move to the area. The land was on the James River and west of the Blue Ridge. Stipulation of the Borden Tract grant was there would be one hundred families settling the area within two years with homes erected to form a town in the center of the county.

A surveyor by the name of John McDowell who had come from Ulster in 1729, first landing in Philadelphia and later moving to Virginia, helped Borden locate the tract of land in 1732 and was rewarded with land of 1000 acres. It was agreed Borden and McDowell would cut a road through the settlement suitable for horses carrying luggage. Among the first settlers on this land was Ephraim McDowell and his family, his sons James and John and his daughter, Mary Greenlee and her husband. The first white man's settlement with a cabin on a farm in Borden Tract belonged to John McDowell.

This tract of land became known as "Borden Tract," and at the time was in Augusta County but later became Rockbridge County.[25] Borden offered 100 acres to anyone who would build a home on the tract and the privilege of purchasing more at fifty shillings per hundred acres. Borden had two years to recruit 100 settlers, and he succeeded. Many men from Ulster settled on Borden Tract. They found themselves free to establish Presbyterian churches. Roads were soon cleared, crops planted, mills built, and homes erected. The tract lay in Indian country and the whites were trespassing. This was land on which the Indians had always hunted and traveled through on expeditions. (By 1778, this land will be called Lexington.)

> *George II By the grace of God of Great Britain, France and Ireland, King, Defender of the faith, etc. to all to whom these presents shall come, greeting know ye that for divers good causes and considerations, but more especially in consideration that Benjamin Borden, Late of Main lately caused to be imported and settled on the land herein after mentioned one family for every 1000 acres, we have given heirs and successors do give, grant and confirm unto the said Benjamin Borden and to his heirs and assigns forever one certain and being on the West side of the Blue Ridge, in the County of Augusta, and on the North and Northeast branches of James River as followeth (To-Wit).*

Many settlers in Virginia lost their lives during Indian attacks by the Pontiac and Shawnee during these years of the French and Indian War (1754 – 1763) in the outlying areas of what at the time was Augusta County. Augusta County covered a great deal of the upper portion of the eastern United States with over seven states, which will take from it in parts. The settlers lived at peace with the Indians until 1754. This war was a conflict between France and England for control of the valuable resources in the new world. The French recruited the Indian tribes to join forces with them to force the British settlers off the land. The Indians considered the settlers as invaders of their land. There were frequent Indian raids during these years with women and children

---

[25] Lyman Chalkley, Lyman, *Chronicles of the Scotch-Irish Settlements in Virginia*, Extracted from the Original Court Records of Augusta County 1745-1800.

35

killed as well as men. Some families built stone houses with fort cellars for protection. Minority group of settlers held their ground backed by a group of small forts ordered to be built by General Washington.

Among those early settlers were William Rhea (Reagh) who purchased 230 acres with title secured in 1750 and later sold the land to his son Archibald Rhea. Archibald Rhea, Jr., brother of William purchased 200 acres with title secured in 1753 (Chalkley's Records indicates deed was dated 1771). Robert Rhea, brother of William, purchased 175 acres (Chalkley's Records indicate 118 acres) with title secured in 1754 and later sold to Archibald Rhea, his brother indicated above. These were the years of the French and Indian War. The land owned by the Rhea brothers were next to each other with Archibald's land lying between Robert and William's land. Robert's land was on Hays Creek and on one side his land touched Archibald's land and on the other side of Robert's land was land belonging to Widow Smiley and land belonging to John Wallace on the back side of Robert's land. Archibald's land also located on Hays Creek and on either side faced Robert's and William's land and on the back side his land adjoined John Wallace's land. William's land adjoined Archibald's, John Wallace's and James Coulter's land and the tip of John Robinson's land. Their lands were located approximately sixteen miles north of what is today Lexington in Rockbridge County.

There were so many settlers who were Scotch-Irish on Bordon Grant the area became known as the "Irish Tract."[26] Most of their early churches were Presbyterian. Their first homes were temporary shelters until they cleared their land and planted crops. They then erected permanent homes. These settlers were mostly farmers and blacksmiths, providing for themselves.[27]

---

[26] Larry Hoefling, *Chasing the Frontier: Scots-Irish in Early America*, iUniverse, 2005, p. 35.

[27] *Early Settlers of Augusta County*, Virginia.

Acquisition of Land from Chalkley's:

Page 10.—2d May, 1758. Robert Reagh (Reah, Reaoh), carpenter and joiner, and Sara to Archibald Reah, Jr., yeoman, £60, 118 acres on Hays Creek; corner widow Smyley. Teste: Win. Reah. Delivered: Archibald Reah, 23d March, 1768. (Note: Robert Rhea was Archibald's brother).

Page 15 - Archebald Reaigh, Jr., 24 acres, Hays Creek. Adjoining Seth Wilson, Burdon [sic, s/b Borden]. February 20, 1762. [Abstract of Land Grant Surveys, 1761-1791, Augusta & Rockingham Counties, Virginia, by Peter Cline Kaylor, pg. 6].

Page 110 - Archibald Raigh, 98 acres, North Mountain. Adjoining Bordens Patent. April 6, 1768. [Abstract of Land Grant Surveys, 1761-1791, Augusta & Rockingham Counties, Virginia, by Peter Cline Kaylor, pg. 40].

Page 48.—2d October, 1771. Borden's executors to Archibald Reah, Jr., corner Archibald Reah, part of 92100. Delivered: Hugh Rhea, 16th December, 1795. Teste: Alexander and Halbert McCluer, William Leakey. (Note: this record shows that Archibald Rhea, Jr. had already acquired the neighboring tract of his brother Robert Rhea in 1758).

From 1753 war raged along the frontier and continued for more than ten years with no peace or security on the frontiers west of the Blue Ridge. In 1754 when the French and Indian War erupted, George Washington, who was 23 years old at the time, was named commander of the Virginia militia. In 1755, Washington determined a chain of fortes and stockades west of the Shenandoah Valley be constructed. These consisted of fortes, stockades and block houses. Fort Dickinson was built by colonial militia in 1756 southwest of current day Millboro Springs and operated until the 1760's. Washington considered Fort Dickinson on the Cowpasture River in what was Augusta County and currently Bath County to be a key stronghold. In Washington's *"A Plan of the Number of Forts, and Strength Necessary to Each Extending Entirely Across our Frontiers, from South to North,"* he wrote:

> *Dickinson's is situated for the defense of a once numerous and fertile settlement, on the Bull, Cow and Calf pastures, and lies directly in the Shawnee path to Ohio, and must be a place of rendezvous if an expedition is conducted against the Ohio Indians below Duquesne.*

It was recommended 250 militiamen be stationed at Fort Dickinson.[28] Although these numbers may have been recommended, it appears the number of men stationed there to man the fort was much lower. In 1756 and 1757, Fort Dickinson was attacked by Indians. In 1755 and 1756, George Washington visited the area and toured the homes and the fort.

The settlers found themselves swept violently into bloody conflict between the British and the French who became an ally with the Indians. In Augusta County, Virginia Militia was compulsory for all free males eighteen to sixty years old within the county during the French and Indian War (1754-1763). Among those exempted were public officers in the civil service, ministers of the Church of England, professors and students of William and Mary College, any person being an overseer of four servants or slaves and actually residing on the plantation where they worked, any miller in charge of a mill, and persons employed in a copper or iron or lead mine. A formal act for better regulating and disciplining the Militia came into effect during the war, excerpts as follows:

> *WHEREAS it is necessary, in this time of danger, that the militia of this colony should be well regulated and disciplined. . .*
>
> *And be it further enacted, by the authority aforesaid, That every person so as aforesaid inlisted (except free mulattoes, negroes, and Indians) shall be armed in the manner following, that is to say: Every soldier shall he furnished with a firelock well fixed, a bayonet fitted to the same, a double cartouch-box, and three charges of powder, and*

---

[28] The Bath County Historical Society, *The Bicentennial History of Bath County, Virginia, 1791-1991*, Heritage House Publishing, Marceline, MO., p. 9.

constantly appear with the same at the time and place *appointed for muster and exercise, and shall also keep at his place of abode one pound of powder and four pounds of ball, and bring the same with him into the field when he shall be required. . .*

And for the better training and exercising the militia, and rendering them more serviceable, Be it further enacted, by the authority aforesaid, That every captain shall, once in three months, and oftner if thereto required by the lieutenant or chief commanding officer in the county, muster, train, and exercise his company, and the lieutenant or other chief commanding officer in the county shall cause a general muster and exercise of all the companies within his county, to be made in the months of March or April, and September or October, yearly; and if any soldier shall, at any general or private muster, refuse to perform the command of his officer, or behave himself refractorily or mutinously, or misbehave himself at the courts martial to be held in pursuance of this act, as is herein after directed, it shall and may be lawful to and for the chief commanding officer, then present, to cause such offender to be tied neck and heels, for any time not exceeding five minutes, or inflict such corporal punishment as he shall think fit, not exceeding twenty lashes. . .[29]

The various tribes were in bloody war with one another and battles were a constant occurrence in the Valley, which was hunting grounds for these tribes. The whole Western Virginia frontier found themselves in constant battles with the Native Americans. How could fear not consume them, I wondered. How terrifying it must have been to fear for your life daily, afraid to step outside your home or work your garden with fringes of fear the enemy lurks in the shadows. The anxiety and nightmares and the bravery required to endure these fears would be all consuming, knowing your child may be killed before your very eyes or dragged off to a strange life or turned into a slave, tortured or scalped, or to see your newborn baby killed. The settlers thought of the enemy as evil monsters who hated them so much they could destroy without

---

[29] *An Act for the better regulating and disciplining the Militia, April 1757,* Militia Act of 1757 at Virginia1774.org.

a conscious; they took and violated and killed. The settlers struggled with this terror daily. The dreams and expectations of a new life had been shattered, and they were left with horrors of what might befall upon their family. These fears and nightmares became a reality to many who were captured and killed. The settlers knew the men who may do this harm to them were ones who hated them for taking their land and home. This hate must have been intense. The Indians looked upon these settlers as unwelcomed invaders who encroached upon their land, selfishly taking what belonged to them.

An excerpt from History of Augusta County pertaining to the years of 1755 or 1756 (years the elder Rhea, the three Rhea brothers and Margaret Rhea resided in the area), states:

> . . . *Some of the settlers fled east of the Blue Ridge, but the vast majority of the inhabitants of Augusta remained at home, prepared for defense, and determined, if necessary, to embrace an honorable death as their refuge against flight. The distresses of the people during this period of war exceed all description. In one of Washington's letters to Gov. Dinwiddle there is a famous passage which brings all this suffering and wretchedness vividly before us. He says: "The supplicating tears of the women, and moving petitions of the men, melt me into such deadly sorrow that I solemnly declare, if I know my own mind, I could offer myself a willing sacrifice to the butchering enemy, provided that would contribute to the people's ease.*[30]

In 1756, Washington returned to the area to once again inspect the frontier. He reported the strongholds,

> *...very weak for want of men, but more so by indolence and irregularity. None I saw in a posture of defense, and few that might not be surprised with the greatest of ease.*[31]

The largest attack in the area lasted for four days, starting on

---

[30] Peyton, Lewis, *History of Augusta County, Virginia*, Samuel M. Yost & Son, MDCCCLXXXII, No. 109.

[31] The Bath County Historical Society, *The Bicentennial History of Bath County, Virginia*, 1791-1991, Heritage House Publishing, Marceline, MO., p. 10.

September 11, 1756 on the Jackson River. It was stated an estimate of 200 Indians committed:

> *Outrages every Minute, Killing the Horses and cattle, and burning the Houses of poor People. Thirteen settlers died, two were wounded, and twenty-nine were taken as prisoners.*[32]

There were other Indian raids in this area, smaller but frequent. The people in this remote location of the frontier stayed in a constant state of fear. There are numerous incidents of attacks and massacres. Among those was the captivity of Mary Draper Ingles during the massacre of Draper's Meadow (located in present day campus of Virginia Tech in Blacksburg, Virginia) by the Shawnee in 1755. There are historical accounts of her escape and her amazing ordeal and journey to return home. These accounts of her escape through the wilderness have become a legend and have inspired books and films. Col. James Patton who had been awarded the original tract of land, which was Drapers Meadow, was killed during this massacre.

The land that had belonged to Colonel James Patton was left to his nephew, William Preston. This land later became Smithfield Plantation. Colonel William Preston was Chairman of the Fincastle County Committee of Safety. James McCorkle, husband of Elizabeth Rhea (B.2. William, A.1. Matthew) also served on this Committee in 1775.

Even after the end of the French and Indian War, the massacres and battles did not stop on either side. It is this life the Rheas of Augusta County lived in these early years, a world once existed with laborious tasks that required hard determination and bravery and futile persistence to survive the rugged and vastness of the mountains and the chaos and fear of attack. The day to day living was certainly a challenge as they had to refrain from unraveling with the fear they must have felt and had to endure.

Today an historical mile marker identifies the general location of where Fort Dickinson once stood. This is the only evidence of the fort. Fort Dickinson not only served as a haven and protection for the settlers but was a meeting place for those headed west and a trading post for hunters and trappers coming from Indian territory and the open hunting range.

---

[32] The Bath County Historical Society, *The Bicentennial History of Bath County, Virginia*, 1791-1991, Heritage House Publishing, Marceline, MO., p. 10.

It is this same land Fort Dickinson was built upon, which over 200 years later Palmer Rhea, Sr. farmed, lived, and raised his family. Horse and wagon gave way to cars and what was a fort became private property and farmland. This land became home to Palmer, Jr. and his siblings and is where they grew to adulthood.

Palmer, Jr. and I visited this same countryside September 2019, 263 years after the four-day attack on the settlers where killings and outrages occurred. Standing there in 2019, we looked around to picturesque views and the gradual onset of dusk as fiery colors of sunset spread across the sky. The land is captivating and rich in scenery. There are no flutters of panic or fear of shadows and terror lurking behind a tree, only vast peacefulness flows through us as we are bewitched by the land. The adventures and dauntless bravery held by the young of those before us allowed us the opportunity to share this same enchanting land today in peace.

WILLIAM RHEA, SR.

THIRD GENERATION

ONE OF THE THREE RHEA BROTHERS OF AUGUSTA COUNTY

DIRECT ANCESTOR TO PALMER RHEA, SR.

WILLIAM RHEA, SR. (C.5.) (B.3. Archibald, A.1. Matthew), (Abt. 1718 1802). William was born about 1718 in Ireland to Archibald Rhea and Ann (last name unknown). He died April 25, 1802 in Bath County, Virginia. William is one of the three Rhea brothers who appeared in Augusta County, Virginia. Researchers and circumstances indicate Archibald is very probable the father of the three Rhea brothers of Augusta County, and for this writing is treated as such unless additional information becomes available.

It is unknown the year when William first came to what was Augusta County, Virginia. About 1740 to 1746, William married Elizabeth Clark, daughter to James and Elizabeth Summers Clark. Elizabeth's father James Clark was a wheelwright and a land agent for William Beverly, who dealt with large parcels of Virginia frontier land. James Clark owned a large plantation of over 800 acres in what was part of Beverly Manor, some nine miles southwest of current-day Staunton near the old Glebe Cemetery. This is near current-day Swoope, Augusta County and near the North Mountain Meeting House. The meeting houses in those early days also served as the churches. In Augusta County Courthouse records, the land was called "James Clark's Old Plantation." Below indicates the land owned by Elizabeth's father James Clark.

Acquisition of Land from Chalkley's:

Page 84.—14th May, 1746. George Hutchinson, of Augusta, yeoman, to James Clarke, wheelwright, £24.10.0; 380 acres in Beverley Manor, corner to land surveyed for John Brown. Witnesses, John Risk, James Brown, James Trimble. Acknowledged, 13th May, 1746, and Eleanor, his wife, relinquishes dower. (Note: later records indicate that this land was patented to James Clarke by Beverley, most likely with George Hutchinson acting as his agent).

Page 93.—1st April, 1755. Jacob Lockhart, plantationer, to James Clerk, wheelwright, £17, 436 acres on which Jacob now lives in Beverley Manor, on Back Creek; said James Clerk's line; corner Glebe land; James Berry's line; James Young's line. Mortgage. Teste: James Goodly, John Jones, William Clerk. Delivered: John Clerk, March, 1758.[33]

William was first of his brothers to purchase land (230 acres) in Borden Grant, known as the "Irish Tract," located south of Beverly Manor. In 1750, William settled on the southeast side of Hays Creek, also known as Walker's Creek. This land in current day is in Rockbridge County about sixteen miles north of Lexington in what is present-day Zack, Virginia and located off Highway 602, about five miles from Brownsburg, Virginia.

William Rhea and family were devoted Presbyterians and their religious beliefs were a significant part of their lives. The first church built was a meeting house of log construction. The settlers relied on visiting ministers until they could secure a settled minister.

William was listed in 1753 as the communicant of Timber Ridge Presbyterian Church according to History of Rockbridge County, and he along with his brother Robert[34] signed the call for the first minister,

---

[33] *Old Augusta*, Early Settlers, www.werelate.org/wiki/Person:James_Clark_%28105%29.
[34] The Bath County Historical Society, *The Bicentennial History of Bath County, Virginia 1701-1991*, Heritage House Publishing, pp.325-331.

John Brown.[35] John Brown was minister to both New Providence and Timber Ridge churches. The log meeting houses at New Providence and Timber Ridge served as houses of worship. On October 11, 1753, Rev. John Brown was ordained as the first minister of New Providence and Timber Ridge at a meeting of New Castle Presbytery and remained there for forty-five years.

John Brown's wife Margaret was sister to Col. William Preston (born in Ireland), one of the leading citizens and political figures in the Virginia colony whose final home was the historical Smithfield Plantation in Blacksburg, Virginia.[36] Current day tours are conducted of the plantation. Descended from the Rev. John Brown and Elizabeth and born and raised in Augusta County, Virginia was John Brown of Kentucky and James Brown of Louisiana, both United States Senators, and James Brown was a Minister to France before retirement.[37]

Among the first families in the valley attending the churches listed in the Journal of the Presbyterian Historical Society were "Alexander, Anderson, Berry, Coulston, Cowden, Campbelll, Eskins, Fulton, Hayes, Henry, Hoover, Gray, Jamison, Kelly, Kennedy, McNutt, McDowell, Montgomery, Patton, Lowry, Robinson, Rhea, Stahlnecker, Stewart, Stephenson, Todd, Thompson, Walker, Wilson."[38] The church of New Providence continued to grow, and the present brick church structure is the fifth sanctuary built, which was completed in 1857 and located at 1208 New Providence Road, Raphine, Virginia.[39]

Timber Ridge Presbyterian Church, in current day, is located at 73 Sam Houston Way, Lexington, Rockbridge County, Virginia. The log meeting house stood north of the present church on rising ground near

---

[35] Foley, Edward, *The Descendants of Matthew "The Rebel" Rhea of Scotland and Ireland*, Heritage Books, 2008, p.5.

[36] Smyth, S. Gordon, *The Pioneer Presbyterians of New Providence, VA.* Part II, 1901-1930, Vol. 11, no. June 6, 1922, p 196.

[37] *Waddell, Joseph Addison, Annals of Augusta County, Virginia, with Reminiscences Illustrative of the Vicissitudes of Its Pioneer Settlers,* 1823-1914, p.32.

[38] *Journal of the Presbyterian Historical Society,*1901-1930, June 1922, VOL. 11, No. 6, p. 193.

[39] Brown, Katharine L., *New Providence Church*, 1746-1996, *A History.*

a log schoolhouse, which is no longer in use. There is an old cemetery nearby, almost indistinguishable. The church building was built in 1756 from the efforts of about fifty families and remodeled as late as 1899 – 1900. John Brown was pastor of this church until 1767. The church is listed on the National Register of Historical Places.[40]

In a cabin on the hilltop just east of this church was the home in which the noted soldier and statesman and Governor of Tennessee and U.S. Senator Sam Houston was born forty years later (1793). The Houston family plantation was in sight of the Timber Ridge Presbyterian Church, and this was the church in which the Houston family worshipped until after the death of Sam Houston's father (1746-1807), who like the Rhea family was also an Ulster Scots person. When Sam was thirteen years old and after his father's death, his family moved to Blount County, Tennessee. Sam Houston's uncle, the Rev. Samuel Houston was involved in the Lost State of Franklin as were the Rhea and Looney families. Other than his five siblings, Houston also had dozens of cousins who lived in this area.

Along with his two brothers, William served in the Augusta County Militia. These were the years of the French and Indian War.

In May 1764, William Rhea had 257 acres conveyed to him on Broad Spring Run (Back Creek). About 1767, William Rhea and family moved to the Upper Mill Creek settlement, a branch of the Calfpasture above Panther's Gap and about four or five miles northeast of present-day town of Millboro. In 1769, William sold to his son Archibald his original land purchase in Borden Grant, which bordered his brothers' land.

In 1773, three-year-old orphan William Wooldridge was "bound out" to William "Reagh" by the church wardens to care for the orphan. (*Bicentennial History of Bath County*). William Rhea's responsibilities to the orphan were:

> *....the said Wm. Reagh shall cause him to be taught to read and write & arithmetic as far as the Rule of Three and to learn him the trade of a*

---

[40] National Park Service (2010-07-09). "National Register Information System", National Register of Historic Places.

farmer and also to furnish and provide sufficient meat, drink, lodging, an apparel fitting an apprentice and shall give him the freedom dues that the law direct..." Augusta County Court Records, Order Book No. XIV, shows on August 19, 1772, that the court was to "bind out" the orphan to "William Reah.

A Presbyterian minister, Philip Vickers Fithian, was visiting the area in December 1775, the day after Christmas and recorded a visit with William Rhea and Elizabeth "Reah" as stated:

. . . Tuesday at Mr. Reahs I passed pleasantly in rural Enjoyment. He owns a very large Farm, it lies by itself three Miles distant from any Neighbor; his Range for Stock is extensive & rich – His stock is large and valuable; Hay in great Quantities. Many Cattle – Many Horses young and old – several fine English Fillies – Mr. Reah is a stiff Quo-He – his Wife is a chatty plain good-humored Body – we supped & breakfasted on buttered Paste, of wheat Meal. . . [41]

Also, in 1775, William deeded tracts of land on Mill Creek to his sons James, William and John. William died on Mill Creek on April 25, 1802 in what is currently Bath County, Virginia.

Parents of William Rhea, Sr.: Thought to be Archibald Rhea and Ann (last name unknown)
Married: Elizabeth Clark in 1740 – 1747.

Known children of William Rhea, Sr. and Elizabeth Clark Rhea (not necessarily in order):[42]

ARCHIBALD RHEA (C.5. William, B.3. Archibald, A.1. Matthew)

---

[41] The Bath County Historical Society, *The Bicentennial History of Bath County, Virginia 1701-1991*, Heritage House Publishing, pp.325-331.
[42] The Bath County Historical Society, *The Bicentennial History of Bath County, Virginia 1701-1991*, The Bath *County Hi*storical *Society*, Heritage House Publishing, pp.325-331.

JAMES RHEA (C.5. William, B.3. Archibald, A.1. Matthew)

WILLIAM RHEA, JR. (C.5. William, B.3. Archibald, A.1. Matthew)

ALEXANDER RHEA (C.5. William, B.3. Archibald, A.1. Matthew)

ROBERT RHEA (C.5. William, B.3. Archibald, A.1. Matthew)

ANN/ANNA RHEA (C.5. William, B.3. Archibald, A.1. Matthew)

JOHN S. RHEA (C.5. William, B.3. Archibald, A.1. Matthew)

(Additional information on children is shown below.)

ARCHIBALD RHEA (C.5. William, B.3. Archibald, A.1. Matthew) (1747/1750 – 1773) Archibald was born about 1747-1750. He died in 1773 in Augusta County, Virginia. Archibald married Margaret (thought to be a Campbell and thought to be a cousin). They settled on property on Walker's Creek.

Known children of Archibald Rhea and Margaret Campbell:

William Rhea (Archibald, C.5. William, B.3. Archibald, A.1. Matthew) (Born abt. 1771) Thought to have died young.

Hugh Rhea (Archibald, C.5. William, B.3. Archibald, A.1. Matthew) (Born abt. 1772) Hugh married Rebecca Smiley. They lived in Tennessee. His second marriage was to Betsy Beck.

John Rhea (Archibald, C.5. William, B.3. Archibald, A.1. Matthew) (Born abt. 1773) John married Mary Deloach. He married again to Mary Smiley, sister to Rebecca Smiley who married his brother Hugh Rhea.

JAMES RHEA (C.5. William, B.3. Archibald, A.1. Matthew) James was born about 1753 in Augusta County, Virginia and died November 27, 1795 in Fayette County, Kentucky. James married Elizabeth Meek in 1772 in Augusta County, Virginia. Elizabeth's sister married James Rhea's brother Robert. James and Elizabeth had nine known children. In 1779, James Rhea sold his property on Mill Creek and moved to the Greenbrier River area, then to Fayette County, Kentucky. After her husband, James Rhea's death, Elizabeth married Newberry Stockton. Robert Rhea became guardian of his brother's four youngest children (Mary "Polly," Hannah, Martha and John).

Known children of James Rhea and Elizabeth Meek:

Nancy Rhea Ritchey (James, C.5. William, B.3. Archibald, A.1. Matthew) Nancy married Joseph Ritchey in Knox County, Tennessee. They lived in Tennessee.

Elizabeth Rhea (James, C.5. William, B.3. Archibald, A.1. Matthew) Elizabeth married her first cousin, Robert Rhea, son of her Uncle William. Robert became guardian of her four youngest siblings after her father died and her mother remarried Newberry Stockton. They lived in Kentucky, then moved to Ohio.

James Rhea, Jr. (James, C.5. William, B.3. Archibald, A.1. Matthew) James was born in what was Greenbrier County, Virginia now West Virginia. James married Rachel Jolliff. They acquired land in Barren County, Kentucky and later moved to Jefferson County, Illinois.

Margaret Rhea Barnett (James, C.5. William, B.3. Archibald, A.1. Matthew) Margaret married William Barnett. In 1803, they lived in Barren County, Kentucky.

Thomas Rhea (James, C.5. William, B.3. Archibald, A.1. Matthew) Thomas was born in what was Greenbrier County, Virginia. Thomas married his cousin Martha Rhea, daughter to his Uncle Robert. They were married in Bath County, Virginia. They moved to Barren County, Kentucky.

Mary "Polly" Rhea Hickman (James, C.5. William, B.3. Archibald, A.1. Matthew) Mary married Thomas Rhea (thought to be a cousin, son of her Uncle Robert Rhea). Her second marriage was to James Hickman in 1819 in Barren County, Kentucky.

Hannah Rhea Hickman (James, C.5. William, B.3. Archibald, A.1. Matthew) Hannah married Noah Hickman.

Martha Rhea (James, C.5. William, B.3. Archibald, A.1. Matthew)

John Rhea (James, C.5. William, B.3. Archibald, A.1. Matthew) John was born in Barren County, Kentucky.

WILLIAM RHEA, JR. (C.5. William, B.3. Archibald, A.1. Matthew) William was born about 1754 in Augusta County, Virginia. He died about 1824 in Green County, Kentucky. William married Mary Gay and had three children. After Mary's death, William married his second wife, Elizabeth Brownlee Nelson (widow of Thomas Nelson, Jr.), and had eight children. In 1781, he was appointed constable in Rockbridge County. William, Jr. sold his property on Mill Creek in 1790 to Samuel McDonald. The house stood one-quarter mile north of the northern end of Bath County Road 654 and was still standing in 1991. In 1795, he sold his property in Rockbridge County. In 1796 to 1798, he moved to Kentucky. It is thought he is buried in the Rhea Cemetery on what was his plantation located several miles northwest of Greensburg, Kentucky.

Known children of William Rhea, Jr. and Mary Gay:

Robert Rhea (William, Jr., C.5. William, B.3. Archibald, A.1. Matthew) Robert was born in Augusta County, Virginia. Robert married his first cousin Elizabeth, daughter of his Uncle James. He became guardian to Elizabeth's four younger siblings when his Uncle James died, and her mother remarried. They moved from Kentucky to Ohio. Robert's second marriage was to Elizabeth Hornbaker. In 1841, he moved to a farm in Jay County, Indiana. His third marriage was to Hannah Peterson. Robert died in Jay County, Indiana.

Agnes Nancy Rhea Wells (William, Jr., C.5. William, B.3. Archibald, A.1. Matthew) Born in Augusta County, Virginia. Agnes married William Wells in Green County, Kentucky.

Archibald Rhea (William, Jr., C.5. William, B.3. Archibald, A.1. Matthew) Archibald was born in Rockbridge County, Virginia. Archibald married Elizabeth (last name unknown). He moved to Green County, Kentucky.

Known children of William Rhea, Jr. and Elizabeth Brownlee Nelson:

John Rhea (William, Jr., C.5. William, B.3. Archibald, A.1. Matthew) Unmarried.

Alexander Rhea (William, Jr., C.5. William, B.3. Archibald, A.1. Matthew) Alexander married Polly/Mary Allen in Green County, Kentucky.

Anne (Anny) Rhea Hutcheson (William, Jr., C.5. William, B.3. Archibald, A.1. Matthew) Born in Rockbridge County, Virginia. Anne married David Hutcheson (Hutchason) in Green County, Kentucky.

William Rhea (William, Jr., C.5. William, B.3. Archibald, A.1. Matthew) Born in Rockbridge County, Virginia. William married Isabella Abney in Green County, Kentucky. His second marriage was to Mrs. Tamer McKinney.

Thomas Rhea (William, Jr., C.5. William, B.3. Archibald, A.1. Matthew) Thomas married Mary Winne (Bullock) in Green County, Kentucky. Thomas died in Green County, Kentucky and is buried in the Rhea Cemetery in Green County.

Elizabeth Rhea Gum (William, Jr., C.5. William, B.3. Archibald, A.1. Matthew) Elizabeth was born in Rockbridge County, Virginia. She married Charles Gum in Green County, Kentucky.

Clarissa Rhea Minton (William, Jr., C.5. William, B.3. Archibald, A.1. Matthew) She was born in Green County, Kentucky. Clarissa married Daniel Minton.

Narcissa Rhea Dills Blakeman (William, Jr., C.5. William, B.3. Archibald, A.1. Matthew) She was born in Green County, Kentucky. Narcissa married William Dills. Her second marriage was to Moses Blakeman. Narcissa is thought to be a twin to Clarissa.

ALEXANDER RHEA (C.5. William, B.3. Archibald, A.1. Matthew) (abt. 1755-1818) Alexander was born about 1755. He died 1818 in Hopkins County, Kentucky. He married Mary Crockett on December 4, 1782 in Augusta County, Virginia. In 1799-1800, Alexander Rhea lived in Henderson County, Kentucky, which later becomes Hopkins County, Kentucky. He was a wheelwright.

Known children of Alexander Rhea and Mary Crockett:

Eleanor Rhea (Alexander, C.5. William, B.3. Archibald, A.1. Matthew)

William Rhea (Alexander, C.5. William, B.3. Archibald, A.1. Matthew) William owned a mill on the Tradewater in Henderson County, Kentucky.

ROBERT RHEA (C.5. William, B.3. Archibald, A.1. Matthew) Robert was born in 1759 in Augusta County, Virginia (now Rockbridge County) and died October 31, 1834 in Pocahontas County, Virginia (now West Virginia). He married his first wife, Martha Meek, in 1781, and his brother James married Martha's sister, Elizabeth. Both families located to Greenbrier County (currently in West Virginia). Robert and Martha had five children. Robert and Martha divorced, and Robert marred his second wife, Catherine Boiler, in 1798. Catherine was a sister to the wife of Robert's son William. At the time of his death, Robert had 575 acres of land in his inventory of property.

Known children of Robert Rhea and Martha Meek:

William Rhea (Robert, C.5. William, B.3. Archibald, A.1. Matthew) (1782-1855) William was born in Greenbrier County, Virginia (later becomes West Virginia). William married Elizabeth Boiler in Bath County, sister to his father's second wife, Catherine. They lived in what is now Pocahontas County, West Virginia and later moved to Ohio. William is buried in Givens Chapel Cemetery, Givens, Pike County, Ohio.

Martha Rhea Rhea (Robert, C.5. William, B.3. Archibald, A.1. Matthew) Martha married Thomas Rhea, son of her Uncle James Rhea. They moved to Barren County, Kentucky.

Thomas Rhea (Robert, C.5. William, B.3. Archibald, A.1. Matthew) Thought to have married his cousin Mary (Polly), daughter to his Uncle James Rhea. Siblings married cousin siblings. Thomas lived in Barren County, Kentucky.

Samuel Rhea (Robert, C.5. William, B.3. Archibald, A.1. Matthew) He was born in Greenbrier County, Virginia (now West Virginia). Samuel died in Pocahontas County, West Virginia.

Robert Rhea, Jr. (Robert, C.5. William, B.3. Archibald, A.1. Matthew) Robert was born in what was Greenbriar County, Virginia (now West Virginia). Robert married Elizabeth Prince in Hopkins County, Kentucky. He died in Hopkins County, Kentucky and is buried in Odd Fellows Cemetery.

Known children of Robert Rhea and Catherine Boiler:

James Rhea (Robert, C.5. William, B.3. Archibald, A.1. Matthew) James was born in Greenbrier County, Virginia (now West Virginia). He married Betty Callison in Pocahontas County, Virginia (now West Virginia). His second marriage was to Sarah Goodwin (Goodman). He moved to Missouri.

Nancy Rhea (Robert, C.5. William, B.3. Archibald, A.1. Matthew) She was born in Greenbrier County, Virginia (now West Virginia). Nancy died at four years old (1801-1805).

Elizabeth Rhea (Robert, C.5. William, B.3. Archibald, A.1. Matthew) Elizabeth was born in Greenbrier County, Virginia (now West Virginia). She died at two years old (1803-1805).

Hannah Rhea Callison (Robert, C.5. William, B.3. Archibald, A.1. Matthew) She was born in Greenbrier County, Virginia (now West Virginia). Hannah married James Callison in 1828 in Pocahontas County, Virginia (now West Virginia).

Anne Rhea Hill (Robert, C.5. William, B.3. Archibald, A.1. Matthew) Anne was born in Greenbrier County, Virginia (now West Virginia). She married William Hill in 1828.

David Rhea (Robert, C.5. William, B.3. Archibald, A.1. Matthew) David was born in Bath County, Virginia. He married Ruth Kinnison in Bath County. By 1836 -1838, he was living in LaGrange County, Indiana. He also lived in Clinton County, Iowa.

Archibald Rhea (Robert, C.5. William, B.3. Archibald, A.1. Matthew) Archibald was born in Greenbrier County, Virginia (now West Virginia). He married Jeanette Beard in 1838. He died in Johnson County, Missouri in 1902.

ANN/ANNA RHEA LOCKRIDGE (C.5. William, B.3. Archibald, A.1. Matthew) Ann was born about 1762 in Augusta County, Virginia. She died November 1837 in Augusta County, Virginia. Ann married John Lockridge.

Known children of Ann Rhea and John Lockridge:

Andrew Lockridge (Ann Lockridge, C.5. William, B.3. Archibald, A.1. Matthew) Born in Augusta County, Virginia. Andrew married Easter Torbett.

William Lockridge (Ann Lockridge, C.5. William, B.3. Archibald, A.1. Matthew) Born in Augusta County, Virginia.

John Lockridge (Ann Lockridge, C.5. William, B.3. Archibald, A.1. Matthew) Born in Augusta County, Virginia. John married Ann Elizabeth Ervine. Their son John Ewing Lockridge was a doctor and married his cousin, Lydia M. Coyner.

James Lockridge (Ann Lockridge, C.5. William, B.3. Archibald, A.1. Matthew) Born in Augusta County, Virginia. James married Eliza Ervine.

Betsy Lockridge (Ann Lockridge, C.5. William, B.3. Archibald, A.1. Matthew) Born in Augusta County, Virginia.

Sarah Lockridge Buchanan (Ann Lockridge, C.5. William, B.3. Archibald, A.1. Matthew). Born in Augusta County, Virginia. Sarah married Hugh P. Weir Buchanan. Sarah died in Ohio.

Ann Lockridge (Ann Lockridge, C.5. William, B.3. Archibald, A.1. Matthew) Born in Augusta County, Virginia.

JOHN S. RHEA (D.8.) (C.5. William, B.3. Archibald, A.1. Matthew) John was born about 1752. **JOHN IS A DIRECT ANCESTOR TO PALMER RHEA, SR. SEE CHAPTER ON JOHN S. RHEA.**

Known children of John Rhea and Margaret Turk were *(According to The Bicentennial History of Bath County, Virginia):*

Elizabeth Rhea Wright (D.8. John, C.5. William, B.3. Archibald, A.1. Matthew) Born about 1775. Elizabeth married Toliver Wright on July 31, 1797.

William Rhea (D.8. John, C.5. William, B.3. Archibald, A.1. Matthew). Moved to Tennessee.

John Rhea (D.8. John, C.5. William, B.3. Archibald, A.1. Matthew) Moved to Tennessee.

Margaret Rhea Wright (D.8. John, C.5. William, B.3. Archibald, A.1. Matthew) She was born about 1781. Margaret married William Wright.

Thomas Turk Rhea (See E.9.) (D.8. John, C.5. William, B.3. Archibald, A.1. Matthew) Thomas was born about 1783 in Augusta County, Virginia. Thomas married Sally (Sarah) Lynch in 1807. He died 1842 in Bath County, Virginia. He was the only child of John and Margaret Turk Rhea who remained in Bath County, Virginia. **THOMAS IS A DIRECT**

ANCESTOR OF PALMER RHEA, SR. SEE CHAPTER ON THOMAS TURK RHEA.

Ann Rhea (D.8. John, C.5. William, B.3. Archibald, A.1. Matthew)

James Rhea (D.8. John, C.5. William, B.3. Archibald, A.1. Matthew)

Jane Rhea (D.8. John, C.5. William, B.3. Archibald, A.1. Matthew)

Polly Rhea (D.8. John, C.5. William, B.3. Archibald, A.1. Matthew)

Known children of John Rhea and Magdalena Dill (*According to The Bicentennial History of Bath County, Virginia*):

Nancy P. Rhea (D.8. John, C.5. William, B.3. Archibald, A.1. Matthew)

Hiram Rhea (D.8. John, C.5. William, B.3. Archibald, A.1. Matthew) Hiram was born 1813 in Bath County, Virginia. He married Hannah Helms.

Sarah Rhea (D.8. John, C.5. William, B.3. Archibald, A.1. Matthew)

Henry Dill Rhea (D.8. John, C.5. William, B.3. Archibald, A.1. Matthew)

Esther J. Rhea (D.8. John, C.5. William, B.3. Archibald, A.1. Matthew)

Mary Rhea (D.8. John, C.5. William, B.3. Archibald, A.1. Matthew)

(Children's names were documented in the wills of both parents in a Chancery Court suit filed in Augusta County on July 19, 1804 (John Rhea vs. Wm. Rhea Heirs).

Names of family members of William Rhea, Sr. were taken from The Bicentennial History of Bath County, Virginia 1701-1991, The Bath County Historical Society, Heritage House Publishing, pp.324-331.

Names confirmed with The Descendants of Matthew "The Rebel" Rhea of Scotland and Ireland by Edward Foley, Heritage Books, 2008.

Names and dates of family members were also confirmed with ancestry. com, court records, family Bibles, and Rhea family researches.)

ROBERT RHEA OF AUGUSTA COUNTY

THIRD GENERATION

ONE OF THE THREE RHEA BROTHERS OF AUGUSTA COUNTY

ROBERT RHEA (C.6.) (Reagh, Reah, Reagh) (B.3. Archibald, A.1. Matthew) (born abt. 1720 – died 1779) Robert is thought to be born about 1720 in Ireland to Archibald Rhea and Ann (last name unknown). He died in 1779 in current day Washington County, Virginia. Robert is one of the three brothers recorded in Augusta County in the mid-1700s. If indeed these three Rheas were brothers as historians have noted, Robert is not a direct ancestor to Palmer Rhea, Sr. but was a great uncle several times removed.

Robert was a carpenter and joiner and owned silversmithing tools. He married Sarah Bingham in Augusta County, Virginia. Sarah was the daughter to John and Sarah Bingham who had a large land grant in Beverly Manor. Robert was first recorded in Augusta County in 1754 when he purchased 118 acres of adjoining land to his brothers in Borden Grant on Hays or Walkers Creek located about sixteen miles north of Lexington. In current day, this land is in Rockbridge County.

Acquisition of Land from Chalkley's:

Page 10.—2d May, 1758. Robert Reagh (Reah, Reaoh), carpenter and joiner, and Sara to Archibald Reah, Jr., yeoman, £60, 118 acres on Hays Creek; corner widow Smyley. Teste: Win. Reah. Delivered: Archibald Reah, 23d March, 1768. (Note: Robert Rhea was Archibald's brother).

Robert was one of six trustees who in 1754 signed the deed for the property of New Providence Church. This was *"organized in 1748 by members of the Pennsylvania congregation."* It is conceivable the Rheas came to Augusta County with the members of the Providence Presbyterian congregation located near Norristown, Pennsylvania.[43]

In 1758, Robert and Sarah sold their land in Borden Grant to Archibald Rhea, Jr., Robert's brother, and left Augusta County, moving to Mecklenburg County, North Carolina where Reverend Alexander Craighead had fled from Windy Cove in what was Augusta County and is now Bath County. Many left the county during these years, fleeing for their lives and those of their children to escape the frequent Indian attacks.

Robert's granddaughter Jane (daughter to Archibald) married Dr. Samuel Sevier, son of John Sevier the first governor of Tennessee. Robert's grandson Archibald (son to Archibald) married (second marriage) Catherine Sevier Campbell, daughter to John Sevier and sister to Samuel Sevier. Robert's granddaughter, Elizabeth Rhea (daughter to Archibald) married a Samuel Houston (unsure of relation in the Houston family) who lived in Roane County, Tennessee. Samuel was a blacksmith and farmer and some sources list him as a Reverend.

Known children of Robert Rhea and Sarah Bingham:

ISABELLA RHEA (C.6. Robert, B.3. Archibald, A.1. Matthew)

JOHN RHEA (C.6. Robert, B.3. Archibald, A.1. Matthew)

---

[43] The Bath County Historical Society, *The Bicentennial History of Bath County, Virginia 1701-1991*, Heritage House Publishing, pp.325-331.

ARCHIBALD RHEA (C.6. Robert, B.3. Archibald, A.1. Matthew)

ANN RHEA (C.6. Robert, B.3. Archibald, A.1. Matthew)

ROBERT RHEA, JR. (C.6. Robert, B.3. Archibald, A.1. Matthew)

ELIZABETH RHEA COYNER (C.6. Robert, B.3. Archibald, A.1. Matthew)

(Additional information on children is shown below.)

ISABELLA RHEA MCCLESKEY (C.6. Robert, B.3. Archibald, A.1. Matthew) (1752-January 20, 1803) Born about 1752 in Augusta County, Virginia. Isabella married a Mr. Paxton about 1772. Her second marriage was to James McCleskey in South Carolina. About 1790, they moved to Elbert County, Georgia where James was a Justice of the Peace. Isabella died January 20, 1803 in Jackson County, Alabama.

Known children of Isabella Rhea and James McCleskey:

Susannah McCleskey (Isabella, C.6. Robert, B.3. Archibald, A.1. Matthew)

David Henderson McCleskey (Isabella, C.6. Robert, B.3. Archibald, A.1. Matthew)

Martha McCleskey (Isabella, C.6. Robert, B.3. Archibald, A.1. Matthew)

James Rhea McCleskey (Isabella, C.6. Robert, B.3. Archibald, A.1. Matthew)

JOHN RHEA (C.6. Robert, B.3. Archibald, A.1. Matthew) (1754-1830) John was born about 1754 in what was at the time Augusta County, Virginia. He married Mary Gay. He fought in

Lord Dunmore's War in 1774. He was the administrator of his father's estate and negotiated the sale of his father's property on Cripple Creek. John moved to Tennessee. In 1830, he died in Roane County, Tennessee.

Known child of John Rhea and Mary Gay:

Mary Agnes Rhea Keagher (John, C.6. Robert, B.3. Archibald, A.1. Matthew) Born about 1781. Mary married Jacob Keagher.

ARCHIBALD RHEA (C.6. Robert, B.3. Archibald, A.1. Matthew) (1756-1793) Archibald was born about 1756 in Augusta County, Virginia. He had property adjoining his father Robert's on Cripple Creek. He married Margaret (last name unsure, some say Campbell). He fought in Lord Dunmore's War in 1774. He sold his land and moved to Knoxville, Tennessee. He operated a ferry and was a church Elder and served regularly on a jury. Archibald died in 1793 in Knoxville, Knox County, Tennessee and buried at Lebanon-in-the Fork Cemetery in Knoxville near the back door of the church, which is five miles east of Knoxville. This cemetery is also known as Three Rivers Cemetery and is a historic cemetery on the National Register of Historic Places. It is located at 2390 Asbury Road, Knoxville.

Among the first members of this Presbyterian church were the families of: James White, James Cozby, John Adair, James Armstrong, Deveraux Gilliam, Archibald Rhea, Sr., Archibald Rhea, Jr., James and Alexander Campbell, Jeremiah Jack, George McNutt, Col. Francis A. Ramsey, Thomas Gillespie, Robert Craighead, Robert Brooks, Joseph Love, Jacob Patton, and Robert Houston.[44]

Archibald was one of the first settlers at Lebanon, Tennessee. His residence was:

> *. . . immediately at Gilliam's, across the French Broad. His house stood about 400 yards from the bank of the river, near to high*

---

[44] Dr. J. G. M. Ramsey's, "History of Lebanon Presbyterian Church "In The Fork": Five Miles East of Knoxville, Tenn. (1918)", Part 3 of 3, 1875.

water mark. There being no spring on that part of the plantation, a well was dug close by the house or station, as it was also called, so that in case of a siege the besieged might still have a supply of water. After peace was made the buildings were moved out to the spring near the residence of Hon. C. Jones. The well was then filled up and can no longer be seen. Mr. Rhea is represented to have been a very worthy and pious man, but as he died in 1793, little is recollected of him. In 1826 a cedar headboard with his name upon it and the date 1793 is still standing, at the head of his grave near the back door of the present church.

His son, Archibald Rhea, Jr., was his successor in the eldership, some several years after. He continued to reside at the same place. He was an excellent man and a devout Christian. He acted as precentor for the congregation; he also taught music as a science and was not only an excellent singer but an experienced and successful teacher. His classes generally met him in the church. The sessions were always opened and closed with prayer by him, or by the minister if present. During recess or intermission of his school Mr. Rhea never allowed his scholars to indulge in any noisy amusements in or around the house of God. He said, «there must be perfect quietness maintained.» This injunction was never allowed to be violated. He had a sweet, clear enunciation and gave out the hymns in public worship with great calmness and precision. I recollect on one occasion at church he came to the stanza:

"There my best friends, my kindred dwell,
There my God, my Saviour reigns."

So impressible was he and his emotional nature so excitable, that his voice trembled, he bursted into tears, handed the book to the preacher and sat down weeping, powerless and subdued by his feelings.

Mr. Rhea was married to one of the daughters of Governor Sevier, and one of the sons of the Governor had married a sister of Mr. Rhea. This relationship brought the two families much together. The Governor's ladies always occupied Mr. Rhea's pew in the church, while the Governor always sat at the head of Dr. Cozby's more fashionable pew at the opposite side of the house. About 1815 Mr. Rhea moved to Knoxville where he became the precentor again for Rev. Thos. Nelson pastor of the Presbyterian church here. He then moved to Alabama, and while there he died. I think I have heard that a son of his, James White Rhea, became a ruling Elder of some church in North Alabama.[45]

His son Archibald married (second marriage) Catherine Sevier Campbell, daughter to John Sevier, the first governor of Tennessee and his daughter Jane married John Sevier's son Dr. Samuel Sevier. Archibald's daughter Elizabeth married a Samuel Houston. (I am unsure if this Samuel Houston is related to the well-known Samuel Houston family, although both families were at one time in Augusta County and it is very likely a relation. I did not research what relationship.)

Known children of Archibald Rhea and Margaret:

Archibald Rhea (Archibald, C.6. Robert, B.3. Archibald, A.1. Matthew) Born 1778. Archibald married Ann Humphreys on October 16, 1798. On February 10, 1803, his second marriage was to Catherine Sevier, widow of Robert Campbell and daughter of John Sevier, first governor of Tennessee.

Robert Rhea (Archibald, C.6. Robert, B.3. Archibald, A.1. Matthew) Born about 1783. Robert married Olivia Connelly on June 6, 1809. Children: Ann Rhea, James White Rhea, William Rhea, John Rhea, Archibald, Robert W. Rhea, Calvin M. Rhea, Hugh G. Rhea, Miller Rhea, Andrew M. Rhea, Mary J. Rhea and Jonathan Rhea.

---

[45] Dr. Ramsey, J.G.M., *Lebanon "in the Fork" Presbyterian Church,* Founded 1791 by Rev. Samuel Carrick.

Ann Rhea Mitchell (Archibald, (C.6. Robert, B.3. Archibald, A.1. Matthew) Born 1783. Ann married Mr. Mitchell and moved to Alabama.

Jane Rhea Sevier (Archibald, C.6. Robert, B.3. Archibald, A.1. Matthew) (1786-1870). Jane married Dr. Samuel Sevier, brother to Catherine Sevier and son of John Sevier, first governor of Tennessee. They moved to Russellville, Alabama.

Sarah Rhea Wear (Archibald, C.6. Robert, B.3. Archibald, A.1. Matthew) Sarah married George Wear.

Elizabeth Rhea Houston (Archibald, C.6. Robert, B.3. Archibald, A.1. Matthew) Elizabeth married Samuel Houston. Children: James Turke Houston, Sarah Houston, Catherine M. Houston, Huldah Cusick Houston, Elvira Mason Houston, Samuel Houston, Jr., Benjamin Franklin Houston, Robert Burns Houston, Margaret Augusta Houston, Martha Willis Houston, Ann Elizabeth Houston, William Francis Houston and Clementine Houston.

Mary Rhea (Archibald, C.6. Robert, B.3. Archibald, A.1. Matthew)

Rebecca Rhea Hamilton (Archibald, (C.6. Robert, B.3. Archibald, A.1. Matthew) Born about 1790 in Knoxville, Tennessee. Rebecca married a Hamilton.

ANN RHEA TURK (C.6. Robert, B.3. Archibald, A.1. Matthew) (1759-1836) Ann was born about 1759 in Mecklenburg County, North Carolina. She married Thomas Turk, Jr (1755-1833) in 1776-1777 in Augusta County, Virginia. Thomas was a Revolutionary War veteran. They spent most of their lives in Augusta County but later moved to Blount County, Tennessee. Ann died in 1836 in Blount County, Tennessee and is buried at the New Providence

Cemetery in Maryville, Blount County, also known as New Providence Presbyterian Church Cemetery. Thomas Turk, Jr. died in 1833 and is also buried at this cemetery.

Known children of Ann Rhea and Thomas Turk, Jr.:

James Turk (Ann, C.6. Robert, B.3. Archibald, A.1. Matthew). (1780–1835) James married Mary Thompson (another source states he married Mary "Polly" Marcland). He died in 1835 and is buried at Bellefonte Cemetery, Bellefonte, Jackson County, Alabama. He was a saddler in the leather industry. He owned a stagecoach inn at Bellefonte, according to ancestor (Sandra Johnson: Find a Grave).

Robert Turk (Ann, C.6. Robert, B.3. Archibald, A.1. Matthew) Robert was born about 1780 in Mecklenburg County, North Carolina.

Thomas Turk III (Ann, C.6. Robert, B.3. Archibald, A.1. Matthew). (1782-1826). Thomas moved to Kentucky. He married his cousin, Margaret "Peggy" Gleaves, daughter of William Geaves and his aunt Elizabeth Turk Gleaves. After his first wife Margaret died, he married a second time to Mary Gleaves (not documented in court records but stated in family Bible.)[46]

Margaret Turk Robertson (Ann, C.6. Robert, B.3. Archibald, A.1. Matthew) Born about 1784. Margaret married William Robertson. They moved to Indiana.

Sally Turk (Ann, C.6. Robert, B.3. Archibald, A.1. Matthew)

Elizabeth Turk Harris (Ann, C.6. Robert, B.3. Archibald, A.1. Matthew) Born about 1792. Elizabeth married Thomas Harris. They moved to Missouri.

Archibald Rhea Turk (Ann, C.6. Robert, B.3. Archibald, A.1. Matthew) (1794-1843) Archibald married Gincy Jane Maupine. He died in McMinn County, Tennessee.

William Turk (Ann, C.6. Robert, B.3. Archibald, A.1. Matthew) William married Sarah H. Harris. They moved to Tennessee.

Hiram Kerr Turk (Ann, C.6. Robert, B.3. Archibald, A.1. Matthew) Hiram was born about 1798.

(Children and birth dates confirmed by "The Bicentennial History of Bath County, Virginia 1791-1991", The Bath County Historical Society.)

---

[46] *The Descendants of Matthew Gleaves*, The Glaves/Gleaves Family in America, The Gleaves Family Association 2009.

ROBERT RHEA, JR. (C.6. Robert, B.3. Archibald, A.1. Matthew). (1763 - February 15, 1850) Robert was born in 1763 in Mecklenburg County, North Carolina (at the time it was Anson County). He lived in Montgomery County, Virginia when he served in the Revolutionary War. He also served in the War of 1812. He married Mary Stephens in 1787. They moved to Knox County, Tennessee in 1790. After several years, they moved to Blount County. He was the first coroner of Blount County in 1795. He died in Blount County, Tennessee on February 15, 1850 at the age of 86. Mary died in Blount County in February 9, 1857. Robert, Jr. is buried in Chilhowee Primative Baptist Church Cemetery (also known as Red Top Primative Baptist Church), 7200 Happy Valley Road, Happy Valley, Blount County, Tennessee. For many years after Robert's death, Happy Valley was known as Rhea's Valley. Happy Valley is located near the Great Smoky Mountains National Park in a narrow valley.

Known children of Robert Rhea, Jr. and Mary Stephens:

Jehu Stephens Rhea (Robert, Jr., C.6. Robert, B.3. Archibald, A.1. Matthew)

Louis L. Rhea (Robert, Jr., C.6. Robert, B.3. Archibald, A.1. Matthew) (1797-1861). Louis married Martha Halloway.

Dillian Rhea (Robert, Jr., C.6. Robert, B.3. Archibald, A.1. Matthew) Dillian was disabled.

Mary Rhea (Robert, Jr., C.6. Robert, B.3. Archibald, A.1. Matthew) Born 1793 in Tennessee.

Elizabeth Rhea (Robert, Jr., C.6. Robert, B.3. Archibald, A.1. Matthew) Born 1804

ELIZABETH RHEA COYNER (C.6. Robert, B.3. Archibald, A.1. Matthew) (November 10, 1765 - August 24, 1841). Elizabeth was born in North Carolina. She died in Augusta County, Virginia. Elizabeth was about fourteen when her father died. She chose William Gleaves as her guardian. He was married to Elizabeth Turk, sister to Thomas Turk, Jr. who was married to Elizabeth Rhea's sister Ann Rhea. Elizabeth Turk was also sister to Margaret Turk, the first wife of Elizabeth's cousin John Rhea (C.5. William, B.3. Archibald, A.1. Matthew), son of William. Elizabeth married Martin Luther Coyner (1771-1842) in 1792 in Augusta County, Virginia and they had nine children. Elizabeth is buried at Mossy Creek Presbyterian Church Cemetery next to her husband at 372 Kyles Mill Road, Mount Salon, Augusta County, Virginia near the Presbyterian Church of which she was a member.

Mossey Creek Presbyterian Church and Cemetery

It was said by Hon. C. Luther Coyner that *"Elizabeth was of pure Scotch Irish blood and was descended on her father's side from Archibald 3rd Duke of Argyle, Scotland, so renowned in that country and England; and on her mother's side from the Binghams of New York, who had founded Binghamton, Broome County, in that State."*

In his book, *"A Historical Sketch of Michael Keinadt and Margaret Diller, his Wife"* he also states on page 109, *"The family of her sister (Mrs. Ann Turk) objected to Elizabeth marrying Martin Coyner, giving as a reason that he was a German and would make her work too hard, as she had been reared tenderly, and raised in the lap of luxury. To which she replied, she would marry Martin Coyner, if she had but one dress to her back."*

Known children of Elizabeth Rhea and Martin Luther Coyner:

John Coyner (Coiner) (Elizabeth, C.6. Robert, B.3. Archibald, A.1. Matthew) (1792/1793 - 1851/1852) John is buried at

East Hickman Cemetery, Nicholasville, Jessamine County, Kentucky.

Robert Crawford Coyner (Elizabeth, C.6. Robert, B.3. Archibald, A.1. Matthew) (1794-July 27, 1874) Robert is buried at South Salem Cemetery, South Salem, Ross County, Ohio.

Archibald Rhea Coyner (Elizabeth, C.6. Robert, B.3. Archibald, A.1. Matthew) (1797-unknown) Archibald was born in Rockingham County, Virginia. Archibald married Mary Brown. He is buried in Fairview Cemetery, Cherryvale, Montgomery County, Kansas.

Margaret Diller Coyner (Elizabeth, C.6. Robert, B.3. Archibald, A.1. Matthew) (1799-1887)

James Burgess Coyner (Elizabeth, C.6. Robert, B.3. Archibald, A.1. Matthew) (1801/1802 – 1864)

Sarah Bingham Coyner Bell (Elizabeth, C.6. Robert, B.3. Archibald, A.1. Matthew) (Born 1803) Sarah married James Bell. They had seven sons, six served in the Confederate Army, three died while in service.

Martin Luther Coyner (Elizabeth, C.6. Robert, B.3. Archibald, A.1. Matthew) (1805-1880) Born in Augusta County, Virginia. He is buried in Crown Hill Cemetery, Indianapolis, Marion Cunty, Indiana.

Rev. David H. Coyner (Elizabeth, C.6. Robert, B.3. Archibald, A.1. Matthew) (1807 - January 21, 1892) Born in Augusta County, Virginia. David was a minister of the Presbyterian Church for over 50 years. He received his education graduating at William and Mary in Virginia. David married Catherine McNeill. After Catherine's death, David married a second time to Catherine Eliza Snodgrass of Hardy County, Virginia. After his second wife's death, he married Frances Snodgrass, sister of his second wife. David was also an author and historian. He died January 21, 1892 in Kilbourne, Ohio. He is buried at Green Mound Cemetery, Kilbourne, Delaware County, Ohio. Chaplain of the 88th OVI Reg. at Camp Chase, Ohio. Known children: Homer, William Summer, Martin Luther, James B., Henry, Charles, Sarah, George, Frank, and Eliza Catherine.

Addison Hyde Coyner (Elizabeth, C.6. Robert, B.3. Archibald, A.1. Matthew) (1809 - November 17, 1856) Born in Augusta County, Virginia. He married Elizabeth Brown. Addison is buried at Rosewood Cemetery, Bloomington, McLean County, Illinois.

(Children and birth dates confirmed by "The Bicentennial History of Bath County, Virginia 1791-1991", The Bath County Historical Society.
(Children and dates confirmed by Ancestry.com and Find A Grave)
(Children and dates confirmed by "Columbia County Historian," History and Genealogy, Columbia County, Oregon, The Augusta Rhea Family)
(Children and birth dates confirmed by "The Descendants of Matthew 'The Rebel' Rhea of Scotland and Ireland," Edward F. Foley)

ARCHIBALD RHEA OF AUGUSTA COUNTY

THIRD GENERATION

ONE OF THE THREE RHEA BROTHERS OF AUGUSTA COUNTY

ARCHIBALD RHEA (C.7.) (B.3. Archibald, A.1. Matthew) (abt. 1725-1804). Archibald was born in Ireland in about 1725. The first record of Archibald was his land purchase in Borden Grant, where he purchased land in 1753 next to his brother William on Hays and Walker's Creeks. This land was approximately sixteen miles north of what was then Augusta County and current day would be near Lexington in Rockbridge County. Today it is known as "Zack." In 1758, Archibald bought his brother Robert's land in Borden Grant.

In 1758, Archibald along with his two brothers, William and Robert, served in the Augusta County Colonial Militia. Archibald married Jean McCausland.

Archibald wrote his Last Will and Testament in 1803 in Amherst County, Virginia and it was recorded on October 1804.

Thought to be children of Archibald Rhea and Jean McCausland:

JOHN S. RHEA (C.7. Archibald, B.3. Archibald, A.1. Matthew) (b. 1776). He married Sarah Scales. He moved to Lincoln County, Tennessee.

ROBERT RHEA (C.7. Archibald, B.3. Archibald, A.1. Matthew)

ANDREW RHEA (C.7. Archibald, B.3. Archibald, A.1. Matthew)

Thought to be children of Archibald Rhea and wife unknown. Wife may have been Jean or another wife:

ISABELLA RHEA (C.7. Archibald, B.3. Archibald, A.1. Matthew) (b. 1758)

ANN RHEA (C.7. Archibald, B.3. Archibald, A.1. Matthew)

JEAN RHEA (C.7. Archibald, B.3. Archibald, A.1. Matthew) (b.1762)

MARTHA RHEA WORKMAN (C.7. Archibald, B.3. Archibald, A.1. Matthew) (b. 1766) Married Samuel Workman

REBECKEA RHEA (C.7. Archibald, B.3. Archibald, A.1. Matthew)

ARCHIBALD RHEA (C.7. Archibald, B.3. Archibald, A.1. Matthew) (b. 1772) He moved to Tennessee.

WILLIAM RHEA (C.7. Archibald, B.3. Archibald, A.1. Matthew)

MARY RHEA ALLEN (C.7. Archibald, B.3. Archibald, A.1. Matthew) (b. 1784) Married Joseph Allen.

MARGARET RHEA
LOONEY RENFRO

THIRD GENERATION

EARLY AUGUSTA COUNTY

MARGARET RHEA (C.8.) (B.4. Matthew, A.1. Matthew) (1722-1803) Margaret lived in Augusta County, Colonial Virginia as early as 1742. Her arrival in America and even Colonial Virginia may have been earlier. This is the same time period as the three Rhea brothers, Robert, Archibald and William lived in the county. (Researchers and family thought they were brothers and considered them as such, so in this writing I will refer to them as brothers).[47] Margaret was near in age as the three brothers and most probably a cousin. There was an elder Archibald Rhea documented as living in Augusta County at the time thought to be the father of the three Rhea brothers.

Margaret was born in 1722 in Fahan Parrish, County Donegal, Ireland.[48] This is a district in the north of County Donegal in Ulster, located three miles south of Buncrana. She was daughter to Matthew Campbell Rhea II (Reagh) who was born in 1689 in Ulster, Ireland[49]

---

[47] The Bath County Historical Society, *The Bicentennial History of Bath County, Virginia,* 1791-1991, pp. 324-331, Heritage House Publishing Marcelina, MO.

[48] *Ancestry.com. U.S., Find A Grave Index, 1600s-Current* [database on-line]. Provo, UT, USA: Ancestry.com Operations, Inc., 2012.

[49] *Ancestry.com.* Global, *Find A Grave Index for Burials at Sea and other Select Burial Locations, 1300s-Current* [database on-line]. Provo, UT, USA: Ancestry.com Operations, Inc., 2012.

and Elizabeth McClain, second wife to Matthew Campbell Rhea II. Margaret Rhea was sister to Rev. Joseph Rhea of Ireland among others and granddaughter to Matthew Rhea of the Campbell Clan of Scotland.

Much has been written of Margaret's older brother Rev. Joseph Rhea and his descendants, one being John Rhea who was chosen the first representative from Sullivan County, Tennessee to the legislature and in 1803 was elected to Congress from the First District.[50]

What is current day Sullivan County, Tennessee is the area Margaret Rhea along with other family migrate to upon leaving their homes in Augusta County, Virginia. At the time they moved to Sullivan County, Tennessee, the land was part of Washington County. Sullivan County was not created until 1779 and was created from Washington District and territory formerly part of Virginia. Margaret Rhea Looney Renfro will spend her elder years in Tennessee, and in 1803 at the age of 81 she died in Kingsport, Sullivan County, Tennessee.

Margaret Rhea left her mark on Colonial Virginia and Tennessee as one of the early frontier women, enduring hardships and maintaining courage. She and her sons, because of their adventurous and bravery deeds, were instrumental in colonial frontier development.

MARGARET RHEA:

Born: 1722 in Fahan Parrish, County Donegal, Ireland

Death: 1803 in Kingsport, Sullivan County, Tennessee

Burial Location: Unknown

Father: Matthew Campbell Rhea II (Reagh), born 1689 in Ireland

Mother: Elizabeth McClain, born about 1690 in Ireland. She was second wife to Matthew Campbell Rhea II.

---

[50] *Foley, Edward F., The Descendants of Rev. Joseph Rhea of Ireland,* Heritage Books 2007.

Siblings: Abraham Rhea, Rev. Joseph Rhea, Agnes Rhea Latta, and James Rhea

Half-Siblings: Matthew Campbell Rhea III, William Rhea, Samuel Rhea, and Isaac Rhea.

Spouse (first): Married about 1742-1743 to Robert Looney, Jr., born about 1721 in Garff, Isle of Man. Robert's death was Feb. 15, 1756 at Reed Creek, located in Augusta County, Virginia. The land at the time of death was Augusta County, but later the land became part of Botetourt County, Virginia.

Spouse (second): Married April - June 1763[51] to Stephen Renfro. This was second marriages for both Stephen and Margaret. Both were widows. Stephen Renfro's oldest daughter, Esther Renfro, married John Looney, younger brother to Robert Looney, Jr. Stephen Renfro's youngest daughter Elizabeth Renfro married Margaret Rhea and Robert Looney, Jr.'s son John (Rhea) Looney, which resulted in Stephen Renfro being both stepfather and father-in-law to John (Rhea) Looney. Stephen Renfro, Sr. was born about 1707 in Fincastle, Botetourt County, Virginia. Stephen's death was 1804 in Knox County, Tennessee.

Children of Margaret Rhea and Robert Looney, Jr.:

JOHN (RHEA) LOONEY (C.8. Margaret, B.4. Matthew, A.1. Matthew) Born about 1744 in Looney Mill Creek, Augusta County, Virginia. Death thought to be about 1819 in Tennessee.

MOSES LOONEY (C.8. Margaret, B.4. Matthew, A.1. Matthew) Born about 1745/1748 in Augusta County, Virginia. Death on July 12, 1824 Knoxville, Tennessee.

---

[51] Source number: *115.000*; Source type: *Electronic Database*; Number of Pages: *1*; Submitter Code: *DNS.* Yates Publishing. *U.S. and International Marriage Records, 1560-1900* [database on-line]. Provo, UT, USA: Ancestry.com Operations Inc, 2004.

BENJAMIN RHEA LOONEY (C.8. Margaret, B.4. Matthew, A.1. Matthew) Born about 1748 in Augusta County, Virginia. Death 1783 near Cumberland Gap (slain by Indians).

SAMUEL RHEA LOONEY (C.8. Margaret, B.4. Matthew, A.1. Matthew) Born about 1754 in Augusta County, Virginia (another source lists birth as 1751). Death May 1779 while fighting Indians in Washington County, Virginia.

MARY LOONEY GRIMES: (C.8. Margaret, B.4. Matthew, A.1. Matthew) Born January 1756 in Augusta County, Virginia.

(Additional information on children is shown below.)

MARGARET RHEA AND ROBERT LOONEY, JR. Robert Looney, Jr. was born in 1721 in Garff, Isle of Man, a self-governing British dependency in the Irish Sea between Great Britain and Ireland. He migrated to Colonial Virginia with his parents, Robert Looney, Sr. and Elizabeth Looney and his siblings. Looney family men were well known as frontiersmen in Colonial Virginia and are mentioned in numerous books and Historical Society writings and ancestry family trees. Robert Looney, Sr. and his wife Elizabeth and children, consisting of at least seven sons, came to America first to Philadelphia in about 1731. They had additional children born in America, having a very large family. Robert Looney, Jr. was about ten years old when they arrived in America.

The Looney family were one of 70 families who formed a major settlement in Virginia, leaving Philadelphia about 1735, as they accompanied Alexander Ross and Morgan Bryan of Providence, Pennsylvania with expectations of a new life. Alexander Ross and Morgan Bryan had petitioned the Council of the Colony of Virginia for land patents for families desiring to settle in Virginia. Records show by 1732, the Looney family settled on a patent of 294 acres on the Cohongoronta River, a variant name for the Potomac River. The patent was near current day Hagerstown, Maryland, although at the time the acreage was part of Virginia. This land was undeveloped and country dark except for fireflies and starry nights and families were greeted with hills, thick trees, winding trails, streams and rivers. The Looney family made their home here for seven to eight years. Robert Looney, Sr. maintained ownership of these 294 acres near the Potomac River even after he and his family moved on to other land. In 1766, the land was sold.

In 1739-1740, seven to eight years after maintaining their home on the land near the Potomac River, Robert, Sr. and family joined an expedition and established their home in Augusta County, Virginia on the James River where he received a grant of 250 acres. As noted previously, Augusta County during those days encompassed numerous acres of land, which later would be divided into other counties as well as parts of other states. The Robert Looney, Sr. family settled on Looney Creek to make their home and raise their family. The land they settled in Augusta County would later become part of Botetourt County.[52]

In 1742, Robert, Sr. gained three more grants of land whereby he became prosperous. He donated land for the county seat. By the same year in 1742, Robert Looney, Sr. and family established the first ferry crossing the James River, built a mill, an orchard and raised livestock and eventually opened an Inn.[53] Because of the strategic location of his property, his home became a trading center and the family became well known in the area. The following sign which currently stands marks the location and establishment of the Looney ferry.

---

[52] Holiday, Donald R., *Ozarks Watch*, "The MacGiolla Dhomhnaights, or MacGillewneys, or Looneys of the Missouri-Arkansas Border", Vol. V, No. 4, Spring 1992.

[53] Kegley, *Virginia Frontier*, P. 163.

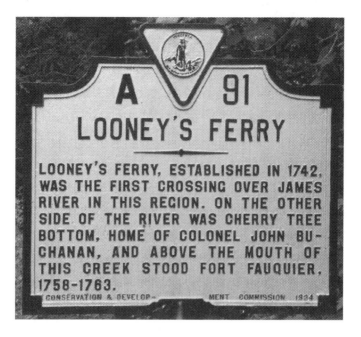

Looney's ferry was a landmark on the Great Wagon Road from Philadelphia leading south through Virginia and the current counties of Augusta, Rockingham and Rockbridge (at the time it was Augusta County) and on to the Carolinas. The Great Wagon Road was the road traveled by the new colonists and was described as follows:

> *Beginning at the port of Philadelphia, where many immigrants entered the colonies, the Great Wagon Road passed through the towns of Lancaster_and York in southeastern Pennsylvania.*
>
> *Turning southwest, the road crossed the Potomac River and entered the Shenandoah Valley near present day Martinsburg, West Virginia. It continued south in the valley via the Great Warriors Trail (also called the Indian Road), which was established by centuries of Indian travel over ancient trails created by migrating buffalo herds. (Also known as the Great Indian War and Trading Path or Seneca Trail.) The Shenandoah portion of the road is also known as the Valley Pike (An Indian trail which is*

now US Route 11). The Treaty of Lancaster in 1744 had established colonists› rights to settle along the Indian Road. Although traffic on the road increased dramatically after 1744, it was reduced to a trickle during the French and Indian War (Seven Years› War) from 1756 to 1763. But after the war ended, it was said to be the most heavily traveled main road in America.

South of the Shenandoah Valley, the road reached the Roanoke River at the town of Big Lick (today, Roanoke). South of Roanoke, the Great Wagon Road was also called the Carolina Road. At Roanoke, a road forked southwest, leading into the upper New River Valley and on to the Holston River in the upper Tennessee Valley. From there, the Wilderness Road led into Kentucky, ending at the Ohio River where flatboats were available for further travel into the Midwest and even to New Orleans.

From Big Lick/Roanoke, after 1748, the Great Wagon Road passed through the Maggoty Gap (also called Maggodee) to the east side of the Blue Ridge Mountains. Continuing south through the Piedmont region, it passed through the present-day North Carolina towns of Winston-Salem, Salisbury, and Charlotte and sites of earlier Indian settlements on the historic Indian Trading Path. The Great Wagon Road ultimately reached Augusta, Georgia, on the Savannah River, a distance of more than 800 miles (1,300 km) from Philadelphia.

Despite its current name, the southern part of this road was by no means passable by wagons until later colonial times. The 1751 Fry-Jefferson map notes the term "Waggon" only north of Winchester, Virginia. In 1753, a group of wagon travelers reported that "the good road ended at Augusta" (now Staunton, Virginia).[54]

---

[54] "Great Wagon Road", Wikimedia Foundation, Inc., last edited 18 December 2018.

The Looney homestead, mill, ferry, and inn were stopping points for travelers and those living in the area. Due to the French and Indian War (1754-1763), it was ordered a fort be built around the Looney homestead. It was named Fort Looney and was at the junction of Looney Creek and the James River. The French and Indian War pitted British American colonies against those of New France. Both were supported by military units from the parent country and by American Indian allies. This war was also known as the Seven Years' War during years 1756-1763. The Looney house and parts of this fort stood until 1914, over one hundred seventy years.

Colonel George Washington visited Fort Looney in 1756 and crossed Looney's ferry during his travels. By 1758, Fort Looney had been renamed to Fort Fauquier in honor of the newly arrived governor of the Colony, Francis Fauquier. Fort Fauquier operated until 1763, the end of the French and Indian War. Today, if still standing, the fort would be located on Looney Creek at the mouth of James River in Buchanan, Virginia in Botetourt County.

Robert Looney, Jr., Margaret Rhea's husband, was a member of the Augusta Virginia Colonial Militia, as were a couple of his brothers. They served under Captain George Robinson's Company No. 8.[55] Others in Company 8 were Pat Shirky, Ensign, James Ranfro, Serj. (brother to Stephen Renfro), James McFeron, Lieut., Dan Mananghan, Mark Eval, Peter Ranfro (brother to Stephen Renfro), George Draper, Robert Roland, Edm. Smith, Francis Kelly, Andrew Gaughagall, Henry Stiles, Henry Philip, Thomas Looney (brother to Robert), Daniel Looney (brother to Robert), Adm. Looney, Mark Joans, John Smith, John Askins, Hugh Caruthers, John Flower, William Bradshay, James Coal, John Coal, Bryan Cass, William Craven, Cornel. Dougherty, Simon Acres, William Acres, Nicolas Horsford, Josh Tasker, Mealore, Henry Brown, Samuel Brown, James Burk, William Bean, Evins, Samuel Martin, Peter Kinder, Stevan Evens, Peter Watkins, Stephen Ranfro,

---

[55] Clearfield, *Virginia Colonial Militia*, Virginia County Records, Vol II, 1651-1776, edited by William Armstrong Crozier.

Benjamin Davis, William Clark, William Sheperd and Benjamin Dearon.[56]

Along with the Looney brothers, serving in this unit were the Renfro brothers (one of which Margaret will marry years following her husband Robert's death). The unit was comprised of men living in the same general area.

During 1742, Margaret's husband Robert Looney, Jr. as did his dad, made a living as a farmer living in Augusta County on a land grant of 213 acres beginning at the South side of Looney's Mill Creek and extended to Beaver Dam Swamp. This was also the year of his marriage to Margaret Rhea. At the ages of 20 and 21 years old, Margaret Rhea and Robert Looney, Jr. married. No records were located as to how Margaret and Robert, Jr. met but as the area was sparsely populated and the Looney families were well established with ferry, mill and inn, and known throughout the area, Margaret and Robert, Jr. could have easily met through mutual friends or family and there is the possibility the families knew one another prior to coming to Virginia.

Although nothing written was discovered about the wedding celebration, whether it be a small or large celebration, there are recorded typical weddings in Augusta County during these colonial days. Men and women married young, even younger than Robert and Margaret. Weddings attracted attention of the entire settlement and as little social life was available, all got involved in the wedding celebration. Weddings were followed with games and dancing and drinking, and the partying could last for days. According to the Annuals of Augusta County, there was no minister of the "Established Church" in the Valley until 1747. Couples who lived there and wished to marry had to travel to Orange or other locations to search for a minister authorized to perform marriages unless a minister traveled through the area.[57]

Margaret Rhea and Robert Looney, Jr. had five children: John

---

[56] *Draper MSS.*, Hist. Soc. of Wisconsin. "Militia Companies in Augusta County", in 1742, The Virginia Magazine of History and Biography, Vol. 8, No. 3 (Jan. 1901), pp. 278-283, Virginia Historical Society.

[57] Waddell, Jos. A., *Annals of Augusta County, Virginia*, p. 383.

Looney, Moses Looney, Benjamin Rhea Looney, Sr., Samuel Rhea Looney, Sr. and Mary Rhea Grimes.

Thirteen to fourteen years after marriage, life for Margaret and her children changed drastically. On February 15, 1756, Robert Looney, Jr. along with a Dutch man by the name of Lieutenant Wright were killed by Indians on Reed's Creek near Alex Sawyer's, which today is in Wythe County, Virginia and was east of Kings Mill, which will later be called Kingsport, Tennessee. Looney's gravesite is unknown.

James Burk also served in the Augusta County Militia under Captain George Robinson's Company along with Looney. It was James Burk who brought word of Looney's killing, and he had one horse shot and five taken away by the Shawnee Indians.[58] An account of Burk's encounter with the Indians during these attacks is as follows:

> *About Valentine's Day 1756, James was still in Burke's Garden but had evidently sent his family out in 1755 when the Indian war began. This February day James discovered Indians near his house, so he mounted one of his horses and tried to avoid them. They shot his horse and he outran them in a foot race. He ran through Walker's Gap, across Poor Valley, through the gap in Brushy Mountain into Bear Garden near Ceres. After crossing Walker's Mountain he went east to the cabin of Alexander Sayers where he learned that Indians had just killed Robert Looney. He hurried on and got to Andrew Lewis's army gathering at Fort Frederick at Dunkard's Bottom on New River (present Claytor Lake). Lewis's force was to march against the Shawnee towns on Ohio. Burk said that Robert Looney had just been killed by Indians on Reed Creek and he himself had lost six horses to them but escaped.[59]*

---

[58] Holliday, Donald R., *Ozarks Watch*, "The MacGiolla Dhomhnaights, or MacGillewneys, or Looneys of the Missouri-Arkansas Border", Vol. V, No. 4, Spring 1992.

[59] William Preston, *Sandy Creek Expedition Journal*, Feb. 1756.

When Robert Looney, Jr. died in 1756 at the age of 35 years old, Margaret was about 34 and left as a widow to care for five children in a hostile frontier land. At the time of Robert's death, their eldest son John would have been about twelve years old, Moses, eleven years old; Benjamin, eight years old; Samuel, two years old; and Mary was a baby. To endure such hardships while living in a tough and unfriendly frontier land would require an exuberant amount of strength and courage, which Margaret apparently possessed. Margaret Looney qualified as Administratrix in court of her deceased husband on March 17, 1756.

Absalom Looney, younger brother to Robert Looney, Jr. and brother-in-law to Margaret Rhea was the fifth son of Robert Looney, Sr. and Elizabeth. Although Absalom Looney is not a member of the Rhea family, he was related to Margaret Rhea through marriage and lived in the same time period and same area. Much has been written about Absalom as a frontiersman, trapping and hunting. While doing so and staying in caves to avoid the Indians, Absalom discovered a fertile valley, rich in pastures, situated between two ridges. He is considered the first white person to explore the area. He later leads his family and others to this new settlement. This valley is located within twenty miles of current day Bluefield, Virginia. Following is a recorded account by a relative Mary Elizabeth Looney.

> Absalom, *fifth son of Robert and Elizabeth, born about 1729 in the Isle of Man, discovered in 1770 what is yet called Abb's Valley while on a hunting and scouting expedition in southwest Virginia, in what is now Tazewell County. Mary Elizabeth Looney notes that "Absolem...led his family and some followers and founded a settlement at least four years before that noted frontier explorer, Daniel Boone, arrived in the same area to build a fort only six miles from Absolem's homestead." Ab, Captain James Moore and his family, and Robert Poage and his family settled in the valley, but during the early part of the Revolution, with Indian attacks continuing and the militia called to the Continental Army, the Poages abandoned the*

*valley; Ab and his family, at his father's insistence, returned
to Fort Looney; and the Shawnee raided the valley and
killed or carried off the remaining Moore family. The
State Historical Society of Virginia has erected a bronze
tablet in memory of the tragedy and to mark the location
of Abb's Valley. It is on Route 85, five miles southwest of
Pocahontas, Virginia.*[60]

**MARGARET RHEA LOONEY AND STEPHEN RENFRO,
SR.** In 1763, seven years after her husband Robert Looney, Jr.'s death,
Margaret Rhea married Stephen Renfro. Stephen was born about 1707
(another source lists birth as 1710) in what will become Fincastle,
Botetourt County, Virginia. Botetourt County was not formed until
1770, so prior to that it was part of Augusta County. Margaret was 41

---

[60] Holliday, Donald R., *Ozarks Watch*, "The MacGiolla Dhomhnaights, or
MacGillewneys, or Looneys of the Missouri-Arkansas Border", Vol. V, No. 4, Spring
1992.

years old and Stephen about 53 years old at the time of their marriage. Like Margaret, Stephen was also a widow, his wife Esther Van Bibber having died in 1755.

As well as stepfather, in years to follow, Stephen will also become the father-in-law of Margaret's son John Looney (son of Robert Looney, Jr. and Margaret Rhea Looney) who married Stephen's younger daughter Elizabeth Renfro in 1773. This marriage took place ten years after Margaret Rhea and Stephen's marriage. Margaret will become stepmother and mother-in-law to Elizabeth Renfro upon Elizabeth's marriage to Margaret's son John. Margaret and Stephen had no children together.

Stephen Renfro had another connection to Margaret Rhea. His eldest daughter, Esther Renfro, married Margaret's brother-in-law John Looney (her husband Robert Looney, Jr.'s younger brother and son to Robert Looney, Sr. and Elizabeth Looney) in 1759 prior to Margaret and Stephen's marriage. It is this John Looney who was stated to have traveled with Daniel Boone for two to three years. Both of Stephen Renfro's daughters were married to a John Looney, one John Looney being an uncle to the other one. Stephen's daughter Esther, born in 1739, may have been the first white female born west of the Blue Ridge Mountains and south of the James River and is said to have been the first white female born in what is today Botetourt County.[61] With families being large in number and many of the children were named after other family members, tracing family roots can be complex and confusing.

Stephen Renfro and his brothers also served on the Augusta militia with Robert Looney, Jr. and his brothers.

In our search of the Rhea family, an interesting article appeared. Having grown up in the mountains myself it was not unusual to hear, "There's gold in them thar hills!" or "There's silver in them thar hills!" There was always the possibility of something being hidden in one of the obscure caves tucked deep into the mountains young and old love

---

[61] *Botetourt County Heritage Book*, 1770 – 2000, pp.153-155. Walsworth Publishing Company, Inc., E. Grose and the Botetourt Heritage Committee.

to explore. The following story about hidden silver involves Margaret Rhea's sister-in-law Mary Randolph who married Joseph Renfro (Stephen's older brother). This story supposedly occurred after Joseph's death. After reading this, you may go in search of the long-lost silver.

From Kingsport Times News, *November 22, 1964*

"Silver In Them Thar Hills?"
By L. F. Addington
Times-News Correspondent
Glamorgan, Virginia

. . . 200 years have thus far failed to reveal Swift's fatal secret that legend says brought sudden, violent death to six men and left the finder crazed. John Swift's story has been told and re-told in song and print until it has become a legend.

The single proven fact is that John Swift did exist, and did live in this mountain country in the mid-1700s. He was said to be a freebooter—mountain talk for a person having "some connection with pirates on the seas," and why he came to the hills has been lost in time.

But come he did, and he supposedly had several silver mines in the vicinity of Pine Mountain at Pound Gap.

Shawnee and Cherokee Indian legend has it that a mammoth cave runs through this portion of Pine Mountain. The area of the mountain above the cave rang hollow when their horses traveled over it, so the Shawnees called the place "Hollow Mountain." The cave was sacred to the Shawnees, for somewhere back in the mists of time they hid their women and children there from the Cherokees during a big battle.

The Shawnees lost the battle, but saved their families. Adding fuel to the big cave legend is the fact that the first road surveys through here called the road up Elkhorn Creek to a gap in Pine Mountain "the road from Pikeville to Sounding Gap."

Then Swift's eyesight began to fail, so he ordered the treasure buried and the small entrance to the cave stopped up and hidden. He went to the home of his lady friend, Mrs. Joseph Renfro at Bean's Station, Tenn., to rest.

Fearing total blindness, he later took four white men and two Shawnees to the Hollow Mountain to remove the silver. That's where greed overcame John Swift. He took his scalping knife and killed all six men. Then, crazed by his crime, he rode out of the wilderness and back to Mrs. Renfro.

The lady wheedled the story out of him, and was so shocked at the killings that she ordered Swift from her home. He left, but he also left his journal and a map with Mrs. Renfro. Fearing scandal, the lady hid the Journal and map and never mentioned them for many year. But she kept the documents, along with directions for finding the treasure cave. Swift? He went completely blind and could never find his silver cavern again, although he spent a lifetime searching for it. Neither has anyone else, although many there are who have tried.[62]

Stephen and Margaret Rhea Renfro, along with family members, including son Moses Looney, David Looney (brother to Robert Looney, Jr.), and some children of Absalom Looney (Robert Looney, Jr.'s brother) migrated to Tennessee. The date they moved was not recorded, but we know David Looney (brother to Robert Looney, Jr.), who accompanied them, was in Fincastle County, Virginia in 1774 as he was Captain of a volunteer militia for Fincastle County, Virginia for the Lord Dunmore's War, a war between the Colony of Virginia and the Shawnee and Mingo Indians. Fincastle County (derived from "Fine Castle," the English country

---

[62] *Kingsport Times News, November 22, 1964, "Silver In Them Thar Hills?" By L. F. Addington.*

estate of Lord Botetourt)[63] was created from Botetourt County in 1772[64] and was abolished in 1776 when it was divided into Montgomery County, Washington County, and Kentucky County. In 1792, these counties became portions of the Commonwealth of Kentucky[65] and two dozen Virginia/West Virginia counties.[66] Among those serving under Captain David Looney's Company for Fincastle County was Moses Looney and the well-known frontiersman Daniel Boone, who served as Lieutenant.[67]

By 1777, Margaret Rhea Renfro, Stephen Renfro, Moses Looney, David Looney, John (Rhea) Looney and some of the children of Absalom Looney were in what is current day Tennessee as they signed a petition as inhabitants of what at the time was lower Washington County, Virginia. The petition protested the erection of a courthouse. This land in current day would be in Sullivan County, Tennessee. These men and women played prominent parts in the defense of settlements against Indians and in the formation of the State of Franklin.

The State of Franklin was created in August 1784 and maintained until December 1788. It was never admitted into the Union as a state. This unrecognized territory was west of the Appalachian Mountains, which at the time was part of North Carolina and today is Northeast Tennessee. The territory had been offered as a cession to Congress by the State of North Carolina to help pay off debts related to the American War for Independence. The State of Franklin was intended to be the fourteenth state of the United States, but it was never admitted. When Congress did not admit Franklin as a state, North Carolina rescinded its offer.

The territory of the State of Franklin consisted of eight counties, which were Blount, Sevier, Caswell (modern Jefferson & Hamblen Counties), Spencer (modern Hawkins County), Greene (includes modern Cocke County), Washington (includes modern Unicoi County), Sullivan and Wayne (modern Johnson and Carter Counties). In modern

---

[63] Iberian Publishing Company's On-Line Catalog: *Fincastle County Virginia*, 2019.

[64] Pendleton, William C. (1920). "History of Tazewell County and Southwest Virginia: 1748-1920", pp. 255-57. W. C. Hill Printing Company.

[65] Kentucky: "Secretary of State - Land Office - Kentucky County Formations".

[66] Iberian Publishing Company's On-Line Catalog: *Fincastle County Virginia*, 2019.

[67] *Soldiers of Fincastle County, Virginia 1774.*

day, these counties are in Tennessee.[68] The President/Governor of the State of Franklin was Col. John Sevier. John Sevier, a tall, handsome and graceful man, was born September 23, 1745 in what was during the time in Augusta County, Virginia (current day it is Rockingham County).[69] John Sevier would have been the same age as Moses Rhea Looney and spent his early days in the same Virginia Valley.

Margaret Rhea's death at 81 years old was recorded as 1803 in Kingsport, Sullivan County, Tennessee, an area where many of her relatives migrated. Stephen Renfro's death at 97 years old was recorded as 1804 in Knox County, Tennessee. Margaret and Stephen were married for 40 years at the time of Margaret's death.

Descendants of Margaret Rhea and Robert Looney, Jr.

JOHN (RHEA) LOONEY (C.8. Margaret, B.4. Matthew, A.1. Matthew) John (Rhea) Looney, eldest son of Robert Looney, Jr. and Margaret Rhea, was born 1744 in Looney's Mill Creek, which at the time the land was in Augusta County, Virginia and later became part of Botetourt County. He was about 12 years old when his dad, Robert Looney, Jr., was killed by Indians.

Information on John Looney was difficult to decipher which John Looney the records pertained to as this John (Rhea) Looney (born 1744) had an Uncle John Looney, Sr. (born 1732), about 12 years his elder. These two John Looneys married sisters, Stephen Renfro's daughters. In our search, it seemed many of these records for both John Looneys were intertwined. Great care was taken to include information on John (Rhea) Looney that pertained to him. Both John Looneys had a father named Robert Looney (one being a Sr. and one a Jr.) and both mothers were named Elizabeth.

John (Rhea) Looney married Elizabeth Renfro (born 1745) on

---

[68] *State of Franklin*, Wikipedia, Feb. 25, 2019. https://en.wikipedia.org/wiki/State_of_Franklin.

[69] Williams, Samuel Cole S., *History of the Lost State of Franklin,* Press of the Pioneers, New York, 1933.

November 1773.[70] Another source indicates they were married in November 1770. [71]He was 26 years old and Elizabeth was about 25 at time of marriage. John migrated with his family to Tennessee along with Margaret Rhea and Stephen Renfro. The year the move took place is unknown, but records indicate that by 1777, a John Looney was among the family who signed a petition as an inhabitant in what was then Virginia but later became Sullivan County, Tennessee. The family may have moved to Sullivan County even years prior to this.

John Looney, Ensign, is among those listed as a Revolutionary Soldier at the battle of Kings Mountain that took place October 7, 1780, on a rocky hilltop nine miles south of present-day Kings Mountain, North Carolina and in what is Cherokee County, South Carolina.[72] Patriots from Southwest Virginia, Northwestern North Carolina, and Eastern Tennessee marched all night through rain to arrive at Kings Mountain. The battle was a bloody life and death struggle that resulted in an important American victory. In current day, there is a Kings Mountain National Military Park where the battle occurred.

MOSES (RHEA) LOONEY (C.8. Margaret, B.4. Matthew, A.1. Matthew) Moses was the second son of Robert Looney, Jr. and Margaret Rhea. He was born about 1745 in Augusta County, Virginia. He married Sarah Holstein (Holston) (1749-1833 or 1838). Sarah's death certificate on *"Find A Grave"* indicates date of death as 1838, but the gravesite stone has death date as 1833. Moses served in the militia, Soldiers of Fincastle County Virginia, as early as 1774. He served under David Looney's Company (his uncle's Company).

Moses Rhea Looney was one of the Overmountain Men, American frontiersmen who took part in the American Revolutionary War. He was listed among those as serving as a Revolutionary Soldier at the battle

---

[70] Yates Publishing. *U.S. and International Marriage Records, 1560-1900* [database on-line]. Provo, UT, USA: Ancestry.com Operations Inc, 2004. Source number: *116.000*; Source type: *Electronic Database*; Number of Pages: *1*; Submitter Code: *DNS*.

[71] Edmund West, comp., *Family Data Collection - Individual Records* [database on-line]. Provo, UT, USA: Ancestry.com Operations Inc, 2000.

[72] *Annals of Southwest Virginia*, 1769-1800, p. 1397.

of Kings Mountain.[73] He served as Lieutenant in the Patriot Militia. This battle took place on October 7, 1780 and was between Patriot and British Loyalist Militias during the Southern Campaign of the American Revolutionary War. His brother John Looney also fought in this battle. The Patriot militia defeated the Loyalist militia.

Moses motioned on behalf of Ann Cross, Administratrix of Samuel Looney, his deceased brother, for the Court to choose Guardians and Settle with the Administratrix on May 22, 1782.[74] During the Colonial period, the death of a husband required that a guardian be named for any minor children, even if the wife was still alive.

A National Register of Historic Places Inventory – Nomination Form filed February 2, 1977 with the United States Department of the Interior National Park Service has listed Moses Looney Fort House at 5436 Old Island Road, Kingsport, Sullivan County, Tennessee as a historic place. Date of the construction of the fort is not known. Moses Looney built his log home on a high ridge above the headwater spring for Fall Creek and beside the Military Road. The date the Military Road was built was 1761. The original log building is encased within the walls of the present home, which is shown below. During a renovation of the current home, the original log fort house was discovered. The original log home consists of a 24 ft. by 15 ft. two-story home built of yellow poplar and hand-hewn oak timbers. The interstices were found filled with a mixture of creek mud, lime, and horsehair mortar. According to the Nomination Form for Historic Places:

> *The earliest records of this area show that Moses and David Looney were among the first pioneer settlers to make homes in the wilderness of Virginia which later became Sullivan County, Tennessee. Recently, historians have found and located the original, 383-acre Moses Looney land grant and they have identified this early, log building as Moses Looney's Fort House. It is the only fort house left standing of the four original forts which were vital to the settlement of Sullivan County before 1776.*[75]

---

[73] *Annals of Southwest Virginia*, 1769-1800, p. 1397.

[74] *Annals of Southwest Virginia*, 1769-1800, p. 1102.

[75] National Register of Historic Places Inventory – Nomination Form, United States Department of the Interior National Park Service, filed Feb. 2, 1977, entered Jan.

National Register of Historic Places, Moses Looney Fort House, 5436 Old Island Road, Kingsport, Tennessee, United States Department of the Interior National Park Service, entered Jan. 18, 1978. (#78002638). Picture of current home. The walls of the original log fort house are encased in the walls of this home.

Moses Looney's log house and fort was an important link for this region of Tennessee. Settlers took refuge at his Fort House during Lord Dunmore's War and the Indian raids of 1774. The first court of Sullivan County, Tennessee was held at the home of Moses Looney in the month of February 1780 when the county was formally organized. Sullivan County was created in 1779 from part of Washington County.

Moses Looney is mentioned in the history of the lost state of Franklin at The First Constitutional Convention – 1784 as a delegate.

Before information reached the Western Country of the repealing act of the North Carolina Assembly, an important and fateful step had been taken. The delegates elected to the second convention met at Jonesborough, December 14, 1784. Among those representing Washington county were John Sevier, William Cocke, John Tipton, Thomas Stewart and Rev. Samuel Houston; from Sullivan County, David Looney, Richard Gammon, Moses Looney, William Cage and John Long; and from Greene county, James Reese, Daniel Kennedy,

John Newman, James Roddy and Joseph Hardin. It is believed that Haywood, followed by Ramsey, gives an incomplete list as above, and that Tirril, Samms, North, Christopher Taylor, Thomas Talbot, Joseph Wilson, William Cox, John Manifee, Gilbert Christian, Carnes, Andrew Taylor, Garrett Fitzgerald, Alexander Cavet, Joshua Gist, Benjamin Gist, Asahel Rawlings, Joseph Bullard, Valentine Sevier, Charles Robertson, Williams Evans, John Maughan, George Maxwell, Vincent, Provincer, William Davis, Samuel Wear, James Wilson, Joseph Tipton, and Captain David Campbell were also delegates. [76]

In 1796, Moses Looney acquired a 700-acre tract of land in what was inhabited by Native Americans as their hunting grounds and is now Sequoyah Hills, a neighborhood in Knoxville, Tennessee. [77] Land along the Holston River of 500 acres was transferred to Moses Looney by a "Deed of Indenture" from Robert King for 115 British pounds. King had acquired the land as a land grant from North Carolina. Moses Looney also received a grant from North Carolina for an additional 200 acres.[78] This area became known as "Looney's Bend" as he and his descendants remained on this land for several decades. In 1798, Moses Looney sells the northern portion of the property along Scenic, previously known as Logan Road and retained the acreage on the west end of Scenic at the southern end of Blow's Ferry and the northern end of Southgate Road. Looney's sons Absalom and Alexander inherit the property at Moses Looney's death.

By mid-1920s, long after Moses Looney's death, major residential development began in Sequoyah Hills on what was farmland and was developed into one of the oldest premiere residential communities of

---

[76] Williams, Samuel Cole, *History of the Lost State of Franklin*, Press of the Pioneers, New York, 1933.

[77] Knoxville-Knox County Metropolitan Planning Commission, "Scenic Drive Area of Sequoyah Hills Neighborhood - Designation Report and Design Guidelines", September 2006. Retrieved: 20 December 2010, wiki/Sequoyah Hills, Knoxville.

[78] Knoxville Historic Zoning Commission, "Designation Report and Design Guidelines, Scenic Drive Area of Sequoyah Hills Neighborhood", Neighborhood Conservation Overlay (NC-1), September 2006.

Knoxville. It is located off Kingston Pike with the entrance gate at the intersection of Kingston Pike, originally part of a Native American Trail, and Cherokee Boulevard between downtown Knoxville and West Knoxville. In early history, the Kingston Road was a dangerous route as many Indian attacks occurred along this road. Sequoyah Hills was one of Knoxville's first suburbs and today continues to be home to some of the city's most affluent residents. It is located on a peninsula created by the bend of the Tennessee River and known as Looney's Bend. The name Sequoyah was taken from the famous Native Indian Chief Sequoyah who invented the Cherokee alphabet.

Moses Looney was buried at Lones Cemetery on Arrowhead Drive, formerly known as Looney Road, located on the western side of Sequoyah Hills in Knoxville, Tennessee. This cemetery is said to hold graves of Civil War soldiers and slaves and earlier settlers.[79] The gravesite shows Moses Looney's death as 1817. Newspaper article from The Knoxville Register dated July 16, 1824 stated Captain Moses Looney died on July 12, 1824 after a lingering illness.

BENJAMIN (RHEA) LOONEY, SR. (C.8. Margaret, B.4. Matthew, A.1. Matthew) Benjamin Rhea Looney, the third son of Robert Looney, Jr. and Margaret Rhea, was born about 1748 in Looney's Creek Mill, Augusta County, Virginia. He was eight years old when his dad, Robert Looney, Jr., was killed by the Indians. At the age of 20, in 1768, he married Mary Johnson in Augusta County, Virginia.

According to a manuscript by Leroy W. Tilton, Benjamin was killed by Indians in 1783 in Cumberland Gap, Tennessee, when he was thirty-five years old. The following is paraphrased from this manuscript.

According to an account by William Gaines Looney (great-great grandson of Absalom Looney, son of Robert Looney (1692-1769)), a group of Looney kin went buffalo hunting northwest of Black Mountain in Harlan County, Kentucky. The group included 32-year

---

[79] Knoxville Historic Zoning Commission, "Designation Report and Design Guidelines, Scenic Drive Area of Sequoyah Hills Neighborhood", Neighborhood Conservation Overlay (NC-1), September 2006.

old Michael Looney, his brother, 22-year old Jonathan Looney, both cousins of Benjamin and 35-year old Benjamin Looney (1748-1783).

On the group's return, when near Cumberland Gap, the group noticed some "whet rocks" that had been exposed by the uprooting of a tree during a storm. It was late in the day and they did not stop, because they suspected the presence of Indians from the behavior of their horses. They pushed on some distance before camping.

The next morning, while backtracking for the whet rocks, the group was attached. Benjamin Looney was wounded, and Jonathan Looney was captured. Michael and Benjamin fled the scene to get help. Sometime later, while Benjamin was resting and, perhaps, mortally wounded, an Indian killed him. Michael Looney escaped with nothing but his flint-lock rifle and one charge, which he needed to get food, during the three day and night return trip on foot.

Jonathan Looney was taken to the Indian village. He escaped, much later, after he was gradually permitted increased liberty of movement. [80]

SAMUEL (RHEA) LOONEY, SR.

SAMUEL (RHEA) LOONEY, SR. (C.8. Margaret, B.4. Matthew, A.1. Matthew) Samuel Looney, fourth son of Margaret Rhea and Robert Looney, Sr. was born about 1754 probably on Looney's Mill Creek, Augusta County, Virginia. Samuel was two years old when his dad was killed by Indians.

He married (her first name was thought to be Nancy) Ann Lane in 1775 and settled on the Holston River. They had two sons, Moses and Samuel. Reference by family relatives indicate Ann was of the Pocahontas Tribe of Cherokee Indians. According to an article dated 1992 in Ozarks Watch by Donald R. Holliday, descendent of the Looney family, a Miss Elizabeth Looney of Washington, D.C. stated, *"Samuel Looney of Robert, Jr. is said to have married a grandchild of Pocahontas, but we have never, never, never been able to prove this."* [81] It

---

[80] Tilton, Leroy W., *Early Looneys in America*, 1949, pp. 16-17, posted ancestry.com on 20 Oct. 2012 by pmhawkins81.

[81] Holliday, Donald R., *Ozarks Watch*, "The MacGiolla Dhomhnaighs, or MacGillewneys, or Looneys of The Missouri-Arkansas Border", Vol. V, No. 4, Spring 1992.

is possible Samuel Looney married an Indian maiden of the same tribe as Pocahontas.

In May 1779, Samuel Looney died while fighting Indians in Washington County, Virginia.

MARY LOONEY GRIMES (C.8. Margaret, B.4. Matthew, A.1. Matthew) Mary, born in Augusta County, Virginia in 1756, was the fifth child of Margaret Rhea and Robert Looney, Jr. and their only daughter. Her father Robert Looney, Jr. was killed by Indians while she was an infant.

It is thought Mary married a man by the name of Grimes, but we located no records indicating if this is true.

JOHN S. RHEA OF BATH COUNTY

FOURTH GENERATION

DIRECT ANCESTOR TO PALMER RHEA, SR.

JOHN S. RHEA (D.8.) (C.5. William, B.3. Archibald, A.1. Matthew) (Born abt. 1752) John S. Rhea is son of William Rhea, Sr. (one of the three Rhea brothers in Augusta and Bath Counties) and Elizabeth Clark. John S. Rhea was born about 1752. He spent most of his life on his parents' farm on Mill Creek in what is currently located in Bath County, Virginia.

His brothers James, William, and Alexander relocated and settled in Green and Adair Counties, Kentucky. His brother Robert settled in Greenbrier County.[82] John stayed and worked the farm and cared for his aging parents. William, his dad, promised John the land, the home plantation and a "Negro boy Tom" if John stayed on the farm and cared for the land and them as they aged. John did so and when he was drafted for the Revolutionary War to help his elderly dad, William, with the farm, John hired a substitute to go to war in his place, which was allowed in those years.

John married his first wife Margaret Turk in 1774 in Augusta County, Virginia. Margaret was daughter to Thomas Turk, Sr. and Margaret Grove Turk and granddaughter to Robert and Mary Turk. Robert Turk had extensive holdings in Orange and Augusta Counties.

---

[82] The Bath County Historical Society, *The Bicentennial History of Bath County, Virginia 1701-1991,* Heritage House Publishing, p 331.

John Rhea had extensive holdings on Mill Creek, Bath County, Virginia and at Painter (Panther) Gap, Rockbridge County, Virginia.

John's wife Margaret died in 1800. On October 18, 1800, John Rhea married his second wife Magdalane (Magdaline) (Magdalene) Dill. Her father had land adjoining John's in Bath County.

After John's parents died (William in 1801 and Elizabeth in 1804), his commitment to care for them ended and he was free to sell his property, his holdings totaling 1,713 acres. The other heirs to the property then living in Virginia, Kentucky and Tennessee gave John clear title to the family land as he was promised and John and Magdalane sold their property in Bath County in 1806. This land was on Mill Creek above Painter Gap. John and Magdalane left Bath County and headed to Tennessee.

In 1814 John received from the United States Land Office at Nashville, Tennessee two quarter sections of land in Madison County, Mississippi Territory (now Alabama).[83]

On August 14, 1814, John Rhea married his third wife, Polly E. Nesmith in what was then Madison County, Mississippi (later Alabama). Polly testified in court she was "nearly seventeen years of age" at the time of marriage. John would have been about 62 years old. He died several months later in the same year (John's daughter Mary Glaves/Gleaves) widow of Eden Ashburn married Thomas H. Nesmith, brother to Polly Nesmith).

Known children of John Rhea and Margaret Turk:

ELIZABETH RHEA WRIGHT (D.8. John, C.5. William, B.3. Archibald, A.1. Matthew) (Born abt. 1775). Elizabeth was born in what is today Bath County, Virginia. In 1797, she married Toliver Wright.

WILLIAM RHEA (D.8. John, C.5. William, B.3. Archibald, A.1. Matthew) (Born abt. 1777). Moved to Tennessee.

---

[83] The Bath County Historical Society, *The Bicentennial History of Bath County, Virginia 1701-1991*, Heritage House Publishing, p 331.

JOHN RHEA (D.8. John, C.5. William, B.3. Archibald, A.1. Matthew) (Born abt. 1779). Moved to Tennessee.

MARGARET RHEA WRIGHT (D.8. John, C.5. William, B.3. Archibald, A.1. Matthew) (Born abt. 1781). Margaret married William Wright.

THOMAS TURK RHEA (See E.9.) (D.8. John, C.5. William, B.3. Archibald, A.1. Matthew) (Abt. 1785 – 1842) Thomas married Sally (Sarah) Lynch in 1807. Thomas died 1842 in Bath County, Virginia. He was the only child of John and Margaret Turk Rhea, who remained in Bath County, Virginia. (**DIRECT ANCESTOR TO PALMER RHEA, SR. SEE CHAPTER ON THOMAS TURK RHEA**).

ANN RHEA (D.8. John, C.5. William, B.3. Archibald, A.1. Matthew)

JAMES RHEA (D.8. John, C.5. William, B.3. Archibald, A.1. Matthew)

JANE RHEA (D.8. John, C.5. William, B.3. Archibald, A.1. Matthew)

POLLY RHEA (D.8. John, C.5. William, B.3. Archibald, A.1. Matthew)

(According to The Bicentennial History of Bath County, Virginia and *The Descendants of Matthew "The Rebel" Rhea of Scotland and Ireland* by Edward F. Foley))

Known children of John Rhea and Magdalena Dill:

NANCY P. RHEA (D.8. John, C.5. William, B.3. Archibald, A.1. Matthew) (Born abt. 1791)

HIRAM RHEA (D.8. John, C.5. William, B.3. Archibald, A.1. Matthew) Born in Bath County, Virginia. Married Hannah Helms. Hiram died about 1850 in Arizona.

SARAH H. RHEA BRASHERS (D.8. John, C.5. William, B.3. Archibald, A.1. Matthew) (Born abt. 1810) Born in Bath County, Virginia. Sarah married Robert L. Brashers.

HENRY DILL RHEA (D.8. John, C.5. William, B.3. Archibald, A.1. Matthew) He was a private in Captain John Harri's Company, 3rd Regmt. Mounted Volunteers of Illinois Militia.

ESTHER J. RHEA (D.8. John, C.5. William, B.3. Archibald, A.1. Matthew)

MARY RHEA (D.8. John, C.5. William, B.3. Archibald, A.1. Matthew)

(According to *The Bicentennial History of Bath County, Virginia*)

(Names confirmed with The Descendants of Matthew "The Rebel" Rhea of Scotland and Ireland by Edward Foley, Heritage Books, 2008 which shows only fourteen children for John S. Rhea with Polly and Jane not listed among his children, and Hiram was mentioned twice.)

THOMAS TURK RHEA

FIFTH GENERATION

DIRECT ANCESTOR TO PALMER RHEA, SR.

THOMAS TURK RHEA (E.9.) (D.8. John, C.5. William, B.3. Archibald, A.1. Matthew) (abt. 1783/1785 – March 1, 1842). Thomas was born about 1783 (another source states 1785) in what was Augusta County and later became Bath County, Virginia. Bath County was formed in 1790 and created from parts of Augusta, Botetourt and Greenbrier Counties. Bath County during much of Thomas Turk's life is referred to as "Greater Bath" as the county embraced a great deal more territory than its current boundaries.

A member of the Rhea family was among the first Grand Jury for the County, as follows:

The members of the first Grand Jury were: Joseph Mayse, foreman. Samuel Black, Thomas Brode, John Dilley, James Hamilton, James Hughart, Owen Kelley. John Lynch, John McClung, Samuel McDonnald, John Montgomery, Joseph Rhea. William Rider, Robert Stuart and Stephen Wilson.[84]

---

[84] Bath County, Virginia Genealogy and History, Genealogy Trails History Group, "Brief History of Bath County Virginia" by Jean Graham McAlister under the auspices of the County School Board and the Board of Supervisors of the County, 1920.

On January 23, 1804, a Thomas Rhea married Martha in Bath County, Virginia. I am unsure if this is the same Thomas Rhea as no other information was located on Martha. At age 22 to 24, Thomas married Sarah (Sally) J. Lynch (May 8, 1785 – June 23, 1856) on September 17, 1807 in Bath County, Virginia. Sarah was born in North Carolina, daughter to Susannah Shaw Lynch Thomas. Sarah's stepfather was Jesse Thomas.

Thomas was the only child of John and Margaret Rhea who remained in Bath County. He was a farmer as was his dad before him. During his lifetime, roads continued to be rough trails, primarily for horseback riders. U.S. Federal Census for 1820 indicates Thomas Turk had one slave, a wife, and five children at home. Thomas died at age 56 in Bath County. Sarah died in Millboro, Bath County, Virginia at age 71. It is unknown where Thomas and Sarah are buried.

Parents of Thomas Turk Rhea: (D.8. John, C.5. William, B.3. Archibald, A.1. Matthew): **John S. Rhea** (C.5. William, B.3. Archibald, A.1. Matthew) and **Margaret Turk**

Known children of Thomas Turk and Sarah Lynch:

JOHN SHAW RHEA (E.9. Thomas Turk, D.8. John, C.5. William, B.3. Archibald, A.1. Matthew)

SUSANNA LUCY RHEA CORLEY (CAULEY) (E.9. Thomas Turk, D.8. John, C.5. William, B.3. Archibald, A.1. Matthew)

MARGARET TURK RHEA KINCAID (E.9. Thomas Turk, D.8. John, C.5. William, B.3. Archibald, A.1. Matthew)

EVALINA (EVELINE/EVELENE) RHEA CARTER (E.9. Thomas Turk, D.8. John, C.5. William, B.3. Archibald, A.1. Matthew)

NANCY RHEA GARVEN (E.9. Thomas Turk, D.8. John, C.5. William, B.3. Archibald, A.1. Matthew)

JAMES THOMAS RHEA (F.10.) (E.9. Thomas Turk, D.8. John, C.5. William, B.3. Archibald, A.1. Matthew)

REBECCA H. RHEA LOAN (E.9. Thomas Turk, D.8. John, C.5. William, B.3. Archibald, A.1. Matthew)

ELIZABETH "BETSY" ANN RHEA LOAN (E.9. Thomas Turk, D.8. John, C.5. William, B.3. Archibald, A.1. Matthew)

(Additional information on children is shown below.)

JOHN SHAW RHEA (E.9. Thomas Turk, D.8. John, C.5. William, B.3. Archibald, A.1. Matthew) (1808 – 1849) John, the first child of Thomas Turk and Sarah Rhea was born in 1808 and lived in Bath County, Virginia. At about age 25, on March 28, 1833, he married Sarah (Sally) Lyle, daughter of Daniel Lyle. John's occupation was a farmer. He died at about age 40 to 41 of "Dropsy." Dropsy is an older term used, which today may be described as "edema" or "congestive heart failure." Sarah was left a widow with several young children.

Known children of John Shaw Rhea and Sarah Lyle:

Sarah Jane Rhea Ratliff (John, E.9. Thomas Turk, D.8. John, C.5. William, B.3. Archibald, A.1. Matthew) (born about 1830). Sarah married James Ratliff (born abt. 1830/1833), a farmer. James Ratliff from Bath County was listed in Twentieth Infantry Regiment (Elmore's Regiment), Confederate Soldiers in 1862. Also, James Ratliff from Shenandoah Mountain enlisted in Company K, Virginia 52nd Infantry Regiment on April 9, 1862 and mustered out on December 31, 1863. James and Sarah made their home in Williamsville, Bath County, Virginia.

Thomas Turk Rhea (John, E.9. Thomas Turk, D.8. John, C.5. William, B.3. Archibald, A.1. Matthew) (abt.

1835/1838 – September 13, 1861)). Thomas was born in Bath County and was named for his grandfather. Thomas was a farmer as was his family before him. On June 6, 1861, Thomas enlisted in the Confederate, Company G, Virginia 25th Infantry Regiment in Bath County. He died in Bath County at age 26. He did not marry.

John Shaw Rhea, Jr. ((John, E.9. Thomas Turk, D.8. John, C.5. William, B.3. Archibald, A.1. Matthew) (Born abt. 1836). On June 6, 1861, a John Shaw Rhea of Bath County, enlisted in Company A, Virginia 62nd Infantry Regiment during Civil War. There was a John S. Rhea, born in 1836 who was in the Twenty-fifth Infantry (Heck's Regiment. There was also a John S. Rhea from Virginia who enlisted in Company G, Virginia 18th Cavalry Regiment during Civil War. At about age 29, on April 27, 1865, John married 19-year old Elizabeth (Betsy) A. McMullin (born abt. 1846), daughter of Sally and James McMullin of Bath County. They were married in Millboro, Bath County, Virginia. John was a farmer and they made their home in Millboro. In 1910, when John was about 73 years old, he and his wife lived on Mill Creek Road, #4.

Angeline (Angelina) Rhea Ayers Smith ((John, E.9. Thomas Turk, D.8. John, C.5. William, B.3. Archibald, A.1. Matthew) (September 28, 1839 – December 8, 1912). Angelina married Stephen P. Ayers in 1860. Stephen died in 1864. On March 16, 1869, at age 28 and a widow, she married Jacob B. Smith, son of William and Alice Smith from Rockbridge County. They were married in Bath County, Virginia. Angeline died at age 73 and is buried at Mingo Cemetery, Mingo, Randolph County, West Virginia.

Lucy E. Rhea Miller (John, E.9. Thomas Turk, D.8. John, C.5. William, B.3. Archibald, A.1. Matthew) (May 20, 1840 – March 28, 1926). Lucy married John N. Miller (December

10, 1835 – September 1915). By 1870, Lucy and John lived in Williamsville, Virginia. They later moved to West Virginia. Lucy died at 85 years old in Mingo, Randolph County, West Virginia. She and John Miller are buried at Mingo Cemetery, Mingo, Randolph County, West Virginia.

James K.P. Rhea (John, E.9. Thomas Turk, D.8. John, C.5. William, B.3. Archibald, A.1. Matthew) (b. abt. 1842)

Charles Andrew Rhea (John, E.9. Thomas Turk, D.8. John, C.5. William, B.3. Archibald, A.1. Matthew) (abt. 1844/1847 - 1907). Charles served as a Private in Bath County Virginia Cavalry. He is buried at Mingo Cemetery, Mingo, Randolph County, West Virginia.

SUSANNA LUCY RHEA CORLEY (E.9. Thomas Turk, D.8. John, C.5. William, B.3. Archibald, A.1. Matthew) On December 16, 1830, Susanna married Thomas Jefferson Corley (Cauley) (May 27, 1802 – June 21, 1862), son of John Manoah Corley (Cauley) and Catherine Snead Corley (Cauley). Thomas was the eldest of twelve children whose family lived in the Falling Springs Valley. In 1840, Susanna and Thomas lived in Stewarts Creek/Green Valley section of Bath County. They later moved to Barbour County, Virginia, which became part of West Virginia. They had eight known children.

Susanna died prior to 1858, and Thomas returned to Bath County with his two youngest surviving children, Jesse and Melvina.

He appointed William Ross as a guardian and joined the county militia known as the 'Bath Rifles.' On April 9, 1862, the 59 officers and men of the militia were enlisted as Company K, 52nd Virginia Infantry, joining Stonewall Jackson, they participated in the Battle of McDowell, and the Valley Campaign. They saw action at Winchester, Cross Keys and Port Republic. In this battle of June 9, 1862, Thomas was wounded in the foot, arm and breast.

> *He died of these wounds on June 21, at the Confederate Hospital, Charlottesville and was buried at the cemetery now on the grounds of the University of Virginia. On June 24, 1989, 127 years after his death a marker was placed on his grave by descendants. A military ceremony was conducted by the 19th Virginia Re-enactment Company.*[85]

The name Corley was throughout the years used interchangeably in county records as Corley and Cauley. Military records and the University of Virginia Confederate Cemetery gravesite for Thomas is spelled as Cauley. Descendants spell the name as Corley. This cemetery located in Charlottesville, Albemarle County, Virginia served as a burial location for soldiers who died at the Charlottesville General Hospital from July 1861 to 1865 with 1,087 Confederate soldiers buried here. This cemetery is contiguous with the University of Virginia Cemetery. A monument stands with bronze plaques, listing the names of those buried.

Known children of Susanna Rhea and Thomas Corley:

John Molen Corley (Susanna, E.9. Thomas Turk, D.8. John, C.5. William, B.3. Archibald, A.1. Matthew) (April 1832 – July 15, 1912). On February 13, 1856, he married Amelia Elizabeth Shomo (1836-1921), daughter of Daniel and Dianna Remaer Shomo. John died in Junior, Barbour County, West Virginia. John and Amelia are buried at Hillyard-Corley Cemetery, Junior, Barbour County, West Virginia.

James Thomas Corley (Susanna, E.9. Thomas Turk, D.8. John, C.5. William, B.3. Archibald, A.1. Matthew) (February 25, 1835 – September 30, 1921). At age 37, James married Armetha Filleathe Daggs (1853 – 1920), daughter of Hiram and Eliza

---

[85] The Bath County Historical Society, *The Bicentennial History of Bath County, Virginia 1701-1991*, Heritage House Publishing, Thomas Jefferson and Susannah Rhea Corley, p.170.

Evans Daggs in Scotland County, Missouri on June 16, 1872. Armetha was born in Memphis, Scotland County, Missouri. Armetha was 19 at time of marriage. James and Armetha are buried at Mount Moriah Cemetery, Azen, Scotland County, Missouri.

Elizabeth "Jane" M. Corley Coffman (Susanna, E.9. Thomas Turk, D.8. John, C.5. William, B.3. Archibald, A.1. Matthew) (November 15, 1837 – December 21, 1910). Elizabeth married Benjamin Franklin Coffman (February 26, 1834 – March 12, 1910), son of Israel and Hester Townsend Coffman, on December 3, 1855. Jane and Benjamin are buried at Coffman Chapel Cemetery, Elkins, Randolph County, West Virginia.

Nancy Corley (Susanna, E.9. Thomas Turk, D.8. John, C.5. William, B.3. Archibald, A.1. Matthew) (1839/1841 – October 10, 1856). Nancy died between age 15 and 17.

Jesse Lee Corley (Susanna, E.9. Thomas Turk, D.8. John, C.5. William, B.3. Archibald, A.1. Matthew) (abt. 1843- abt. 1874). Jesse was a farmer. Jesse is listed among Confederate Soldiers as Enl. Company G, 11th Virginia Cav. September 8, 1862, POW on April 8, 1865 and released on oath in Clarksburg, West Virginia on April 10, 1865. On March 13, 1866, he married Jemima Jane Vanscoy, daughter of William and Sarah Hart Vanscoy in Randolph County, West Virginia. His father, Thomas Jefferson Corley, also served in the Confederate Army and died from his wounds in battle. Jesse died at about age 31.

Malinda Corley (Susanna, E.9. Thomas Turk, D.8. John, C.5. William, B.3. Archibald, A.1. Matthew) (April 1, 1844 – April 2, 1859). Malinda died at age 15.

Allen (Ellen) Corley (Susanna, E.9. Thomas Turk, D.8. John, C.5. William, B.3. Archibald, A.1. Matthew) (b. 1845)

Melvina Corley Goddin (Susanna, E.9. Thomas Turk, D.8. John, C.5. William, B.3. Archibald, A.1. Matthew) (October 19, 1848 – February 9, 1923). On November 6, 1866, Melvina married Judson C. Goddin (1841-1923), son of Thomas and Rachel Chenoweth Goddin. Melvina and Judson are buried at Chenoweth Cemetery (also known as Daniels Graveyard), Elkins, Randolph County, West Virginia.

MARGARET TURK RHEA KINCAID (E.9. Thomas Turk, D.8. John, C.5. William, B.3. Archibald, A.1. Matthew) (March 18, 1813 – July 28, 1888). On October 1, 1832 at about age 19, Margaret married Willis Kincaid (March 1811- June 6, 1887), son of William and Rebecca Lockridge Kincaid. In 1850, they lived in Bath County, and in 1870 and 1880, they lived in Williamsville, Bath County, Virginia. Margaret died at age 75, and she and Willis are buried at Woodland Union Church, 347 McClung Drive (Rt. 629), Millboro, Bath County, Virginia. They had nine known children:

James Nelson Kincaid (Margaret, E.9. Thomas Turk, D.8. John, C.5. William, B.3. Archibald, A.1. Matthew) (April 25, 1830 – March 5, 1911) James married Amanda Ellen Gwin (Grimm) (1834-1897). He served in the Confederate Virginia militia. James and Amanda are buried at Rocky Spring Presbyterian Church Cemetery, 567 Marble Valley Road (Rt. 600), Deerfield, Augusta County, Virginia.

Floyd Kincaid (Margaret, E.9. Thomas Turk, D.8. John, C.5. William, B.3. Archibald, A.1. Matthew) (July 21, 1833 – August 23, 1914). On December 3, 1862, Floyd enlisted at Camp Washington for the duration of the war. He was in 1st Company E, 18th Virginia Cavalry as Quartermaster Sergeant. This company became 2nd Company G, 18th Virginia Cavalry. He was POW on June 29, 1863 at McConnellsburg, Pennsylvania and sent to Harrisburg, Pennsylvania, then Philadelphia. He was sent to Ft. Delaware and then Pt. Lookout on October 27, 1863. He was paroled on January 17, 1865 and arrived at Camp Lee on January 25, 1865. Floyd married Elizabeth L. Stewart (1841-1913) on October 15, 1862 in Highland, Virginia. Floyd and Elizabeth are buried at Woodland Union Church Cemetery, 347 McClung Drive (Rt. 629), Millboro, Bath County, Virginia.

Charles Kincaid (Margaret, E.9. Thomas Turk, D.8. John, C.5. William, B.3. Archibald, A.1. Matthew) (Born abt. 1837)

Martha Kincaid Dill (Margaret, E.9. Thomas Turk, D.8. John, C.5. William, B.3. Archibald, A.1. Matthew) (May 3, 1838 – July 8, 1903). On December 6, 1881, Martha married James M. Dill (born abt. 1819), son of Jacob and Lenore Dill. Marriage records indicate she was a widow. If so, previous husband is unknown. Martha is buried at Woodland Union Church Cemetery, Cemetery, 347 McClung Drive (Rt. 629), Millboro, Bath County, Virginia.

Joseph B. Kincaid (Margaret, E.9. Thomas Turk, D.8. John, C.5. William, B.3. Archibald, A.1. Matthew) (November 11, 1840 – May 26, 1887). At age 27, Joseph married Catherine Jane Armentrout (1849-1908), daughter of Joel and Mary Armentrout, on November 20, 1867 in Millboro, Virginia. He served in the Civil War in Company G, 11th Virginia Cavalry, Dearing's Brigade, Rosser's Division, Cavalry, Army of Northern Virginia, C.S.A. Joseph lived in Millboro Springs, Virginia. He died at age 46. He and Catherine are buried at Woodland Union Church Cemetery, 347 McClung Drive (Rt. 629), Millboro, Bath County, Virginia. Catherine died at age 59 and is also buried at Woodland Union Church Cemetery.

Elizabeth H. Kincaid Cleek (Margaret, E.9. Thomas Turk, D.8. John, C.5. William, B.3. Archibald, A.1. Matthew)

(1842 – March 6, 1890). On November 17, 1864 at age 22, Elizabeth married Pvt. Eli Cleek (January 28, 1840 – October 17, 1902) in Bath County. Eli enlisted on May 14, 1861 and mustered into Bath Virginia Cavalry Company. Elizabeth died at age 48. She and Eli are buried at Woodland Union Church Cemetery, 347 McClung Drive (Rt. 629), Millboro, Bath County, Virginia.

Margaret Ellen Kincaid Guinn (Margaret, E.9. Thomas Turk, D.8. John, C.5. William, B.3. Archibald, A.1. Matthew) (1845 - 1931) At about age 20, Margaret married Pvt. George Hamilton Guinn (Gwin) (1836-1929) on December 21, 1865 in Bath Alum Springs, Bath County, Virginia. George served in Co. A, 52nd Virginia Infantry Regt. Margaret died at about age 86. She and George are buried at Goshen Baptist Church Cemetery (also known as Riverview Cemetery) in Goshen, Rockbridge County, Virginia.

John Willis Kincaid (Margaret, E.9. Thomas Turk, D.8. John, C.5. William, B.3. Archibald, A.1. Matthew) (May 28, 1849 – August 2, 1925). John married Amanda Warfield (1857 – February 16, 1920). In 1900, John and Amanda lived in Baltimore, Maryland. John died widowed at age 76 In Rockbridge, Virginia. He and Amanda are buried at Loudon Park Cemetery, 3801 Frederick Avenue, Baltimore, Maryland.

Rachel Virginia Kincaid Campbell (Margaret, E.9. Thomas Turk, D.8. John, C.5. William, B.3. Archibald, A.1. Matthew) (July 2, 1858 – April 23, 1937). At age 25, Rachel married Thomas L. Campbell (1855-1913) on December 20, 1883 in Bath County, Virginia. In 1900, they lived in Walker's Creek, Rockbridge County, Virginia. Rachel died a widow at age 78 in Waynesboro, Virginia.

EVALINE (EVELINE) (EVELENE) RHEA CARTER (E.9. Thomas Turk, D.8. John, C.5. William, B.3. Archibald, A.1. Matthew) (Abt. 1821 – July 7, 1856) Evaline was born on Pig Run, Millboro, Virginia. In April 1840, she married William M. Carter in Bath County and they lived on Pig Run. Evaline died at age 35.

Known children of Evaline Rhea and William Carter:

Thomas H. Carter (Evaline, E.9. Thomas Turk, D.8. John, C.5. William, B.3. Archibald, A.1. Matthew) (August 18, 1840 – September 17, 1872). Thomas married Sophia Ann Burns on February 3, 1863 in Bath County, Virginia. By 1870 U.S. Federal Census, Thomas and Sophia Ann lived in Wayne, Iowa. Thomas died at age 32 in Melrose, Monroe County, Iowa. Thomas and Sophia are buried at Prather Cemetery (also known as Martin Cemetery), Melrose, Iowa. This cemetery has been vandalized and many gravestones broken beyond repair.

Margaret "Maggie" Angeline Carter Thomas (Evaline, E.9. Thomas Turk, D.8. John, C.5. William, B.3. Archibald, A.1. Matthew) (August 1848 – October 1919). At age 21, Margaret married John Martin Thomas, Sr. (1844-1924) on November 10, 1868 in Bath County, Virginia. Margaret and John are buried at Revercomb Family Cemetery (formerly Cloverdale Chapel Cemetery), Deerfield Valley Road, Millboro Springs, Bath County, Virginia. They do not have headstones in this cemetery.

Marcus Carter (Evaline, E.9. Thomas Turk, D.8. John, C.5. William, B.3. Archibald, A.1. Matthew)

Wilson Carter (Evaline, E.9. Thomas Turk, D.8. John, C.5. William, B.3. Archibald, A.1. Matthew) (January 1, 1852 – May 1, 1933). Wilson married Eva Lee Logan (1861-1933) on October 18, 1888. U.S. Federal Census for 1900 indicate they lived in Millboro,

Virginia. Wilson died at age 81 in Natural Bridge, Virginia. Wilson and Eva are buried at Broad Creek ARP Church Cemetery, Broad Creek Church Road, Rockbridge County, Virginia.

Harriet Anne Carter Newcomer (Evaline, E.9. Thomas Turk, D.8. John, C.5. William, B.3. Archibald, A.1. Matthew) (August 11, 1855 – June 11, 1929). At age 19, Harriett married John William Newcomer (March 7, 1851 – July 17, 1926) on December 24, 1874 in Bath County, Virginia. Harriet died at age 73 in Bath County, Virginia.

NANCY RHEA GARVEN (E.9. Thomas Turk, D.8. John, C.5. William, B.3. Archibald, A.1. Matthew) (b. abt. 1815/1822). Nancy married John Garven.

JAMES THOMAS RHEA (F.10.) (E.9. Thomas Turk, D.8. John, C.5. William, B.3. Archibald, A.1. Matthew) (abt. 1823 – July 16, 1890) (Other source has birthdate as 1832.) On December 26, 1850, James married Malinda Smith in Rockbridge County. **SEE CHAPTER ON JAMES THOMAS RHEA, GRANDDAD TO PALMER RHEA, SR.**

REBECCA H. RHEA LOAN (LOWEN) (E.9. Thomas Turk, D.8. John, C.5. William, B.3. Archibald, A.1. Matthew) (b. abt. 1825/1828). On April 9, 1838, Rebecca married John Lewis Loan (Lowen) in Bath County, Virginia. The 1860 U.S. Federal Census lists them as living in Millboro Springs, Virginia and by the 1870 Census, they lived in Cedar Creek, Virginia. Rebecca's sister Elizabeth also married a Loan, thought to be related.

Known children of Rebecca H. Rhea and John Lewis Loan:

Elizabeth Loan (Rebecca, E.9. Thomas Turk, D.8. John, C.5. William, B.3. Archibald, A.1. Matthew) *The Bicentennial History of Bath County, Virginia* lists Elizabeth as a child of

Rebecca and John Loan (Lowen). I discovered no additional information on Elizabeth.

Sarah S. Loan Gillispie (Rebecca, E.9. Thomas Turk, D.8. John, C.5. William, B.3. Archibald, A.1. Matthew) (abt. 1840 - unknown). Sarah married Gilbreth (Gillie) Hamilton Gillispie (1837-1920) on March 14, 1867 in Germantown, Bath County, Virginia. In 1900, they lived in Cedar Creek, Virginia. Gillie was widowed at time of his death in 1920, so Sarah died after 1900 and prior to 1920. Gilbreth (Gillie) died in Healing Springs, Virginia. Death records indicate Gillie is buried at Mustoe Family Cemetery in Hot Springs, Virginia. This cemetery is located on private property and located behind Mustoe House Antiques at 1277 Sam Snead Highway in Hot Springs.

Rachel Loan Carter (Rebecca, E.9. Thomas Turk, D.8. John, C.5. William, B.3. Archibald, A.1. Matthew) (abt. 1848 – November 5, 1893). Rachel married John W. Carter on December 19, 1878 at Cowpasture River, Bath County, Virginia. Rachel died at about 45 years old in Bath County.

Nancy Jane Loan Ray ((Rebecca, E.9. Thomas Turk, D.8. John, C.5. William, B.3. Archibald, A.1. Matthew) (b. abt. 1850/1851 – d. unknown). Nancy married Henry Boyd Ray in Bath County on October 5, 1869. By 1900, they lived in Millboro, Virginia.

William L. Loan (Rebecca, E.9. Thomas Turk, D.8. John, C.5. William, B.3. Archibald, A.1. Matthew) (b. abt. 1850/1852 – d. unknown). At about age 26, William married Mary Ann Lawson on February 12, 1878 in Alleghany County, Virginia. William is buried at Windy Cove Presbyterian Church Cemetery, Millboro Springs, Bath County, Virginia.

John Samuel Loan (Lowen) (Rebecca, E.9. Thomas Turk, D.8. John, C.5. William, B.3. Archibald, A.1. Matthew) (February 14, 1853 – June 10, 1923). John married Bettie B. Cash, (1851-1912) daughter of John and Elizabeth Cash, on December 24, 1879 in Bath County, Virginia. John died at age 70 in Millboro, Virginia. John and Bettie are buried under the name of Lowen at Horeb Baptist Church Cemetery, 5742 Cowpasture River Highway (Rt. 42), Millboro, Virginia.

Porter Loan (Rebecca, E.9. Thomas Turk, D.8. John, C.5. William, B.3. Archibald, A.1. Matthew), (b. June 1, 1856). In 1880, at about age 24, Porter was single and lived in Millboro, Virginia.

Charles Loan (Rebecca, E.9. Thomas Turk, D.8. John, C.5. William, B.3. Archibald, A.1. Matthew) (b. February 25, 1859). Charles married Rebecca (last name unknown) on October 11, 1881 in Bath County, Virginia.

Joseph Loan (Rebecca, E.9. Thomas Turk, D.8. John, C.5. William, B.3. Archibald, A.1. Matthew) (abt. 1860/1861 – November 8, 1881). Joseph died at 19 years old and is buried at Windy Cove Presbyterian Church Cemetery, Millboro Springs, Bath County, Virginia.

ELIZABETH (BETSY) ANN RHEA LOAN (E.9. Thomas Turk, D.8. John, C.5. William, B.3. Archibald, A.1. Matthew) (abt. 1829/1830 – February 2, 1879). Elizabeth married Samuel Loan (Lowen) (born about 1824). Samuel served in the Confederate Army, enlisting in Valley Mills, Virginia on April 26, 1862. He enlisted in Company K, Virginia 52nd Infantry Regiment and mustered out on February 4, 1863. He enlisted again on April 15, 1864. (*The Virginia Regimental Histories Series*). Elizabeth "Betsy" and Samuel lived in Millboro, Virginia. Betsy died at age 49/50 in Bath County, Virginia.

Known children of Elizabeth Rhea and Samuel Loan:

John William Loan (Lowen) (Elizabeth, E.9. Thomas Turk, D.8. John, C.5. William, B.3. Archibald, A.1. Matthew) (May 23, 1845 – May 13, 1935). John served in the Confederate Army, Company K, 20th Virginia Calvary, Jackson's Brigade, Lomax's Division, Valley District, Virginia. He married Mary Ellen Welch on August 12, 1868 in Mill Creek, Virginia. In 1880, they lived in Millboro, Virginia. John died in Clifton Forge, Virginia. He is buried at Cedar Hill Cemetery, 1521 S. Carpenter Drive, Covington, Virginia.

James Lewis Loan (Elizabeth, E.9. Thomas Turk, D.8. John, C.5. William, B.3. Archibald, A.1. Matthew) (October 27, 1848 – October 10, 1917). James married Estaline Francis Ellinger (1850-1925) on February 26, 1874 in Bath County. He died at age 69 and he and Estaline are buried at Lyle Chapel Cemetery, Bath County, Virginia.

Frances (Fannie) Loan (Elizabeth, E.9. Thomas Turk, D.8. John, C.5. William, B.3. Archibald, A.1. Matthew) (abt. 1852 - unknown)

Floyd Samuel Loan (Elizabeth, E.9. Thomas Turk, D.8. John, C.5. William, B.3. Archibald, A.1. Matthew), (b. August 6, 1854). Floyd married Martha Margaret Randolph on June 22, 1880 in Bath County, Virginia. In 1900, Floyd and Martha lived in Millboro, Virginia.

Rebecca S. Loan McMullin (Elizabeth, E.9. Thomas Turk, D.8. John, C.5. William, B.3. Archibald, A.1. Matthew), (abt. 1858 - unknown). According to *The Bicentennial History of Bath County, Virginia*, Rebecca married (first name unknown) McMullin.

Andrew W. Loan (Elizabeth, E.9. Thomas Turk, D.8. John, C.5. William, B.3. Archibald, A.1. Matthew) (abt. 1862 - unknown)

Charles Joyce Loan (Elizabeth, E.9. Thomas Turk, D.8. John, C.5. William, B.3. Archibald, A.1. Matthew) (May 4, 1865 – December 20, 1933). Charles married Mary Margaret Ayers (1868-1950) on September 18, 1884 in Bath County, Virginia. Charles died in Hot Springs, Virginia at age 69. Charles and Mary are buried at Woodland Union Church Cemetery, 347 McClung Drive (Rt. 629), Millboro, Virginia.

Mary V. Loan Phillips (Elizabeth, E.9. Thomas Turk, D.8. John, C.5. William, B.3. Archibald, A.1. Matthew) (b. abt. 1867). On April 6, 1882 at about age 15, Mary married William A. Phillips (1860 – 1935), son of James and Nancy Phillips. They were married in Green Valley, Virginia. In 1900, they lived in Indian Valley, Floyd, Virginia. William is buried at Green Valley Cemetery, Bath County, Virginia.

JAMES THOMAS RHEA

SIXTH GENERATION

DIRECT ANCESTOR TO PALMER RHEA, SR.

JAMES THOMAS RHEA (F.10.) (E.9. Thomas Turk, D.8. John, C.5. William, B.3. Archibald, A.1. Matthew) (Born abt. 1823 – July 16, 1890) (Another source lists dates as 1821-1888 and another lists birth as 1832.). James was born in Bath County, Virginia. About age 27 or 28, he married Malinda Ann Smith (born 1836 according to death records and 1832/1835 according to U.S. Federal Census records – died 1911), Malinda was daughter to Henry and Angelina Smith. James and Malinda were married in Rockbridge County, Virginia on January 1, 1851. (Another source lists marriage date as December 26, 1850). Malinda's age at time of marriage would have been 15 to 18 years old. James was Palmer Rhea, Sr.'s paternal grandfather.

James grew to adulthood in the mountainous Bath County with his parents, Thomas Turk Rhea and Sarah Lynch Rhea, and his siblings. As an adult, James was a farmer and owned his own farm on Pig Run in Millboro, Bath County, Virginia. The Bath County land is beautiful with surrounding mountain ridges. Bath County is divided into two main valleys and then sub-valleys. His farm was in the Cowpasture River Valley. This area is currently located near the central western border of the Commonwealth of Virginia. However, prior to West Virginia being formed in 1863, Bath County lay near the center of the State of Virginia. James would have been about 40 years old when this division of land occurred.

At about age 67, James was killed by lightning on his farmland on

Pig Run while walking home carrying a bucket. According to family, James, along with others, had been timbering his land. This land later became known as "Beatty's Ridge," named after John Andrew Beatty, Sr., who was a neighbor to the Rhea family. James and his sons often timbered the land, selling the timber, as well as farming. His son James William Rhea was accompanying him at the time of the lightening incident and was unharmed.

It is unknown where James Thomas Rhea is buried. His wife Malinda died at about age 75 and is buried at Rehobeth Community Church Cemetery, 3785 Pig Run Road, Millboro, Bath County, Virginia.

James Thomas Rhea

Parents of James Thomas Rhea: Thomas Turk Rhea (D.8. John, C.5. William, B.3. Archibald, A.1. Matthew) and **Sarah (Sally) J. Lynch**

Known Children of James Thomas Rhea and Malinda Ann Smith:

THOMAS "PAP" HENRY RHEA (G.11.) (F.10. James, E.9. Thomas Turk, D.8. John, C.5. William, B.3. Archibald, A.1. Matthew) **FATHER TO PALMER RHEA, SR.**

NANCY (NANNIE) ENORA RHEA WADE BRINKLEY (F.10. James, E.9. Thomas Turk, D.8. John, C.5. William, B.3. Archibald, A.1. Matthew)

MARTHA A. RHEA WOOD (F.10. James, E.9. Thomas Turk, D.8. John, C.5. William, B.3. Archibald, A.1. Matthew)

JOHN A. W. (WILSON) RHEA (F.10. James, E.9. Thomas Turk, D.8. John, C.5. William, B.3. Archibald, A.1. Matthew)

JAMES WILLIAM RHEA (F.10. James, E.9. Thomas Turk, D.8. John, C.5. William, B.3. Archibald, A.1. Matthew)

SHAW ALEXANDER RHEA (F.10. James, E.9. Thomas Turk, D.8. John, C.5. William, B.3. Archibald, A.1. Matthew)

GEORGE BEATY RHEA (F.10. James, E.9. Thomas Turk, D.8. John, C.5. William, B.3. Archibald, A.1. Matthew)

(Additional information on children is shown below.)

Rhea Brothers: Thomas Henry Rhea, John (A.W.) Wilson
Rhea, James William Rhea, Shaw Alexander Rhea, and
George Beaty Rhea (Photo courtesy of Gloria Deitz)

THOMAS "PAP" HENRY RHEA (G.11) (F.10. James, E.9.
Thomas Turk, D.8. John, C.5. William, B.3. Archibald, A.1.
Matthew) (1853-1938). Thomas was son of James Thomas Rhea
and Malinda Ann Smith Rhea. Thomas married Elizabeth Vest
(Vess) and after her death he married Mamie Gear. **THOMAS
IS FATHER TO PALMER RHEA, SR. SEE CHAPTER ON
THOMAS HENRY RHEA.**

Known children of Thomas Henry Rhea and Elizabeth Vest:

John Wilson Rhea (G.11. Thomas, F.10. James, E.9. Thomas
Turk, D.8. John, C.5. William, B.3. Archibald, A.1. Matthew)

Nellie Rhea Hysong (G.11. Thomas, F.10. James, E.9. Thomas
Turk, D.8. John, C.5. William, B.3. Archibald, A.1. Matthew)

Garnett Sutton Rhea (G.11. Thomas, F.10. James, E.9. Thomas
Turk, D.8. John, C.5. William, B.3. Archibald, A.1. Matthew)

Mollie Mae Rhea Perkinson Lyon (G.11. Thomas, F.10. James, E.9. Thomas Turk, D.8. John, C.5. William, B.3. Archibald, A.1. Matthew)

Harry Tucker Rhea (G.11. Thomas, F.10. James, E.9. Thomas Turk, D.8. John, C.5. William, B.3. Archibald, A.1. Matthew)

James Tally Rhea (G.11. Thomas, F.10. James, E.9. Thomas Turk, D.8. John, C.5. William, B.3. Archibald, A.1. Matthew)

Mattie Myrtle Rhea Coleman (G.11. Thomas, F.10. James, E.9. Thomas Turk, D.8. John, C.5. William, B.3. Archibald, A.1. Matthew)

Henry McKinley Rhea (G.11. Thomas, F.10. James, E.9. Thomas Turk, D.8. John, C.5. William, B.3. Archibald, A.1. Matthew)

Alice Beatty Rhea Brown Russell (G.11. Thomas, F.10. James, E.9. Thomas Turk, D.8. John, C.5. William, B.3. Archibald, A.1. Matthew)

Known children of Thomas Henry Rhea and Mamie Gear:

Stoney Eckle (Echols) Rhea (G.11. Thomas, F.10. James, E.9. Thomas Turk, D.8. John, C.5. William, B.3. Archibald, A.1. Matthew)

Courtney Russell Rhea (G.11. Thomas, F.10. James, E.9. Thomas Turk, D.8. John, C.5. William, B.3. Archibald, A.1. Matthew)

Palmer B. Rhea (See H.12.) (G.11. Thomas, F.10. James, E.9. Thomas Turk, D.8. John, C.5. William, B.3. Archibald, A.1. Matthew)

Helen Virginia Rhea Campbell (G.11. Thomas, F.10. James, E.9. Thomas Turk, D.8. John, C.5. William, B.3. Archibald, A.1. Matthew)

Clarence Rhea (G.11. Thomas, F.10. James, E.9. Thomas Turk, D.8. John, C.5. William, B.3. Archibald, A.1. Matthew)

Baby Rhea (Died at birth) (G.11. Thomas, F.10. James, E.9. Thomas Turk, D.8. John, C.5. William, B.3. Archibald, A.1. Matthew)

NANCY (NANNIE) ELNORA RHEA WADE BRINKLEY (F.10. James, E.9. Thomas Turk, D.8. John, C.5. William, B.3. Archibald, A.1. Matthew) (December 11, 1853 according to death record. According to Bath County birth records, she was born on December 1853/1854 - March 14, 1938). Nancy, the daughter of James and Malinda Rhea, was born in Bath County and lived her young days with family in Millboro, Virginia. She married Reuben A. Wade (born abt. 1851) on January 2, 1873 in Millboro Springs, Virginia. Nancy was about 20 years old and Reuben was about 22 years old when married. In 1880, Nancy was living with her parents James and Malinda along with her two children. On April 24, 1881, at age 28, she married 31-year old Charles Francisco Brinkley (March 15, 1850 – March 31, 1922), son of John and Eliza Brinkley. They lived in Williamsville, Bath County, Virginia. Nancy was a widow at time of her death. She died from "myocarditis," which is a cardiovascular disease. Nancy and husband Charles Brinkley are buried at Woodland Union Church Cemetery, 347 McClung Drive (Rt. 629), Millboro, Virginia. According to 1900 census, Nancy had 10 children between both husbands.

MARTHA A. RHEA WOOD (F.10. James, E.9. Thomas Turk, D.8. John, C.5. William, B.3. Archibald, A.1. Matthew) (September 25, 1857 – April 20, 1883). Martha was the third child of James and Malinda Rhea and was born in Bath County, Virginia. About age

22, Martha married 24-year-old John Wood (b. 1855), son of James M. and Mary J. Wood, on April 3, 1879 in Bath County, Virginia. John was a farmer. Martha died in Bath County, Virginia at about age 25. John remarried in 1887 to Annie J. Vess. Martha and John had one known child:

Harry Gratton Wood (Martha, F.10. James, E.9. Thomas Turk, D.8. John, C.5. William, B.3. Archibald, A.1. Matthew) (February 6, 1880 – February 27, 1926). Harry died at the age 45 to 46 years. Harry married Annie Lee Burgess (1888-1961). He worked as a conductor for the railroad. Harry and Annie are buried at Crown Hill Cemetery, Clifton Forge, Alleghany County, Virginia.

JOHN A.W. (WILSON) RHEA (F.10. James, E.9. Thomas Turk, D.8. John, C.5. William, B.3. Archibald, A.1. Matthew) (June 4, 1863 – March 15, 1952). John was the fourth child of James and Malinda Rhea. He lived in Millboro, Virginia with his family. About age 23, he married 31-year old Mary Elizabeth (Eliza Beth) (Lizzie) Brooks (March 6, 1855 – January 9, 1927) on April 16, 1886. By 1900 and 1910, John and "Lizzie" lived in Williamsville, Virginia. He worked as a farmer on his own farm. John died as a widow at age 88. He and "Eliza Beth," who died at age 71, are buried at Rocky Spring Presbyterian Church Cemetery, 567 Marble Valley Road (Rt. 600), Deerfield, Augusta County, Virginia. U.S. Federal Census show Elizabeth and John had seven known children.

Known children of John Rhea and Elizabeth Brooks:

Earnest E. Rhea (John, F.10. James, E.9. Thomas Turk, D.8. John, C.5. William, B.3. Archibald, A.1. Matthew) (February 24, 1887 – June 30, 1913). Earnest is the first known child of John and Mary Elizabeth Rhea. Earnest died at 26 years old of tuberculosis. He was single at time of death and is buried as are his parents John and Eliza Beth at Rocky Spring Presbyterian Church Cemetery, 567 Marble Valley Road (Rt. 600), Deerfield, Virginia.

Ella Houston Rhea Zimbro (John, F.10. James, E.9. Thomas Turk, D.8. John, C.5. William, B.3. Archibald, A.1. Matthew) (December 6, 1889 – May 11, 1979). Ella is the second child of James and Malinda Rhea. She married Lilburn T. Zimbro (1889-1975). At time of death, Ella's last address was in Fishersville, Virginia. She was 89 years old and a widow. Ella is buried at Rocky Spring Presbyterian Church Cemetery, 567 Marble Valley Road, Deerfield, Virginia as are her parents, John and Eliza Beth, and her husband Lilburn.

Zora Lee Rhea Rowe ((John, F.10. James, E.9. Thomas Turk, D.8. John, C.5. William, B.3. Archibald, A.1. Matthew) (September 10, 1891 – June 28, 1982). Zora is the third child of John and Mary Rhea. Zora married Wesley Romer Rowe (1897-1984). Zora died of leukemia at the age of 90. Zora and Wesley are buried at Oak Lawn Mausoleum and Memory Gardens, 1921 Shutterlee Mill Road, Staunton, Virginia.

Okley Rhea Shinault (John, F.10. James, E.9. Thomas Turk, D.8. John, C.5. William, B.3. Archibald, A.1. Matthew) (November 25, 1892 – February 27, 1980). Okley is the fourth child of John and Mary Rhea. She married Walter R. Shinault (October 9, 1890 – February 4, 1946), son of George and Maggie Shinault. Okley was a widow at time of death. Death records indicate Okley and Walter are buried at Windy Cove Cemetery, Millboro Springs, Bath County, Virginia.

Forrest Kincaid Rhea (John, F.10. James, E.9. Thomas Turk, D.8. John, C.5. William, B.3. Archibald, A.1. Matthew) (November 24, 1894 – September 2, 1979). Forest was known as "Pop" by family. At age 23, Forrest married 19-year old Ida Mae Myers (abt. 1898 – abt. 1984) on January 4, 1917 in Washington, D.C. Ida was known by her family as "Nanny." Forrest worked as an inspector for the Sun Oil Company. He died of "cardiorespiratory arrest" due to "cardiovascular disease."

Forrest died in Woodstock, Virginia at the age of 85. Forrest and Ida are buried in Green Hill Cemetery, Fairfax Street, Stephens City, Frederick County, Virginia.

JAMES WILLIAM RHEA (F.10. James, E.9. Thomas Turk, D.8. John, C.5. William, B.3. Archibald, A.1. Matthew) (April 13, 1866 – December 12, 1957) James was born in Millboro, Bath County, Virginia. He was the fifth child of James and Malinda. James who was about 20 years old was accompanying his dad at the time lightning stuck his dad as they returned home from timbering their land on Pig Run, Millboro.

James married Emma Lee Shanks (October 30, 1870 – April 8, 1953) on December 18, 1890 when he was about 24 years old and Emma was about 20. His wife Emma and three of their children died before he died of cancer at the age of 91. Emma died of "coronary occlusion" at the age of 83. James and Emma are buried at Rehobeth Community Church Cemetery, Millboro, Virginia.

James William Rhea
(Courtesy of Gloria Deitz)

Known children of James William Rhea and Emma Lee Shanks:

Mazie Brown Rhea Loan (James, F.10. James, E.9. Thomas Turk, D.8. John, C.5. William, B.3. Archibald, A.1. Matthew) (August 13, 1892 – April 2, 1966). Mazie was born in Bath County, Virginia and lived on Pig Run in Millboro. She was the first child of James William and Emma Rhea. Mazie married Howard Mitchell Loan (October 15, 1885 – May 15, 1963). Mazie died at 74 years old in Mount Solon, Augusta County, Virginia. Mazie and Howard are buried at Alleghany Memorial Park, (Garden of the Cross, Section IV), Low Moore, Alleghany County, Virginia.

Known children of Mazie Rhea and Howard Mitchell Loan:

Earl Leslie Loan (Mazie, James, F.10. James, E.9. Thomas Turk, D.8. John, C.5. William, B.3. Archibald, A.1. Matthew) (February 1, 1914 – April 1, 1973) At the age of 30, Earl married Juanita Elsie Brinkley (1923-1974) on September 26, 1944. Earl died at the age of 59, and he and Juanita are buried at Calvary Baptist Church Cemetery, 429 Crooked Spur Road (Rt. 633), Millboro Springs, Virginia.

Anna Lee Loan Fultz (Mazie, James, F.10. James, E.9. Thomas Turk, D.8. John, C.5. William, B.3. Archibald, A.1. Matthew) (December 31, 1915 – May 31, 2003) At the age of 25, Anna married Sidney Vernon Fultz (1901-1965) at Nimrod Hall, Virginia on December 31, 1940.

Claude Mitchell Loan (Mazie, James, F.10. James, E.9. Thomas Turk, D.8. John, C.5. William, B.3. Archibald, A.1. Matthew) (August 31, 1918 – May 24, 2009) Claude received a Bronze Star Medal from U.S. Army, World

War II. At the age of 26, Claude married Violet Christine Linkswiler on February 3, 1944 in Clifton Forge, Virginia. Claude died at age 91 and is buried at Alleghany Memorial Park, Low Moore, Alleghany County, Virginia.

Homer Rhea Loan, Sr. (Mazie, James, F.10. James, E.9. Thomas Turk, D.8. John, C.5. William, B.3. Archibald, A.1. Matthew) (October 2, 1920 – March 31, 1985). Homer married Dorothy Leona Downey (1922-2001). Homer died at age 65, and he and Dorothy are buried at Alleghany Memorial Park (Garden of Reformation, Section H), Low Moore, Alleghany County, Virginia.

Ernest Hollis Loan, Sr. (Mazie, James, F.10. James, E.9. Thomas Turk, D.8. John, C.5. William, B.3. Archibald, A.1. Matthew) (April 19, 1923 – December 17, 1988). Ernest was born in Nimrod Hall, Virginia. Ernest served in the Air Force from 1943- 1969. He served also for the U.S. Postal Service in Roanoke, Virginia. Ernest married Betty J. Giles (1926-2008). He died at the age 65, and he and Betty are buried at Clover Hill United Methodist Church Cemetery, 3457 Fulton School Road, Dayton, Rockingham County, Virginia.

James Delemo (Delenio) "Doots" Loan, Sr. (Mazie, James, F.10. James, E.9. Thomas Turk, D.8. John, C.5. William, B.3. Archibald, A.1. Matthew) (August 8, 1925 – December 19, 1997) James married Annie Bayne (1928-2016). He died at 72 years old, and he and Annie are buried at Horeb Baptist Church Cemetery, 5742 Cowpasture River Highway (Rt. 42), Millboro, Bath County, Virginia.

Leola Argenbright Rhea Roach (James, F.10. James, E.9. Thomas Turk, D.8. John, C.5. William, B.3. Archibald, A.1. Matthew) (June 28, 1894 – March 22, 1947). Leola was born in Millboro, Virginia. Death records indicate she was born in 1894 but grave records indicate 1896. Birth records for Allie indicate Allie is the third child born to James and Emma Rhea and Allie was born in 1895, so it appears the 1894 birth date for Leola would be the correct date. She married John Beverly Roach (November 21, 1880 gravesite shows birth date as 1879 – December 13, 1952). In 1930, they lived in Richmond, Virginia. Leola died at 52 years old of "cardiac failure." Leola and John are buried at Rehobeth Community Church Cemetery, 3785 Pig Run Road, Millboro, Bath County, Virginia. Known children:

> **James Beverly Roach** (Leola, James, F.10. James, E.9. Thomas Turk, D.8. John, C.5. William, B.3. Archibald, A.1. Matthew) (October 30, 1918 – April 22, 1986). James was born in Bath County, Virginia. At age 24, James married Eulallia Ernestine Dodd (1920-2002) in 1942 in Clifton Forge, Virginia. Eulallia was a nurse for Medical College of Virginia Hospitals. At time of death, James lived in Richmond, Virginia. James is buried at Signal Hill Memorial Park, 12360 Hanover Courthouse Road, Hanover, Virginia.

Allie Mae Rhea (James, F.10. James, E.9. Thomas Turk, D.8. John, C.5. William, B.3. Archibald, A.1. Matthew) (October 17, 1895 – February 3, 1981). Virginia Health records indicate Allie was the third child of James William and Emma Rhea. Allie was a retired nurse. She did not marry and no known children. Allie is buried at Rehobeth Community Church Cemetery, 3785 Pig Run Road, Millboro, Bath County, Virginia.

Octave Thannet Rhea Hinton (James, F.10. James, E.9. Thomas Turk, D.8. John, C.5. William, B.3. Archibald, A.1. Matthew) (December 17, 1897 – February 18, 1982). Octave was the fourth child of James and Emma and was born in Bath County, Virginia. Octave married Charles James Hinton, Jr (May 29, 1905 – November 14, 1934). Charles died at the age of 29. Octave worked as a seamstress at Sweetbrier College. She died in Harrisonburg, Virginia of "congestive heart failure" due to pneumonia. Octave is buried at Rehobeth Community Church Cemetery, 3785 Pig Run Road, Millboro, Bath County, Virginia. Charles is buried at Mount Pleasant United Methodist Church Cemetery, Alleghany County, Virginia.

Known children of Octave Rhea and Charles James Hinton:

Charles James Hinton, III, (Octave, James, F.10. James, E.9. Thomas Turk, D.8. John, C.5. William, B.3. Archibald, A.1. Matthew), Charles married Edna Gilma Plecker of Bath County, Virginia.

Ruth Thanet Hinton Cupp (Octave, James, F.10. James, E.9. Thomas Turk, D.8. John, C.5. William, B.3. Archibald, A.1. Matthew), (June 13, 1930 – June 14, 1980) Ruth married Oscar Frederick Cupp of Augusta County, Virginia on January 18, 1952 (Jan. 23, 1952). Ruth died in Staunton, Virginia. She is buried at Pleasant View Lutheran Church Cemetery, 2733 Spring Hill Road (Rt. 613), Verona, Augusta County, Virginia.

Christine Lee Hinton St. Claire (Octave, James, F.10. James, E.9. Thomas Turk, D.8. John, C.5. William, B.3. Archibald, A.1. Matthew) February 15, 1933 – April 30, 1960). Christine is buried at Rehobeth Community Church Cemetery, 3785 Pig Run Road, Millboro, Bath County, Virginia.

Boyd Edmond Rhea (James, F.10. James, E.9. Thomas Turk, D.8. John, C.5. William, B.3. Archibald, A.1. Matthew) (October 8, 1900 – October 14, 1948). Boyd's U.S. World War II draft records indicate he had brown hair with blue eyes and was about 5 ft. 8 inches. Boyd died at the age of 48 of "chronic nephritis," which is a "condition in which the functional units of the kidneys become inflamed." Death records and U.S. Federal Census indicate Boyd was single and lived with his parents James and Emma. He is buried at Rehobeth Community Church Cemetery, 3785 Pig Run Road, Millboro, Bath County, Virginia.

James Floyd Rhea (James, F.10. James, E.9. Thomas Turk, D.8. John, C.5. William, B.3. Archibald, A.1. Matthew) (December 5, 1902/1903 – November 4, 1918). Death records indicate death was in 1903 and gravesite indicates death was 1902.) Floyd, as he was called, died at age 15 of "Spanish Influenza and pneumonia." He is buried at Rehobeth Community Church Cemetery, 3785 Pig Run Road, Millboro, Bath County, Virginia.

David Franklin Rhea (James, F.10. James, E.9. Thomas Turk, D.8. John, C.5. William, B.3. Archibald, A.1. Matthew) (July 29, 1906 – February 10, 1973). At age 45, David married 18-year old Frances Arlene "Sassy Jo" Mines (1934-2013) on January 4, 1952 in Bath County, Virginia. David served in the U.S. Army during World War II. "Sassy Jo" was active in the Millboro Volunteer Fire Department, working the Bingo and Fireman's carnivals. She was a cook at Ted's Place restaurant. David died at 67 years old and is buried at Rehobeth Community Church Cemetery, 3785 Pig Run Road, Millboro, Bath County, Virginia. Frances lived to 79 years old and is buried at Horeb Baptist Church Cemetery, Millboro, Virginia. Known children:

> **James Franklin Rhea** (David, James, F.10. James, E.9. Thomas Turk, D.8. John, C.5. William, B.3. Archibald, A.1. Matthew) (December 14, 1959 – December 18, 1974). James died of a gunshot wound at 15 years old. He is buried at Rehobeth Community Church Cemetery, 3785 Pig Run Road, Millboro, Bath County, Virginia.

Other Children: PRIVATE

James William Rhea Family
First Row: James Floyd Rhea, Boyd Rhea and David Rhea
Second Row: James and Emma Shanks Rhea
Third Row: Daughters Mazie, Leola, Allie, and Octave (unsure of order)
(Photo courtesy of Gloria Deitz)

SHAW ALEXANDER RHEA (F.10. James, E.9. Thomas Turk, D.8. John, C.5. William, B.3. Archibald, A.1. Matthew) (August 11, 1868 – January 27, 1944) Shaw was born in Bath County, Virginia and raised in Millboro, Virginia, living at home with his parents until he married. At 28 years old, on May 7, 1896, Shaw married 17-year-old Nannie Virginia Rapp of Kerr's Creek, Rockbridge County. In 1900, Shaw was divorced and lived with his brother Thomas and family. At 38 years old, he married 17-year old Fannie Lillian Baber (February 20, 1889 – October 21, 1965) on November 25, 1906 in Albemarle County, Virginia. They lived in Millboro, Virginia. Shaw died of "hypertensive cardiorenal disease" at the age of 75. Shaw and wife Fannie are buried at Windy Cove Cemetery, Millboro Springs, Bath County, Virginia.

Known children of Shaw Rhea and Lillian Baber:

Henry A. Rhea (Shaw, F.10. James, E.9. Thomas Turk, D.8. John, C.5. William, B.3. Archibald, A.1. Matthew) (1907-1984) Henry was the first child of Shaw and Fannie Rhea. The family lived in Millboro, Virginia. Henry married Mary Louise Lowen (October 17, 1912 – December 1987). In 1935, they lived in Covington, Virginia. They lived in Berkeley, South Carolina by 1940. Henry and Mary are buried in Carolina Memorial Park, 7113 Rivers Avenue, North Charleston, South Carolina.

Garnett Roosevelt Rhea (Shaw, F.10. James, E.9. Thomas Turk, D.8. John, C.5. William, B.3. Archibald, A.1. Matthew) (January 30, 1910 – April 4, 1993) Garnett was born in Millboro Springs, Virginia. He married Pauline Elizabeth Bazemore (February 22, 1920 – March 10, 1957) At 83 years old, Garnett died, and he and Pauline are buried in Carolina Memorial Park, 7113 Rivers Avenue, North Charleston, South Carolina.

Percy Coleman Rhea (Shaw, F.10. James, E.9. Thomas Turk, D.8. John, C.5. William, B.3. Archibald, A.1. Matthew) (July 7, 1912 – February 16, 1979) Percy was born in Millboro Springs, Virginia. His World War II draft card indicates he was blond hair, blue eyes and 198 pounds and 6 foot 2 inches. He married Mary Margaret Ingram (October 4, 1916 – February 28, 1945). Percy died of lung cancer. At time of death, he lived in Lynchburg, Virginia. Percy is buried at Windy Cove Cemetery, Millboro Springs, Bath County, Virginia.

(Virginia) Pattie Rhea Curry (Shaw, F.10. James, E.9. Thomas Turk, D.8. John, C.5. William, B.3. Archibald, A.1. Matthew) (November 12, 1914 – March 17, 2015) Pattie was born in

Bath County, Virginia. At age 23, she married Rev. Joseph Curry (1914-1980) on June 23, 1938. Pattie and Joseph served in the Virginia United Methodist Conference. Pattie was a member of Cave Spring United Methodist Church, served on the administrative board of the guild, organized junior choirs at five churches in the conference, an elected member of the conference from 1980-2004, served on the District Church and Building Location Committee, served on the board for Camp Alta Mons for 17 years, served on the Mission Education Cultivation Team for the conference, and an officer of the Roanoke District United Methodist Women. She was a former schoolteacher, a hairdresser and a ceramics instructor for 29 years. Patty was recipient of the Roanoke United Methodist Home "Volunteer of the Decade" award from 1990-2000 and received the 1997 Distinguished Service Award from The Hermitage Guild Virginia for the United Methodist Homes. Patty died at age 100. She is buried at Windy Cove Cemetery, Millboro Springs, Bath County, Virginia.

Lillian "Jo" Elizabeth Rhea Michael (Shaw, F.10. James, E.9. Thomas Turk, D.8. John, C.5. William, B.3. Archibald, A.1. Matthew) (June 12, 1917 – April 1, 1997) At the age of 21, Lillian married Virgil Hamlin Michael (1918-1995) on January 5, 1939. Lillian was born in Bath County, Virginia and died at her home in North Charleston, South Carolina. She was a member of the Aldersgate United Methodist Church, where she served on the administration board and several committees. She graduated from Rice Business College and was said to be involved in the founding of the City of North Charleston in 1972-1973. She was inducted into the Charlie Hall of Fame in 1993 for Golden Deeds of Kindness and appointed by Mayor Bourne to serve on Coliseum Advisory Board. She was former owner of Artistic Florist and Gift Shop in North Charleston and a member of Trident Chamber of Commerce Task Force in the 1990s and charter member of North Charleston Choral

Society. Lillian is buried at Carolina Memorial Park, 7113 Rivers Avenue, North Charleston, South Carolina.

Luther Martin Rhea (Shaw, F.10. James, E.9. Thomas Turk, D.8. John, C.5. William, B.3. Archibald, A.1. Matthew) (August 17, 1919 – February 17, 1979) Luther served as a private in WWII. He married Jessie Prosser (February 9, 1924 – December 11, 2007). U.S. World War II Army Enlistment Records indicate Luther was divorced and enlisted on April 3, 1942. Luther (or Martin as he was sometimes called) and Jessie are buried in Glen Haven Memorial Park and Mausoleum, 2300 Temple Drive, Winter Park, Orange County, Florida.

GEORGE BEATY RHEA (F.10. James, E.9. Thomas Turk, D.8. John, C.5. William, B.3. Archibald, A.1. Matthew) (January 27, 1875 – February 6, 1939) George was the seventh child of James and Malinda Rhea. He married Ruth Naomi Rucker (December 17, 1879 – November 26, 1918). Ruth died at age 39 of influenza. By 1930, George had remarried Esther Gentry (another source has her name as Esther Holbert) (May 18, 1895 – August 9, 1975) who was twenty years younger than George. George worked as a farmer on his own farm and later as a bus operator. After George's death, Esther married Thomas T. Holbert. At time of death, George was 64 years old and lived at Sweet Briar, Amherst, Virginia. George and Ruth are buried at Amherst Cemetery, 513 Grandview Drive (Rt. 1108), Amherst, Virginia.

Known children of George Rhea and Ruth Rucker:

Theresa Marie "Tessie" Rhea Lawhorne (George, F.10. James, E.9. Thomas Turk, D.8. John, C.5. William, B.3. Archibald, A.1. Matthew) (October 5, 1900 – June 14, 1966) Theresa married Elmo Thurston Lawhorne, Sr. (June 22, 1903 – April 4, 1993). Theresa and Elmo are buried at Amherst Cemetery,

513 Grandview Drive (Rt. 1108), Amherst, Virginia. Known children are:

Elizabeth Ruth Lawhorne Turner Hatchell (Theresa, George, F.10. James, E.9. Thomas Turk, D.8. John, C.5. William, B.3. Archibald, A.1. Matthew) (1923–2006) Elizabeth died in Louisville, Kentucky. She married Norman Albion Turner (1913-1976) on April 3, 1948 when she was 24 years old. They divorced on February 25, 1965. On March 18, 1966, Elizabeth married Ollen Herbert Hatchell, Jr. (1926-1972). They divorced on July 15, 1969. Elizabeth worked as a postal clerk and lived in Sweet Briar, Virginia. She was a retired postal clerk of 47 years. Elizabeth and Norman Albion are buried at Amherst Cemetery, 513 Grandview Drive (Rt. 1108), Amherst, Virginia.

Margrite Irene Lawhorne Merkey (Theresa, George, F.10. James, E.9. Thomas Turk, D.8. John, C.5. William, B.3. Archibald, A.1. Matthew) (1926-1987). Margrite married Gerald Alan Merkey. Margrite is buried at Amherst Cemetery, 513 Grandview Drive (Rt. 1108), Amherst, Virginia.

Eleanor Mae "Peggy" Lawhorne Johnson (Theresa, George, F.10. James, E.9. Thomas Turk, D.8. John, C.5. William, B.3. Archibald, A.1. Matthew) (1930 – 2015). Eleanor married Malcolm Hill Johnson (1928-2005) on July 30, 1950 at the age of 20. They divorced on February 9, 1979. She is buried at Amherst Cemetery, 513 Grandview Drive (Rt. 1108), Amherst, Virginia.

Elmo Thurston Lawhorne, Jr. (Theresa, George, F.10. James, E.9. Thomas Turk, D.8. John, C.5. William, B.3. Archibald, A.1. Matthew) (1933-2008) Elmo married Hazel Wylene Dalton. On August 5, 1958, Elmo married Jeannette

Frances Reynolds. On March 13, 1962 Elmo and Jeannette Frances divorced. Elmo lived in Sweet Briar, Virginia. Elmo and Wylene are buried at Briarwood Memorial Gardens, 1823 S. Amherst Highway (Rt. 29 Bus.), Amherst, Virginia.

Georgie Naomi Rhea Davis (George, F.10. James, E.9. Thomas Turk, D.8. John, C.5. William, B.3. Archibald, A.1. Matthew) (October 8, 1901 – June 15, 1984) Georgia married Raymond "Ray" Lester Davis (1903 – 1964). Georgie and Ray lived in Madison Heights, Virginia. Georgie died at age 82. She and Ray are buried at Amherst Cemetery, 513 Grandview Drive (Rt. 1108), Amherst, Virginia.

Lonnie Burnette Rhea, Sr. (George, F.10. James, E.9. Thomas Turk, D.8. John, C.5. William, B.3. Archibald, A.1. Matthew) (December 13, 1904 – March 12, 1966) Lonnie was born in Bath County. Lonnie married Elsie Jane Blankenbaker on December 19, 1921 when he was 17 years old. Lonnie and Elsie divorced on February 13, 1950. Later, Lonnie married Evelyn Mae Johnson (1911-1973). Lonnie worked as a Chief Laboratory Operator for the U.S. Federal Government. He lived in Alexandria, Virginia. Lonnie and Evelyn are buried at Mount Comfort Cemetery, 6600 S. Kings Highway, Fairfax County, Virginia. Known children of Lonnie Rhea and Elsie Blankenbaker:

> **Lonnie Burnette Rhea, Jr.** (Lonnie, George, F.10. James, E.9. Thomas Turk, D.8. John, C.5. William, B.3. Archibald, A.1. Matthew), (1923–1923). Lonnie died at 5 days old from an unknown cause.

> **Ruth Rhea Neas** (Lonnie, George, F.10. James, E.9. Thomas Turk, D.8. John, C.5. William, B.3. Archibald, A.1. Matthew) (1924-2006) Ruth married Calvin Franklin Neas (1924-1997) on May 3, 1944 at age 20. Ruth died at

age 82. She and Calvin are buried at Amherst Cemetery, 513 Grandview Drive (Rt. 1108), Amherst, Virginia.

Myrle Rhea Wood (Lonnie, George, F.10. James, E.9. Thomas Turk, D.8. John, C.5. William, B.3. Archibald, A.1. Matthew) (1926-2012) Myrle married Otis Odell Wood on July 29, 1944 at the age of 18. Myrle died at age 86 and is buried at Amherst Cemetery, 513 Grandview Drive (Rt. 1108), Amherst, Virginia.

Mable L. Rhea Burley (George, F.10. James, E.9. Thomas Turk, D.8. John, C.5. William, B.3. Archibald, A.1. Matthew) (November 27, 1909 – June 28, 1950) Mable married Joseph Edward Burley (1907-1979). Mable died at 40 years of age, and she and Joseph are buried at Amherst Cemetery, 513 Grandview Drive (Rt. 1108), Amherst, Virginia.

Helen Hunt Rhea Edgemon Keyser (George, F.10. James, E.9. Thomas Turk, D.8. John, C.5. William, B.3. Archibald, A.1. Matthew) (August 7, 1913 – September 4, 1976). Helen married Walter Wilson Keyser (1918 – 1966) on September 24, 1943. Walter served as a Sgt. In the U.S. Army during World War II. Helen worked as a postal clerk at Sweet Brian Post Office. Helen was 63 years old at time of death. Helen and Walter are buried at Amherst Cemetery, 513 Grandview Drive (Rt. 1108), Amherst, Virginia.

THOMAS HENRY "PAP" RHEA

SEVENTH GENERATION

FATHER TO PALMER RHEA, SR.

THOMAS HENRY "PAP" RHEA (G.11.) (F.10. James, E.9. Thomas Turk, D.8. John, C.5. William, B.3. Archibald, A.1. Matthew) (1853-1938). **Thomas was father to Palmer Rhea, Sr.** Siblings of Thomas Henry Rhea and Elizabeth Vest are Palmer Rhea Sr.'s half siblings and those of Thomas and Mamie Gear are Palmer Rhea Sr.'s siblings.

Thomas was born in Virginia. He died in 1938 in Bath County, Virginia. "Pap," as he was called, married Elizabeth Vest (Vess) (1860 according to gravestone - died 1905) on December 21, 1876 in Millboro, Virginia. Elizabeth was about 16 years old at time of marriage and Thomas was about 23. Elizabeth's parents were Andrew J. Vest (Vess) and Melvina Vest (Vess). Elizabeth was born in Rockbridge County, Virginia.

Thomas was a Constable for the fourth Magisterial District in 1885 and in 1887. He was a tax collector in 1886 for the Millboro District. Thomas lived on Pig Run in Millboro. Some of their neighbors were Vess, Beatty, and Shanks.

Elizabeth died in 1905 at the age of 45. After Elizabeth's death, Thomas married Mamie Gear (1891/1892-1919). Mamie was born in West Virginia. I'm unsure of the year they were married, but they had their first child in 1909.

In 1919, Mamie and the baby died during childbirth. Mamie

was only 27 or 28 at time of her death. Thomas died in Lynchburg Memorial Hospital, Virginia at the age of 86 and is buried in Rehobeth Community Church Cemetery, 3785 Pig Run, Millboro, Bath County, Virginia. Elizabeth Vest Rhea and Mamie Gear Rhea are also buried at Rehobeth Community Church Cemetery.

Parents of Thomas Henry "Pap" Rhea: James Thomas Rhea and Melinda Ann Smith Rhea

Known children of Thomas Henry Rhea and Elizabeth Vest:

JOHN WILSON RHEA (G.11. Thomas, F.10. James, E.9. Thomas Turk, D.8. John, C.5. William, B.3. Archibald, A.1. Matthew)

NELLIE RHEA HYSONG (G.11. Thomas, F.10. James, E.9. Thomas Turk, D.8. John, C.5. William, B.3. Archibald, A.1. Matthew)

GARNETT SUTTON RHEA (G.11. Thomas, F.10. James, E.9. Thomas Turk, D.8. John, C.5. William, B.3. Archibald, A.1. Matthew)

MOLLIE MAE RHEA PERKINSON LYON (G.11. Thomas, F.10. James, E.9. Thomas Turk, D.8. John, C.5. William, B.3. Archibald, A.1. Matthew)

HARRY TUCKER RHEA (G.11 Thomas, F.10. James, E.9. Thomas Turk, D.8. John, C.5. William, B.3. Archibald, A.1. Matthew)

JAMES TALLY RHEA (G.11. Thomas, F.10. James, E.9. Thomas Turk, D.8. John, C.5. William, B.3. Archibald, A.1. Matthew)

MATTIE MYRTLE RHEA COLEMAN (G.11. Thomas, F.10. James, E.9. Thomas Turk, D.8. John, C.5. William, B.3. Archibald, A.1. Matthew)

HENRY MCKINLEY RHEA (G.11. Thomas, F.10. James, E.9. Thomas Turk, D.8. John, C.5. William, B.3. Archibald, A.1. Matthew)

ALICE BEATTY RHEA BROWN RUSSELL (G.11. Thomas, F.10. James, E.9. Thomas Turk, D.8. John, C.5. William, B.3. Archibald, A.1. Matthew)

Known children of Thomas Henry Rhea and Mamie Gear:

STONEY ECKLE RHEA (G.11. Thomas, F.10. James, E.9. Thomas Turk, D.8. John, C.5. William, B.3. Archibald, A.1. Matthew)

COURTNEY RUSSELL RHEA (G.11. Thomas, F.10. James, E.9. Thomas Turk, D.8. John, C.5. William, B.3. Archibald, A.1. Matthew)

PALMER B. RHEA (SEE H.12) (G.11. Thomas, F.10. James, E.9. Thomas Turk, D.8. John, C.5. William, B.3. Archibald, A.1. Matthew)

HELEN VIRGINIA RHEA CAMPBELL (G.11. Thomas, F.10. James, E.9. Thomas Turk, D.8. John, C.5. William, B.3. Archibald, A.1. Matthew)

CLARENCE RHEA (G.11. Thomas, F.10. James, E.9. Thomas Turk, D.8. John, C.5. William, B.3. Archibald, A.1. Matthew)

BABY RHEA (Died at birth) (G.11. Thomas, F.10. James, E.9. Thomas Turk, D.8. John, C.5. William, B.3. Archibald, A.1. Matthew)

(Additional information on children is shown below.)

Millboro, Virginia, 1864

JOHN WILSON RHEA (G.11. Thomas, F.10. James, E.9. Thomas Turk, D.8. John, C.5. William, B.3. Archibald, A.1. Matthew) (1878-1909). John was the first child of Thomas and was born in Bath County, Virginia. His mother Elizabeth was about 18 years old at his birth, and his dad Thomas was about 25 years old. At about age 26, John married Bessie (Bettie) J. Lewis (1889- October 30, 1957), daughter of William and Bessie Lewis, on April 26, 1905 in Charlottesville, Virginia. John Wilson died at 31 years old. He is buried at Rehobeth Community Church Cemetery, 3785 Pig Run, Millboro, Bath County, Virginia. Bessie Lewis Rhea who lived in Staunton, Virginia died October 30, 1957 and is buried at Thornrose Cemetery, 1041 West Beverley Street, Staunton, Virginia. Known child:

Bernard M. Rhea (John Wilson, G.11. Thomas, F.10. James, E.9. Thomas Turk, D.8. John, C.5. William, B.3. Archibald, A.1. Matthew) (1908- March 31, 1927). In 1924, Bernard lived in Staunton with his family and worked as a clerk. He was unmarried. He died at 19 years old from tuberculosis and is buried at Thornrose Cemetery, 1041 West Beverley Street, Staunton, Virginia.

NELLIE RHEA HYSONG (G.11. Thomas, F.10. James, E.9. Thomas Turk, D.8. John, C.5. William, B.3. Archibald, A.1. Matthew) (1882 - February 1, 1940). Nellie was born in Bath County, Virginia. When she was 26 years old, she married Martin Wellington Hysong (1880-1959) on January 27, 1908. Martin Hysong was born in Westmoreland, Pennsylvania and had attended college, at least two years. He became president and founder of Hysong's Funeral Home in Washington, D.C., where he served as funeral director. The four-story townhouse was located at 1014 Massachusetts Avenue, N.W., Washington, D.C.

Nellie died in 1940 and was buried at Abbey Mausoleum in Arlington, Virginia, which once overlooked the Pentagon. The Mausoleum is now torn down. This mausoleum was founded in 1924 and was one of the most luxurious burial places in Washington, D.C. metropolitan area for Washington, D.C.'s elite. Many famous individuals and political leaders were buried here. The structure was a Romanesque style with granite exterior, marble interior and stained-glass windows, high ceilings, and skylights.

The Mausoleum encountered financial difficulties and declared bankruptcy in 1966. Abbey Mausoleum had been vandalized at least six times between 1979 and 1994, with vandals opening and desecrating remains, pouring ashes on the floor. Crypts were broken into with coffins removed and remains decapitated and skulls put on broomsticks. Finally, prior to closing the mausoleum, remains buried there were disinterred, some by family members and buried elsewhere. A U.S. federal court approved the burial relocation plan in December 2000. The mausoleum was demolished in 2001. The Corps of Engineers reinterred any remaining bodies that had not already been removed to a mausoleum at National Memorial Park, a cemetery near Falls Church, Virginia. Nellie is not listed among those buried at National Memorial Park. I am unsure where her remains were taken after the closing of the Abbey Mausoleum.

In 2004, three Tiffany windows were rescued from the Abby Mausoleum and installed at the Arlington Art Center, 3550 Wilson Boulevard, Arlington, Virginia. These have become part of Arlington Public Art's Permanent Collection. There had been thirteen of the stained-glass windows slated for demolition and rescued by Arlington County staff. Twelve of the windows were of a "simple geometric/floral composition." The thirteenth and largest stain glass window rescued portrayed Christ extending his hand in benediction and a signature pane of artist "Louis C. Tiffany, NY." These stained windows were created in 1930s. Six of the windows were damaged beyond repair. These were used to restore the other seven. Four of these rescued windows were installed at the Westover Branch Library, 1644 N. McKinley Road, Arlington, Virginia in 2010.

Nellie's husband, Martin Hysong, died in Miami, Florida in 1959. He is buried at Fort Lincoln Cemetery, 3401 Bladensburg Road, Brentwood, Prince George's County, Maryland. They had two sons who both had died by the time of the burial relocation of Abbey Mausoleum.

Known children of Nellie Rhea and Martin Hysong:

Thomas Martin Hysong (Nellie, G.11. Thomas, F.10. James, E.9. Thomas Turk, D.8. John, C.5. William, B.3. Archibald, A.1. Matthew) (1914-1972). Married Mary Parke Colston. Buried at Fort Lincoln Cemetery, 3401 Bladensburg Road, Brentwood, Prince George's County, Maryland.

Jerry Edgar Hysong (Nellie, G.11. Thomas, F.10. James, E.9. Thomas Turk, D.8. John, C.5. William, B.3. Archibald, A.1. Matthew) (1917-1969). Buried at Fort Lincoln Cemetery, 3401 Bladensburg Road, Brentwood, Prince George's County, Maryland. He never married.

GARNETT SUTTON RHEA (G.11. Thomas, F.10. James, E.9. Thomas Turk, D.8. John, C.5. William, B.3. Archibald, A.1. Matthew) (January 24, 1884 - January 21, 1956). Garnett was the third child of Thomas and Elizabeth Rhea. He was born and raised in Bath County, Virginia. In 1903, he married Laura May Landes, daughter of John and Willie Landes, in Bath County, Virginia. Garnett and Laura divorced. In 1920, he and his wife, Mathilda Thylia, lived with his sister Nellie Rhea Hysong in Washington, D.C. He worked as an undertaker at his brother-in-law Martin Hysong's funeral home. U.S. Federal Census shows him as widowed by 1940. He died in Washington, D.C. and is buried at Cedar Hill Cemetery (also known as Forest Lake Cemetery), 4111 Pennsylvania Avenue, Suitland, Prince George's County, Maryland.

MOLLIE MAE RHEA PERKINSON LYON (G.11. Thomas, F.10. James, E.9. Thomas Turk, D.8. John, C.5. William, B.3. Archibald, A.1. Matthew) (December 28, 1886/1887 - June 2, 1965). Gravesite shows death as 1887 and death records lists death as 1886. Mollie was born in Bath County, Virginia. She married George Worthington Perkinson (born 1876/1877) on April 16, 1903 in Richmond, Virginia when she was about 17 and he was about 26. Her second marriage was to Edgar Lyon (1873-1943) on June 26, 1912 who was widowed. Mollie died at about age 79 in Clifton Forge, Virginia of "pyelonephritis," a type of urinary tract infection that affects the kidneys. Mollie was a widow at time of her death. She is buried at Rehobeth Community Church Cemetery, 3785 Pig Run Road, Millboro, Bath County, Virginia. Known child between Mollie and George Perkinson:

Mabel Esther Perkinson Conner (Mollie, G.11. Thomas, F.10. James, E.9. Thomas Turk, D.8. John, C.5. William, B.3. Archibald, A.1. Matthew) (June 15, 1904 – December 7, 1978). Mabel was born in Millboro, Bath County, Virginia. She married Tazewell Reece Conner, Sr. (October 13, 1906 – December 8, 1977). At time of her death, Mabel resided in Clifton Forge, Virginia. Mabel is buried at Rehobeth Community Church Cemetery, 3785 Pig Run Road, Millboro, Bath County, Virginia. Tazewell, Sr. is buried at Union Chapel Cemetery, Healing Springs, Bath County, Virginia.

HARRY TUCKER RHEA (G.11. Thomas, F.10. James, E.9. Thomas Turk, D.8. John, C.5. William, B.3. Archibald, A.1. Matthew) (October 11, 1888/1889 – February 19, 1946). Harry Tucker is the fifth child of Thomas and Elizabeth Rhea. Harry married Mabel whose last name is unknown. At age 21, U.S. Federal Census indicate "Tucker" as he was called, was a mail carrier. World War I Draft Registration shows his address as 1014 Mass Avenue, Washington, D.C. In 1920, Harry Tucker lived in Monterey, California. He was a chauffeur for a hotel. In 1940-1946, his residence is California. No known children. He is buried at Rehobeth Community Church Cemetery, 3785 Pig Run Road, Millboro, Bath County, Virginia.

JAMES TALLEY RHEA (G.11. Thomas, F.10. James, E.9. Thomas Turk, D.8. John, C.5. William, B.3. Archibald, A.1. Matthew) (December 18, 1892 – December 31, 1970). James was born on Pig Run, Millboro in Bath County, Virginia. He married Catheren Ann Matheney (1903-1991). James Talley was a carpenter and a stone mason. He served in the U.S. Army, discharged at the end of World War I. He purchased about 100 acres in 1927 on the Cowpasture River. This land was originally a portion of the Fort Dickinson land.[86] Palmer Rhea, Jr. recalls James Talley being a skilled carpenter and Palmer's dad Palmer Rhea, Sr., brother to James Talley, took his wooden boat to James for repair on several occasions. James Talley died at the age of 78 of "cardiac rupture," a medical term for heart attack. He is buried in Rehobeth Community Church Cemetery, 3785 Pig Run Road, Millboro, Bath County, Virginia. Catheren is buried at Horeb Baptist Church Cemetery, 5742 Cowpasture River Highway (Rt. 42), Millboro, Bath County, Virginia.

---

[86] *The Bicentennial History of Bath County, Virginia 1701-1991,* The Bath *County Hist*orical *Society,* Heritage House Publishing, pp.330-331.

Known children of James Talley Rhea and Catheren Matheney:

James Wilson Rhea (James Talley, (G.11. Thomas, F.10. James, E.9. Thomas Turk, D.8. John, C.5. William, B.3. Archibald, A.1. Matthew) (1921-2001) James was born in Millboro Springs, Bath County, Virginia. He married Hattie Mae Lutes. He served in the U.S. Marines in World War II. He died in Rockville, Maryland at the age of 80.

William Gratton "Bill" Rhea (James Talley, G.11. Thomas, F.10. James, E.9. Thomas Turk, D.8. John, C.5. William, B.3. Archibald, A.1. Matthew) (March 20, 1924 – July 5, 1996) Bill was born in Bath County, Virginia. At age 21, he married Clara Lucille Plecker (1926-2017) on May 9, 1945. He served in the U.S. Army Air Corps in World War II. The Rhea family recalls Bill owned an auto repair shop in Bath County. Bill and Clara Lucille are buried at Woodland Union Church Cemetery, 347 McClung Drive (Rt. 629), Millboro, Virginia. Known child:

> **Karen Lucille Rhea Capley** (William, James Talley, G.11. Thomas, F.10. James, E.9. Thomas Turk, D.8. John, C.5. William, B.3. Archibald, A.1. Matthew) (b. May 17, 1946) Karen married Thomas Morton Capley in 1964. Thomas was Principal of the Cheatham County High School in Ashland City, Tennessee. Thomas previously worked in the Bath County school system. Karen and Thomas Capley died in an auto-truck accident in November 1968. Karen was 22 years old and Thomas 35. Otis Mabrey, a science teacher and assistant coach with whom they were riding, also died in the accident. Thomas and Karen's young child and pet dog survived the accident.

Mollie Marie Rhea Clark. (James Talley, G.11. Thomas, F.10. James, E.9. Thomas Turk, D.8. John, C.5. William, B.3. Archibald, A.1. Matthew) Mollie was born in Bath County, Virginia. She married James Andrew Clark (1931-2004) in 1955. Mollie was a registered nurse. Known children:

> **Brenda Marie Clark Fowler** (Mollie, James Talley, G.11. Thomas, F.10. James, E.9. Thomas Turk, D.8. John, C.5. William, B.3. Archibald, A.1. Matthew) (1957-2001) Brenda was born in Clifton Forge, Virginia. She is buried at Calvary Baptist Church Cemetery, 429 Crooked Spur Road (Rt. 633), Millboro Springs, Bath County, Virginia.

> **Other: Private**

Mary Ann Rhea Salter (James Talley, G.11. Thomas, F.10. James, E.9. Thomas Turk, D.8. John, C.5. William, B.3. Archibald, A.1. Matthew) Mary was born in Bath County, Virginia. She married Ray Lewis Salter in 1957.

MATTIE MYRTLE RHEA COLEMAN (G.11. Thomas, F.10. James, E.9. Thomas Turk, D.8. John, C.5. William, B.3. Archibald, A.1. Matthew) (June 28, 1900 - January 19, 1974 per death certificate). Mattie was born in Bath County, Virginia. She married William E. Coleman. In 1935 - 1940, Mattie and William lived in Washington, D.C. Her husband William's profession in 1940 was listed in U.S. Federal Census as upholstering. Mattie lived in Arlington, Virginia at time of death. She was a retired apartment resident manager. Mattie died of "acute coronary insufficiency." She was taken to Hysong's Funeral Home (her brother-in-law's funeral home), 1300 N Street, N.W., Washington, D.C. According to her death certificate, she is buried at Fort Lincoln Cemetery, 3401 Bladensburg Road, Brentwood, Maryland. We were unable to locate her memorial records at this cemetery.

HENRY MCKINLEY RHEA (G.11. Thomas, F.10. James, E.9. Thomas Turk, D.8. John, C.5. William, B.3. Archibald, A.1. Matthew) (August 1, 1900 according to U.S. World War I draft registration and his tombstone also has 1900, but his death records indicate birth date as 1902 – October 23, 1929). Henry was born in Bath County, Virginia. He married Kathleen Augusta (1910-1998). Henry worked as a bus driver. He was about 27 years old and was living in Roanoke, Virginia when he died of pneumonia. Kathleen was 18 or 19 at the time of Henry's death. Six years later in 1935, Kathleen remarried Richard Lee "Bill" Funkhouser. Henry is buried at Rehobeth Community Church Cemetery, 3785 Pig Run Road, Millboro, Bath County, Virginia. Kathleen Augusta Rhea Funkhouser is buried at Mount Crawford Cemetery, Mount Crawford, Rockingham County, Virginia. Known child:

> **Nolen Elwood Rhea.** (Henry, G.11. Thomas, F.10. James, E.9. Thomas Turk, D.8. John, C.5. William, B.3. Archibald, A.1. Matthew) (1927 – unknown). Nolen was born in Rockingham County, Virginia. In 1945 at age 18, he was at the U.S. Maritime Service Training Station in Washington, D.C. He married Mattie Lee Montgomery in 1948 in Washington, D.C. and they divorced in 1971. Nolen is buried at Mount Crawford Cemetery, Crawford Street, Rockingham County, Virginia. Children not listed for privacy.

ALICE BEATTY RHEA BROWN RUSSELL. (G.11. Thomas, F.10. James, E.9. Thomas Turk, D.8. John, C.5. William, B.3. Archibald, A.1. Matthew) (born abt. 1897- other sources state birth date as 1902 or 1903, which should be the correct date if she was indeed the last child born of Elizabeth.). Alice was born in Millboro. She was the last child of Elizabeth and Thomas. Elizabeth was about 37 years old at Alice's birth and Thomas was about 44. In 1920, Alice lived in Washington, D.C. with her sister Nellie Rhea Hysong and worked as a manicurist. She married Rex J. Brown in 1923 in Washington, D.C. Alice remarried George Allen Russell in Detroit, Michigan in 1932.

Children of Thomas Henry Rhea and Mamie Gear Rhea:

ECHOLS RHEA (STONEY ECKLE RHEA) (G.11. Thomas, F.10. James, E.9. Thomas Turk, D.8. John, C.5. William, B.3. Archibald, A.1. Matthew) (Born abt. 1909 – April 26, 1932) Stoney, as he was called, was born in Bath County. He was the first child of Thomas and Mamie. Mamie was about 17 years old and Thomas was about 56 years old. Mamie died when Stoney was about ten years old. Stoney was about 23 years old at time of his death. He is buried in Rehobeth Community Church Cemetery, 3785 Pig Run Road, Millboro, Bath County, Virginia. No known wife or children.

COURTNEY RUSSELL RHEA (G.11. Thomas, F.10. James, E.9. Thomas Turk, D.8. John, C.5. William, B.3. Archibald, A.1. Matthew) (May 6, 1911 – November 26, 1990). Russell as he was called was born in Millboro Springs, Bath County, Virginia, the second child to Thomas and Mamie. He went by his middle name Russell. Russell was about eight years old when his mother Mamie died and about 27 when his dad died. By the 1930 U.S. Federal Census, Russell was nineteen years old and was a boarder with the Dill family in Millboro. The World War II draft records indicate he had blue eyes and brown hair. According to family, his physical appearance almost duplicated those of his brother Palmer Rhea. His death certificate shows his name as Russell Courtney Rhea, and he was 79 years old and divorced at time of death. He is buried in Rehobeth Community Church Cemetery, 3785 Pig Run Road, Millboro, Bath County, Virginia.

PALMER B. RHEA, SR. (See H.12.) (G.11. Thomas, F.10. James, E.9. Thomas Turk, D.8. John, C.5. William, B.3. Archibald, A.1. Matthew) (July 26, 1913 according to a delayed birth certificate – February 3, 1989). **See chapter on Palmer B. Rhea, Sr.**

HELEN VIRGINIA RHEA CAMPBELL (G.11. Thomas, F.10. James, E.9. Thomas Turk, D.8. John, C.5. William, B.3. Archibald,

A.1. Matthew) (April 9, 1915 according to tombstone and burial records. Delayed birth certificate shows birth date as July 22, 1915. She died on September 25, 1970). Helen was born in Millboro Springs, Virginia. She was four years old when her mother died. Her father Thomas would have been 66 years old at this time. Her dad Thomas died when she was about 23 years old.

According to the 1930 U.S. Federal Census, Helen was living with the Porter family at sixteen years old. She may have lived with them even earlier. At age 31, Helen married Clarence Bransford Campbell, Sr. (May 21, 1894 – March 16, 1966) on June 15, 1946 in Clifton Forge, Virginia. Helen died at age 55 from "adenocarcinoma of left breast with multiple metastasis of bone, liver, brain," the medical term for breast cancer. She was a widow at the time of her death. Helen and Clarence are buried at Central Advent Christian Church Cemetery, 3515 Longdale Furnace Road (Rt. 269), Clifton Forge, Alleghany County, Virginia. Known children. If other children, it is private information.

Betty Jean Campbell Hague (Helen, G.11. Thomas, F.10. James, E.9. Thomas Turk, D.8. John, C.5. William, B.3. Archibald, A.1. Matthew) (June 15, 1948 – April 14, 2016) Betty died at age 68 and is buried at Central Advent Christian Church Cemetery, 3515 Longdale Furnace Road (Rt. 269), Clifton Forge, Alleghany County, Virginia.

Clarence Bransford Campbell, Jr. (Helen, G.11. Thomas, F.10. James, E.9. Thomas Turk, D.8. John, C.5. William, B.3. Archibald, A.1. Matthew) (March 4, 1950 – March 15, 2012). Clarence died at age 65 and is buried at Central Advent Christian Church Cemetery, 3515 Longdale Furnace Road (Rt. 269), Clifton Forge, Alleghany County, Virginia.

CLARENCE RHEA (G.11. Thomas, F.10. James, E.9. Thomas Turk, D.8. John, C.5. William, B.3. Archibald, A.1. Matthew) (June 18, 1917 - unknown). Clarence was born in Millboro Springs, Bath County, Virginia. He was two years old at the time of his mother's death and his dad, Thomas, was 66 years old. In 1930 U.S. Federal Census, Clarence, who was about 12 years old, lived with Madge Douglass, a widow, and her brother. By age 22, Clarence lived with the Conner family as a hired-hand laborer. Clarence served in the military, enlisting on January 2, 1943. He was single at enlistment. Clarence died in active military duty as a Private in the U.S. Army in World War II. No known wife or children.

BABY RHEA (G.11. Thomas, F.10. James, E.9. Thomas Turk, D.8. John, C.5. William, B.3. Archibald, A.1. Matthew) (1919-1919) Baby Rhea died at birth as did his mother Mamie Rhea. Mamie was about 27 or 28 years old at time of death. Baby Rhea is buried at Rehobeth Community Church Cemetery, 3785 Pig Run Road, Millboro, Bath County, Virginia.

Rehobeth Community Church Cemetery, 3785 Pig
Run Road, Millboro, Bath County, Virginia.

This country church borders what was once Rhea family land. According to family, the land the church sits upon was donated generations ago by the Rhea family for the building of the church. The building was remodeled, but the land is much the same other than the paved road. Many of the gravesites in the background are those of the Rhea family, spouses and descendants, dating back to 1905.

We stood over the gravesites, looking across the land in its tranquility as the Rhea family had most likely done over 100 years ago. This stretch of land beyond the church had been the Thomas Rhea family's home for many years. This peaceful little church and the land beyond holds numerous memories as it listened to generations of Rhea family voices in both happy and sad times. The shadows of the past seem to cling near us as if they understood our desire to know their history and pass it on to others. It was here that I felt a connection to the Rhea ancestors. Throughout this research and writing, Palmer and I visited this church cemetery on numerous occasions. Each time, I looked across the land with the thought "If only the ghostly shadows could talk." (Photo by Lillian "Sissy Crone" Frazer, June 2019)

Acreage on Pig Run Road, Millboro, Bath Cunty, Virginia across from the Rehobeth Community Church According to information from family and records, this was once among the Rhea family land.
(Photo by Lillian "Sissy Crone" Frazer, June 2019)

Pig Run Elementary School (closed Spring 1933 with 18 students that year.) Once known as New Hope School. This school was located about a mile from Rehoboth Church. J.W. Rhea purchased this building on November 14, 1933 for $49.50. According to Rhea family, David Rhea later lived in this home.

Children at New Hope School (also known as Pig Run School)
(Photo courtesy of Gloria Deitz)

Children at New Hope School (also known as Pig Run School)
(Girls with same dresses were sisters.)
(Photo courtesy of Gloria Deitz)

PALMER B. RHEA, SR.

EIGHTH GENERATION

PALMER B. RHEA, SR. (H.12.) (G.11. Thomas, F.10. James, E.9. Thomas Turk, D.8. John, C.5. William, B.3. Archibald, A.1. Matthew) (July 26, 1913 according to a delayed birth certificate – February 3, 1989). On July 26, 1913, Palmer was born in Bath County, Virginia, the third son to Thomas and Mamie Gear Rhea. At birth, Palmer, Sr. was given a middle initial "B" but no middle name. Family was unaware of his middle initial until many years later when they obtained a copy of his birth certificate.

Burial Location: Central Advent Christian Church Cemetery, 3515 Longdale Furnace Road (Rt. 269), Clifton Forge, Alleghany County, Virginia

Parents: Thomas "Pap" Henry Rhea (James, E.9. Thomas Turk, D.8. John, C.5. William, B.3. Archibald, A.1. Matthew) and **Mamie Gear Rhea**

Siblings: Stoney Echols Rhea, Courtney Russell Rhea, Helen Virginia Rhea, Clarence Rhea and Baby Rhea

Half-Siblings: John Wilson Rhea, Nellie Rhea, Garnett Sutton Rhea, Mollie Mae Rhea, Harry Tucker Rhea, James Tally Rhea, Mattie Myrtle Rhea, Henry Mckinley Rhea, Alice Beatty Rhea

Spouse: Mary Margaret Clark Nicely (Mother: Arvilla Reynolds, Father: Luman Curtis Clark)

Children of Palmer Rhea, Sr. and Mary Margaret Clark: Palmer Rhea, Jr. and Jo Ann Rhea

Stepchildren (Children of Mary Margaret Clark and Guy Jackson Nicely): Mitchell Eugene Nicely, Barbara Ellen Nicely, Geneviee Murle Nicely, Randolph Jackson Nicely, Roxie Lou Nicely, Margaret Christine Nicely, Edith Pauline Nicely

Palmer Sr.'s dad Thomas was previously married to Elizabeth Vest (Vess) and they had nine children from this marriage. After Elizabeth died, Thomas married Mamie Gear. Thomas and Mamie had six children, one who died at childbirth as did Mamie. Palmer was six years old when his mother died. Thomas had 15 children in total, three children younger in age than Palmer. Thomas was 66 years old and found himself widowed in his senior years with the responsibility for the care of five young children from ages ten to toddler, Palmer Sr. being one of them. Census indicate the young children lived at home with Thomas initially and then records list each young child as living with another family, some unrelated but neighbors living nearby. Palmer, Sr. lived with a neighbor, the John Beatty family in his teenage years and the years of 1930 and 1940 (according to U.S. Federal Census) and perhaps even earlier. The Rhea family thought he may have once lived with another family as well. As a teenager and young adult, Palmer worked on the Beatty farm.

Palmer, Sr. served in World War II in the U.S. Army from November 6, 1941 to December 2, 1944. Enlistment records indicate Palmer, Sr. was 5 feet 9 inches and 184 pounds in 1940 at 27 years old and was single.

Palmer's roots run deep in this mountainous county of the Allegheny Mountains. There was no city buzz, but there was and continue to be breathtaking views among the strong and enduring mountains and their blanket of trees. Palmer was born a mountain boy and a farm boy. His great granddad many times removed migrated to this nearby land sometime between the years of 1740 and 1750. By the 1950s and 1960s, 200 years later, Palmer Rhea, Sr. would spend his life farming land among the same mountain ranges that his forefathers once trotted, hunted and farmed. This timeless place was his home and home to generations of his family, and he loved it.

Palmer was called "Paul" by friends and family. In his mid-30's, "Paul" began working on a farm owned by Dr. John M. Emmitt, and years later the land was sold to another individual, Harry Walton. The land was a dairy farm with over 600 acres located in Crizer's Gap, Millboro, Bath County, Virginia (family referred to it as being in the Nimrod Hall area). The farm was known as the Molen Farm. There were several tenant homes on the property, Palmer, Sr. lived in a tenant home on one end of the property and other tenant families lived in the other homes. Palmer, Sr.'s. responsibilities were the growing and cutting of hay and grains and other farm duties while others working on the farm dealt with the caring and milking of the cows. In the years to follow, Dr. Emmitt, owner of the farm, sold the Molen Farm to Harry Walton and Palmer, Sr. continued to work for Mr. Walton.

After collection of the milk, it was taken to Covington to Peerless Creamery for pasteurization and processing. Once processed, the milk was distributed in bottles labeled as White Oak Dairy. Mr. Walton who now owned the farm also owned a farm on Potts Creek in Covington, Virginia, which was called White Oak Dairy Farm.

Milk bottle from the 1950s of White Oak Dairy milk

Palmer, Jr. and I recently visited the land that was once the Molen Farm, looking for signs of what was home to him in his early youth. Palmer, Jr., now in his mid-60's, with face illuminated with passion of days gone by, pointed out the location of where the big white two-story farmhouse in which he was born once stood. He proudly directed my view to other areas of what was portions of the farm, obviously picturing those early days. I had a desire to envision what he was seeing and smell the ghostly scents but as I looked over the land, I saw overgrown farmland and trees tangled with thick weeds. As we walked the area, Palmer, Jr. pointed out a tree hit by lightning in his youth and the long stretch of road they walked to retrieve their mail. Life would have been isolated with all this land other than the families living and working the farm. I imagined when night crept in this quiet green land would be dark, so dark it would be difficult to see in front of you, unless the moon and stars were shining bright. The dark may bring the sounds of the howl of a wolf. Yes, it was a remote location but today with the sky a bright blue as we look over the land, I see vibrant wildflowers in the distance, and we are surrounded by nature in its awesome glory.

On August 5, 1952 at age 39, Palmer, Sr. married for the first and only time to Mary Margaret Clark Nicely (March 9, 1916 – January 2, 1998), daughter to Luman Curtis Clark and Arvilla (Arvella) Reynolds.

They were married by Pastor Saunders, the pastor of the Baptist Church in Millboro.

Standing on his old homeplace must have stirred memories in Palmer, Jr. as he continued enthusiastically describing his first home. On the front of the old white farmhouse was a porch that ran the length of the front of the house, one door leading to the kitchen where most often he would find his mother cooking, canning, or baking. There was no bathroom but there was running water. There was no easy twist of a faucet to get that water, but a hand pump was in the kitchen. The other door, on the front of the home, entered the living area. Along the back of the house was another porch that ran almost the length of the rear of the house with a door entrance to Palmer, Sr. and Mary's bedroom. Their source of heat was wood burning stoves, and although there was a fireplace, Palmer, Jr. doesn't recall it ever holding a fire. He smiled as he recalled the fireplace was once briefly a home to a family of snakes. That ended one evening as two black snakes crawled out of the brick fireplace. The unwelcomed guests were quickly removed from the home. Palmer, Jr's bedroom was a small room leading off his parent's bedroom and upstairs housed two bedrooms for the other children. After Palmer's sister Jo Ann was born, Palmer moved upstairs, and Jo Ann stayed in the little bedroom next to Palmer, Sr. and Mary. Many of the older siblings had married and already moved.

Unfortunately, we located no pictures of the house or dairy of the Molen Farm. Cameras and development of pictures were luxuries in those days, so few pictures were taken. Even without the pictures to view, slowly the overgrown farmland we looked upon began taking form as I envisioned the outhouses and sheds behind the house, two small buildings inhabited by the chickens at night and who ran freely across the land during the day. In the far distance was the barn and silo. Roaming the land were the many head of dairy cows grazing leisurely. On the other side of the house set back somewhat stood the pig pen full of grunting and squealing pigs. If Palmer, Jr. or one of his siblings could only draw, the picture of the Molen Farm would not be lost. Perhaps someone has a photo to share someday.

Prior to Palmer, Sr.'s marriage to Mary, she was a widow to Guy

Jackson Nicely. Guy worked on the dairy portion of the Molen farm. Palmer, Sr. became acquainted with the family at that time. During their marriage, Mary and Guy Nicely had seven children: Mitchell Eugene, Barbara Ellen, Geneviee Murle, Randolph Jackson, Roxie Lou, Margaret Christine and Edith Pauline. Upon Guy Nicely's death, Mary was left a widow with children ranging in ages from 16 to a baby. Guy Nicely is buried at Central Advent Christian Church Cemetery.

Palmer and Mary Margaret Clark Nicely, as mentioned, would later marry and had two children by their marriage, a son named after him, Palmer Rhea, Jr. and a daughter, Jo Ann Rhea. Palmer, Sr. and Mary also raised Mary's children from her marriage with Guy Nicely, so they had a family of nine children.

As we stood amid the overgrown weeds looking out to the land beyond of what was once an active farm, a gentle breeze flows across our faces and my thoughts go to those who once roamed the land, ones I had never met but felt as if I knew them. As Palmer's arm stretched out to show the location of where once stood the barn, he told me a story of an evening years ago. He was still a young boy. His dad came in for dinner and quietly told his wife he needed to go back to the dairy barn. Palmer, Jr. overheard and insisted he accompany his dad. His dad didn't want him along but finally agreed, sternly informing his son, "Boy, if you go with me, you'll have to be quiet."

Excited to be allowed to go, Palmer, Jr. nodded in agreement and scuttled out behind his dad and in silence followed him. After a brisk walk they met up with another farm worker and instead of heading to the barn they proceeded to the field where a buck laid sprawled out in the high grass. Someone had shot the deer and now his dad and the other worker were dragging it back to the barn when they saw vehicle lights headed their direction. The farm had over 600 acres of land, which they often hunted but it was not deer hunting season. Palmer, Sr. with a sternness to his voice, instructed Palmer, Jr. to lie down in the high grass. Palmer, Sr. and the other man crouched down in the grass as well. A tingle of fear ran up Palmer, Jr.'s back wondering why it was necessary to be so quiet. The vehicle stopped very close to them and a man stepped out, leaving on his car lights. Palmer, Jr. could smell the cigar the man had in his hand and each time he took a puff, Palmer could see the tip end light up. He heard his dad and the other man say it was the game warden. Palmer, Jr. was a bit edgy, but his dad laid a hand firmly on his shoulder. Finally, the game warden finished his cigar and took a final look around. Apparently satisfied, he jumped back into his vehicle and headed away from them. Once the vehicle was out of sight, Palmer, Sr. offered no explanation, simply told Palmer, Jr. to help pull the buck to the barn. Palmer, Jr. followed through with no hesitation.

Some days and some things just cannot be forgotten even if we would like to, and Palmer proceeded to tell me about one of those days as he looked at where the barn once stood. Again as a young lad, he had done some mischief, which now escaped his memory of what it might have been, but he was attempting to escape his mother's punishment by fleeing to the direction of the barn in hopes she would forget his mischief. His sisters Margaret and Edith chased after him to bring him back to face his due punishment. (As I listened intently, I knew I would never flee my punishment as that would only make things worse with my mother but then again it was the brothers in our family that were full of mischief, not we girls.) Palmer continues his story. In his fleeing, his steps took on speed and he ran as swiftly as his little legs would carry him toward the barn with both sisters in high chase behind him.

As they neared the barn, they saw black smoke rising from the barn. With eyes intense and a twinge of fear and forgetting all else, all three stopped to watch as they saw men hustling to get the cows out of the barn, men and cows hollering, fire ablaze and black smoke circling overhead. Soon the firetruck arrived, but water had to be pumped from the nearby river, a good distance from the barn. In the excitement of freeing the cows, some cows escaped trying to get back into the barn near their young ones. Although all attempts were made to free all the animals, the barn was full of hay and the fire grew and moved faster than the men making it impossible to reenter the barn. Palmer, Jr. recalled the horrendous smell of burning cow flesh as over 30 cows, young and old, died that day. The barn fell in burned rubble so quickly, never to be rebuilt.

Not long after, Dr. Emmitt, who once owned The Molen Farm,

purchased a 536-acre farm known as Fort Dickinson Farm located on the Cowpasture River in Bath County, Virginia. Dr. Emmitt offered Palmer, Sr. the opportunity to manage the working farm and Palmer, Sr. accepted this offer.

The Molen Farm, which Palmer, Sr. previously worked, in years to come was sold to the government and became known as the Walton Tract on the Cowpasture River and is managed by the Virginia Department of Game & Inland Fisheries offering access to the Cowpasture River for canoeing or fishing or to venture through the acres of fields and woodland for an opportunity to view wild turkeys and local habitats.

Palmer, Sr.'s new management and home at Fort Dickinson became the home and the farmland that Palmer, Jr., and some of his siblings so fondly recall as their home place. Even though the farm did not belong to them, they loved it as though it was their own. The family lived in the three-story farmhouse located on the property. The home was three levels with only two living levels as the basement was unfinished, the walls were of plaster as homes were in those days and their sources of heat were wooden stoves, much as it was in their home at the Molen Farm. Unlike the Molen Farm, this farmhouse had two bathrooms.

A historical marker stood on the edge of the property then and continues to stand today. This land was one of a chain of defense forts established in 1756 under the direction of Colonel George Washington to counter the Indian attacks. Colonel Washington inspected this fort during his travels in 1755 – 1756 about the same time that the three Rhea brothers came to what was then the Augusta County area. There were no remains of the fort when Palmer's family lived there, only the sign indicating it was once a fort. Random people often stopped by trying to locate or view relics of the old fort. There was a large antique dinner bell on the property. The land and mountains that Palmer and his family roamed, was the same land that held threads of history for his family and for so many others who protected Fort Dickinson in those colonial days.

Following is an excerpt from *A History of Windy Cove Presbyterian Church* regarding the home on Fort Dickinson:

This house stands on the original site of Fort Dickinson. It stands on a small plateau in the midst of the river bottoms. One-half mile north of Nimrod Hall, and about one mile from the first house of worship of Windy Cove congregation. It is about three miles from the present church building by the road. This ancient Fort is intimately connected with the history of Windy Cove. It was named for the first Adam Dickinson, the leading pioneer on the Cowpasture River, and on a part of whose land the first church building stood. Of the first Indian raids into Bath County, the earliest we can locate took place near the middle of September, 1756. During this raid occurred the first attack on Fort Dickinson. Captain Dickinson was away at a general muster. When Washington came along about seven weeks later, he remarked that the stockade was in need of improvement. He also remarked that at the time of attack, the Indians crept close to the enclosure without being discovered and captured several children.[87]

The primary crops of the farm were cows and hogs. Once old enough, the cows and hogs would be taken to the livestock market in Staunton, Virginia to be sold. Hay and grains were grown on the farm to feed the livestock. For Palmer, Sr. and family farming held laborious tasks and routine of daily chores as well as the simple pleasures in life.

The family also raised milking cows. These were not sold but used for fresh milk and to make butter. Chickens were raised on the farm to supply fresh eggs as well as an occasional dinner. Palmer's family canned vegetables from the garden to sustain them during the winter months. Farming was difficult work with grueling hours and little monetary money for the family, but they loved the farm. It was home.

When the youth, Palmer Rhea, Jr. with the mass of blond hair and blue eyes, wasn't assisting his dad on the farm, he was active on the school team sports (football, baseball and track) or would trample through the woods hunting for whatever was in season whether it be deer, wild turkey, quail, rabbit and even groundhog and squirrel.

---

[87] *A History of Windy Cove Presbyterian Church*, Millboro Springs, Virginia 1749-1976, History Committee, McClure Printing Co., Inc., Verona, Virginia, pp. 22-23.

Hunting was not for the sport as much as it was a way of life for his family. Palmer's dad hunted before him and his dad before him. They supplemented the family's food with the wild mountain game brought home.

Palmer, Jr. got his first deer at 11 years old. He helped his dad skin the deer meat at this early age. Before his teen years, he would adventure in the woods alone at times and other times with a family member or his life-long friends to shoot a deer and drag it back home. He began fishing the river and trout streams beginning at six years old. On occasion today, Palmer with enthusiasm and pride in his voice states, "Bath County has the best hunting and fishing a body can find!" Palmer, as does his family, holds tight to those cherished memories.

In Palmer, Sr.'s retirement years, Fort Dickinson Farm was sold, and Palmer Sr. and Mary moved from the farm. Their children had grown to adulthood having families of their own. On February 3, 1989, Palmer, Sr. died of "myocardial infarction," medical term for heart attack. Palmer is buried at Central Advent Christian Church Cemetery, 3515 Longdale Furnace Road (Rt. 269), Clifton Forge, Alleghany County, Virginia. He was 75 years old at death. Almost nine years later, on January 2, 1998, Mary died and is also buried at Central Advent Christian Church Cemetery.

The children and stepchildren of Palmer Rhea, Sr. have children and grandchildren but only one son, one male grandchild and one male great-grandchild at this time can carry on the Rhea family name. Names of grandchildren and great grandchildren are not included for privacy.

Palmer Rhea, Sr. and family moved into this farmhouse about 1963, living there until the early 1980's. The home was one of two tenant homes located on what was part of the original Ft. Dickinson land. This was a 10-room, three-story home (basement level unfinished) built in 1835 and owner was Warwick Gatewood. This home was about a mile north of Nimrod Hall. At the time Palmer Rhea, Sr. lived in the home, the land was privately owned and served as a working farm, primarily livestock. The farm was operated and managed by Palmer Rhea, Sr. This home served as the Palmer Rhea, Sr. family home during his term of management of the property and is the home that Palmer Rhea, Jr. calls his home place. This home no longer stands.

Distant view of the Fort Dickinson Farm buildings and home. The farm buildings continue to stand today but the three-level home no longer stands. Photo courtesy of Jo Ann Rhea Irvine

Palmer Rhea, Sr. and Mary Rhea in their senior years (first row)
Children: Roxie, Jo Ann, Margaret (second row)
Photo courtesy of Charles Putnam

Palmer Rhea, Sr.at a family wedding.
(Photo courtesy of Jo Ann Rhea Irvine)

Palmer Rhea, Jr., 2019

Calfpasture River, Bath County, Virginia
Photo by Lillian "Sissy Crone" razer, June 2019

Bull Pasture River, Bath County, Virginia.
Photo by Lillian "Sissy Crone" Frazer, August 2019

The Junction of the Bullpasture River and Cowpasture River
where the Bullpasture joins the Cowpasture River (originally
named "Wallawhatoola" interpreted as "winding waters")
south of what was the Town of Williamsville, Virginia.
Photo by Lillian "Sissy Crone" Frazer, August 2019

An excerpt from *A History of Windy Cove Presbyterian Church* regarding
the Cowpasture River:

*About this time a number of enterprising and hardy families, seeking a
home in the wilderness, came and settled in this neighborhood on this
river, and changed its beautiful Indian name of Wallawhatoola into
that of Cowpasture River. They were soon afterwards joined by other
families. They were the descendants of those who had suffered so much
in the Old Country under Claverhouse, the bloodhound of persecution
in Scotland. Their fathers and mothers had been shut up for eight
months in the siege of Derry. It is stated in the history of that day of
blood, that about twenty-seven thousand persons were shut up in the
walls of that town, of whom about one thousand perished in the siege,
when James the II was endeavoring to bring them into subjection, and
establish over them in all the realm, the Roman Catholic religion. They
came to this broad land in the hope of enjoying that civil and religious
liberty which neither they nor their fathers could enjoy at home.* [88]

---

[88] *A History of Windy Cove Presbyterian Church*, Millboro Springs, Virginia 1749-1976,
History Committee, McClure Printing Co., Inc., Verona, Virginia, pp. 20-2

Slim's Grocery, Williamsville, Bath County, Virginia
This was an operating store in days of some of the Rhea family,
who lived and shopped in this area. Today this store is shuttered
with dilapidated boards and faded memories remaining.
Photo taken by Lillian "Sissy Crone" Frazer," July 2019

Another fort established centuries ago located in what is current day Bath County is Fort Lewis. This fort tucked in the mountains was among the series of fortifications established to protect the Shenandoah Mountain pass from Indian attacks during the French and Indian War. Colonel Charles Lewis built a small stockade on his 3,200-acre plantation farm in 1750, which served as the Fort. This enchanting land is still known as the Fort Lewis Farm, and the farm itself has seen little change throughout the years, appearing mostly untouched with all its scenic spender. Fort Lewis Lodge is privately owned and serves as a country inn and cabins with fishing and hiking. The gristmill which had been built in 1850s has been remodeled and serves as a dining room. We recently accompanied Palmer Jr's. childhood friends and residents of the County, Clara and Jimbo Tennant, to tour the Lodge and Silo, enjoy a fabulous dinner and relax on the pavilion looking upon breathtaking views. One could not possibly view these mountains and be oblivious to the surroundings. I was absorbed in the beauty as I thought of a bygone era. We later dined in the restored countryside gristmill dining room and relished a magnificent meal.

Deitz Store, Millboro Springs, Virginia

Palmer, Jr. fondly recalls the Deitz Store. He laughs as he tells of an afternoon years ago in his early youth. Palmer, Jr. was standing outside the barn at Fort Dickinson with his dad and other farm workers, one being Wendell Luckett, when a mother skunk and her babies crossed the field. Mr. Luckett told young Palmer that if he caught one of the baby skunks, he would take him to Deitz Store and buy him all the ice cream he could eat. Palmer gladly agreed already craving the ice cream that he would get as payment.

Young Palmer ran to the skunks, slowly approached them and, as he reached down to get one of the babies, he was sprayed by the mother. Palmer covering his face ran as quickly as he could to Mr. Luckett. Mr. Luckett was unable to refrain from laughing as young Palmer stood silently watching. After uncontrollable laughter, Mr. Luckett said, "Get in the truck, boy. A deal is a deal."

Palmer leaped in the truck while Mr. Luckett drove with his head hung out the window. Once at Deitz Store, they both hopped out and headed inside. The nasty smell arrived ahead of them as Mr. Deitz looked up and yelled, "You smell like a skunk, boy! Get out of here."

Palmer, Jr. got his ice cream and learned the ghastly odor of a skunk does not go away easily.

Windy Cove Church, Millboro Springs
Photo taken by Lillian "Sissy Crone" Frazer, May 2019

Woodland Union Church, Millboro
Photo taken by Lillian "Sissy Crone" Frazer, May 2019

The Homestead, Hot Springs, Bath County, Virginia. The original lodge was built in 1766 by Thomas Bullitt. The modern resort dates from 1888 and was rebuilt by J.P. Morgan and investors. Palmer Rhea, Jr. has affectionate memories of this spectacular resort as he recalls a couple fall seasons during high school working in the dining room. Upon graduation, Palmer, Jr. recalls the resort graciously allowed the local Bath County High School to host their prom. When in the area, Palmer, Jr. and I have a fondness for driving by The Homestead even when time does not allow us to tour. (Photo taken by Lillian "Sissy Crone" Frazer, May 2019)

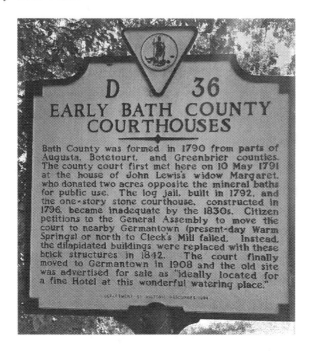

"*December 14, 1790 the Virginia Assembly passed an act- which created Bath County (act found in Morton's History.) The first court in Bath County convened on May 10, 1791 at the home of Margaret Lewis, widow of Captain John Lewis, at Warm Springs. The justices present on the opening day were the following: John Bollar, I. Dean, J. Poage. William Poage, Samuel Vance and John Wilson. The first sheriff was Sampson Matthews and Charles Cameron, the first clerk. Their bond was set at 1,000 lbs. ($3,333.33). William Poage: was the first surveyor and Samuel Vance the first coroner. The Attorneys were John Cotton, James Reed, and Archibald Stuart. The members of the first Grand Jury were: Joseph Mayse, foreman. Samuel Black, Thomas Brode, John Dilley, James Hamilton, James Hughart, Owen Kelley. John Lynch, John McClung, Samuel McDonald, John Montgomery, **Joseph Rhea**. William Rider, Robert Stuart and Stephen Wilson.*"

(Prepared by Jean Graham McAlister Under the auspices of the County School Board and the Board of Supervisors of the County, 1920, Transcribed by N. Piper)

RHEAS

A.1. MATTHEW CAMPBELL RHEA (abt. 1665 – unknown)
Children of **MATTHEW CAMPBELL RHEA** and Janet Baxter:
> **B.2. WILLIAM RHEA** (A.1. Matthew)
> **B.3. ARCHIBALD RHEA** (A.1. Matthew)
> **B.4. MATTHEW CAMPBELL RHEA** (A.1. Matthew)

B.2. WILLIAM RHEA (A.1. Matthew) (abt. 1687 - abt. 1777)
> Children of **WILLIAM RHEA** (A.1. Matthew) and Elizabeth:
> **MARY RHEA BROWN** (B.2. William, A.1. Matthew)
> **ELIZABETH RHEA MCCORKLE** (B.2. William, A.1. Matthew)
> Children of Elizabeth Rhea McCorkle and James McCorkle:
> **James McCorkle** (Elizabeth, B.2. William, A.1. Matthew)
> **William McCorkle** (Elizabeth, B.2. William, A.1. Matthew)

B.3. ARCHIBALD RHEA (A.1. Matthew): (b. abt. 1688)
(THOUGHT TO BE DIRECT ANCESTOR TO PALMER RHEA, SR. ACCORDING TO RESEARCHERS UNLESS OTHER INFORMATION BECOMES AVAILABLE.)
> Children of **ARCHIBALD RHEA** (A.1. Matthew) and Ann:
> **C.5. WILLIAM RHEA, SR.** (B.3. Archibald, A.1. Matthew **(DIRECT ANCESTOR TO PALMER RHEA, SR)**
> **C.6. ROBERT RHEA** (B.3. Archibald, A.1. Matthew)
> **C.7. ARCHIBALD RHEA** (B.3. Archibald, A.1. Matthew)

B.4. MATTHEW CAMPBELL RHEA II (A.1. Matthew) (b. abt. 1689)

Children of **MATTHEW RHEA CAMPBELL II** (A.1. Matthew) and Elizabeth McClain:

> **ELIZABETH MCCLAIN RHEA** (B.4. Matthew. A.1. Matthew)
>
> **ABRAHAM RHEA** (B.4. Matthew. A.1. Matthew)
>
> **JAMES RHEA** (B.4. Matthew. A.1. Matthew)
>
> **MARGERY RHEA** (B.4. Matthew. A.1. Matthew)
>
> **JOSEPH RHEA** (B.4.Matthew. A.1. Matthew) (1715-1777)
>
> Children of **JOSEPH RHEA** and Elizabeth McIlwaine:
>
> > **John Angus Rhea** (Joseph, B.4. Matthew. A.1. Matthew)
> >
> > **Matthew Rhea** (Joseph, B.4. Matthew. A.1. Matthew)
> >
> > **Margaret Rhea Preston** (Joseph, B.4. Matthew. A.1. Matthew)
> >
> > **William Rhea** (Joseph, B.4. Matthew. A.1. Matthew)
> >
> > **Joseph C. Rhea** (Joseph, B.4. Matthew. A.1. Matthew)
> >
> > **Elizabeth Rhea Rhea** (Joseph, B.4. Matthew. A.1. Matthew)
> >
> > **Samuel Rhea** (Joseph, B.4. Matthew. A.1. Matthew)
> >
> > **James Rhea** (Joseph, B.4. Matthew. A.1. Matthew
>
> **AGNES RHEA** (B.4. Matthew. A.1. Matthew)
>
> **MARGARET RHEA LOONEY RENTFRO (See C.8.)** (B.4. Matthew. A.1. Matthew)

Children of **MATTHEW CAMPBELL RHEA II** (A.1. Matthew) and Mary Lockhart:

> **SAMUEL RHEA (REA)** (B.4. Matthew. A.1. Matthew)
>
> Children of **SAMUEL RHEA (REA):**
>
> > **Ann Rhea (Rea)** (Samuel, B.4. Matthew. A.1. Matthew)
> >
> > **John Rhea (Rea)** (Samuel, B.4. Matthew. A.1. Matthew)
> >
> > **William Rhea (Rea)** (Samuel, B.4. Matthew. A.1. Matthew)
> >
> > **Sarah Rhea (Rea)** (Samuel, B.4. Matthew. A.1. Matthew)
> >
> > **Samuel Rhea (Rea)** (Samuel, B.4. Matthew. A.1. Matthew)
> >
> > **Hannah Rhea (Rea)** (Samuel, B.4. Matthew. A.1. Matthew)
> >
> > **James Rhea (Rea)** (Samuel, B.4. Matthew. A.1. Matthew)

ISAAC RHEA (B.4. Matthew. A.1. Matthew)

MATTHEW RHEA III (B.4. Matthew. A.1. Matthew)

WILLIAM RHEA (B.4. Matthew. A.1. Matthew)

Children of **WILLIAM RHEA:**

    Matthew Rhea (William, B.4. Matthew. A.1. Matthew)

    Jennie Rhea (William, B.4. Matthew. A.1. Matthew)

    Joseph Rhea (William, B.4. Matthew. A.1. Matthew)

    William Rhea (William, B.4. Matthew. A.1. Matthew)

    Sarah Rhea (William, B.4. Matthew. A.1. Matthew)

    Elizabeth Rhea (William, B.4. Matthew. A.1. Matthew)

    Robert "Major" Rhea (William, B.4. Matthew. A.1. Matthew)

C.5. WILLIAM RHEA, SR. (C.5.) (B.3. Archibald, A.1. Matthew) (1718-1802) **(DIRECT ANCESTOR TO PALMER RHEA, SR.)**

Children of **WILLIAM RHEA, SR.** (B.3. Archibald, A.1. Matthew) and Elizabeth Clark Rhea (not necessarily in order):

ARCHIBALD RHEA (C.5. William, B.3. Archibald, A.1. Matthew) (abt. 1747/1750 – 1773)

Children of **ARCHIBALD RHEA:**

    William Rhea (Archibald, C.5. William, B.3. Archibald, A.1. Matthew)

    Hugh Rhea (Archibald, C.5. William, B.3. Archibald, A.1. Matthew)

    John Rhea (Archibald, C.5. William, B.3. Archibald, A.1. Matthew)

JAMES RHEA (C.5. William, B.3. Archibald, A.1. Matthew) (abt. 1753-1795)

Children of **JAMES RHEA** (C.5. William, B.3. Archibald, A.1. Matthew) and Elizabeth Meek:

    Nancy Rhea Ritchey (James, C.5. William, B.3. Archibald, A.1. Matthew)

    Elizabeth Rhea Rhea (James, C.5. William, B.3. Archibald, A.1. Matthew)

James Rhea, Jr. (James, C.5. William, B.3. Archibald, A.1. Matthew)

Margaret Rhea Barnett (James, C.5. William, B.3. Archibald, A.1. Matthew)

Thomas Rhea (James, C.5. William, B.3. Archibald, A.1. Matthew)

Mary "Polly" Rhea Rhea Hickman (James, C.5. William, B.3. Archibald, A.1. Matthew)

Hannah Rhea Hickman (James, C.5. William, B.3. Archibald, A.1. Matthew)

Martha Rhea (James, C.5. William, B.3. Archibald, A.1. Matthew)

John Rhea (James, C.5. William, B.3. Archibald, A.1. Matthew

WILLIAM RHEA, JR. (C.5. William, B.3. Archibald, A.1. Matthew) (abt. 1754-1824)

Children of **WILLIAM RHEA, JR.** and Mary Gay:

Robert Rhea (William, Jr., C.5. William, B.3. Archibald, A.1. Matthew)

Agnes Nancy Rhea Wells (William, Jr., C.5. William, B.3. Archibald, A.1. Matthew)

Archibald Rhea (William, Jr., C.5. William, B.3. Archibald, A.1. Matthew)

Known children of **WILLIAM RHEA, JR.** and Elizabeth Brownlee Nelson:

John Rhea (William, Jr., C.5. William, B.3. Archibald, A.1. Matthew)

Alexander Rhea (William, Jr., C.5. William, B.3. Archibald, A.1. Matthew)

Anne (Anny) Rhea Hutcheson (William, Jr., C.5. William, B.3. Archibald, A.1. Matthew)

William Rhea (William, Jr., C.5. William, B.3. Archibald, A.1. Matthew)

Thomas Rhea (William, Jr., C.5. William, B.3. Archibald, A.1. Matthew)

Elizabeth Rhea Gum (William, Jr., C.5. William, B.3. Archibald, A.1. Matthew)

Clarissa Rhea Minton (William, Jr., C.5. William, B.3. Archibald, A.1. Matthew)

Narcissa Rhea Dills Blakeman (William, Jr., C.5. William, B.3. Archibald, A.1. Matthew

ALEXANDER RHEA (C.5. William, B.3. Archibald, A.1. Matthew) (abt. 1755-1818)

Known children of **ALEXANDER RHEA** and Mary Crockett:

Eleanor Rhea (Alexander, C.5. William, B.3. Archibald, A.1. Matthew)

William Rhea (Alexander, C.5. William, B.3. Archibald, A.1. Matthew)

ROBERT RHEA (C.5. William, B.3. Archibald, A.1. Matthew) (1759-1834)

Known children of **ROBERT RHEA** and Martha Meek:

William Rhea (Robert, C.5. William, B.3. Archibald, A.1. Matthew)

Martha Rhea Rhea (Robert, C.5. William, B.3. Archibald, A.1. Matthew)

Thomas Rhea (Robert, C.5. William, B.3. Archibald, A.1. Matthew)

Samuel Rhea (Robert, C.5. William, B.3. Archibald, A.1. Matthew)

Robert Rhea, Jr. (Robert, C.5. William, B.3. Archibald, A.1. Matthew

Known children of **ROBERT RHEA** and Catherine Boiler:

James Rhea (Robert, C.5. William, B.3. Archibald, A.1. Matthew)

Nancy Rhea (Robert, C.5. William, B.3. Archibald, A.1. Matthew)

Elizabeth Rhea (Robert, C.5. William, B.3. Archibald, A.1. Matthew)

Hannah Rhea Callison (Robert, C.5. William, B.3. Archibald, A.1. Matthew)

Anne Rhea Hill (Robert, C.5. William, B.3. Archibald, A.1. Matthew)

David Rhea (Robert, C.5. William, B.3. Archibald, A.1. Matthew)

Archibald Rhea (Robert, C.5. William, B.3. Archibald, A.1. Matthew)

ANN/ANNA RHEA LOCKRIDGE (C.5. William, B.3. Archibald, A.1. Matthew) (abt. 1762-1837)

Known children of **ANN/ANNA RHEA LOCKRIDGE** and John Lockridge:

Andrew Lockridge (Ann Lockridge, C.5. William, B.3. Archibald, A.1. Matthew)

William Lockridge (Ann Lockridge, C.5. William, B.3. Archibald, A.1. Matthew)

John Lockridge (Ann Lockridge, C.5. William, B.3. Archibald, A.1. Matthew)

James Lockridge (Ann Lockridge, C.5. William, B.3. Archibald, A.1. Matthew)

Betsy Lockridge (Ann Lockridge, C.5. William, B.3. Archibald, A.1. Matthew)

Sarah Lockridge Buchanan (Ann Lockridge, C.5. William, B.3. Archibald, A.1. Matthew).

Ann Lockridge (Ann Lockridge, C.5. William, B.3. Archibald, A.1. Matthew)

JOHN S. RHEA (D.8.) (C.5. William, B.3. Archibald, A.1. Matthew) (b. abt. 1752) **(DIRECT ANCESTOR TO PALMER RHEA, SR.)**

Known children of **JOHN S. RHEA** and Margaret Turk were:

Elizabeth Rhea Wright (D.8. John, C.5. William, B.3. Archibald, A.1. Matthew)

William Rhea (D.8. John, C.5. William, B.3. Archibald, A.1. Matthew

John Rhea (D.8. John, C.5. William, B.3. Archibald, A.1. Matthew)

Margaret Rhea Wright (D.8. John, C.5. William, B.3. Archibald, A.1. Matthew)

THOMAS TURK RHEA (E.9.) (D.8. John, C.5. William, B.3. Archibald, A.1. Matthew) **(DIRECT ANCESTOR TO PALMER RHEA, SR.)**

Ann Rhea (D.8. John, C.5. William, B.3. Archibald, A.1. Matthew)

James Rhea (D.8. John, C.5. William, B.3. Archibald, A.1. Matthew)

Jane Rhea (D.8. John, C.5. William, B.3. Archibald, A.1. Matthew)

Polly Rhea (D.8. John, C.5. William, B.3. Archibald, A.1. Matthew)

Known children of **JOHN S. RHEA** and Magdalena Dill:

Nancy P. Rhea (D.8. John, C.5. William, B.3. Archibald, A.1. Matthew)

Hiram Rhea (D.8. John, C.5. William, B.3. Archibald, A.1. Matthew

Sarah H. Rhea (D.8. John, C.5. William, B.3. Archibald, A.1. Matthew)

Henry Dill Rhea (D.8. John, C.5. William, B.3. Archibald, A.1. Matthew)

Esther J. Rhea (D.8. John, C.5. William, B.3. Archibald, A.1. Matthew)

Mary Rhea (D.8. John, C.5. William, B.3. Archibald, A.1. Matthew)

C.6. ROBERT RHEA (B.3. Archibald, A.1. Matthew) (abt. 1720-1779)

Known children of **ROBERT RHEA** and Sarah Bingham were:

ISABELLA RHEA MCCLESKEY (C.6. Robert, B.3. Archibald, A.1. Matthew) (1752-1803)

Children of **ISABELLA RHEA MCCLESKEY** and James McCleskey:

Susannah McCleskey (Isabella, C.6. Robert, B.3. Archibald, A.1. Matthew)

David Henderson McCleskey (Isabella, C.6. Robert, B.3. Archibald, A.1. Matthew)

Martha McCleskey (Isabella, C.6. Robert, B.3. Archibald, A.1. Matthew)

James Rhea McCleskey (Isabella, C.6. Robert, B.3. Archibald, A.1. Matthew)

JOHN RHEA (C.6. Robert, B.3. Archibald, A.1. Matthew) (1754-1830)

Known children of **JOHN RHEA** and Mary Gay:

Mary Agnes Rhea Keagher (John, C.6. Robert, B.3. Archibald, A.1. Matthew)

ARCHIBALD RHEA (C.6. Robert, B.3. Archibald, A.1. Matthew) (1756-1793)

Known children of **ARCHIBALD RHEA** and Margaret were:

Archibald Rhea (Archibald, C.6. Robert, B.3. Archibald, A.1. Matthew)

Robert Rhea (Archibald, C.6. Robert, B.3. Archibald, A.1. Matthew)

Ann Rhea Mitchell (Archibald, C.6. Robert, B.3. Archibald, A.1. Matthew)

Jane Rhea Sevier (Archibald, C.6. Robert, B.3. Archibald, A.1. Matthew)

Sarah Rhea Wear (Archibald, C.6. Robert, B.3. Archibald, A.1. Matthew)

Elizabeth Rhea Houston (Archibald, C.6. Robert, B.3. Archibald, A.1. Matthew)

Mary Rhea (Archibald, C.6. Robert, B.3. Archibald, A.1. Matthew)

Rebecca Rhea Hamilton (Archibald, C.6. Robert, B.3. Archibald, A.1. Matthew)

ANN RHEA TURK (C.6. Robert, B.3. Archibald, A.1. Matthew) (1759-1836)

Known children of **ANN RHEA TURK** and Thomas Turk, Jr. are:

James Turk (Ann, C.6. Robert, B.3. Archibald, A.1. Matthew).

Robert Turk (Ann, C.6. Robert, B.3. Archibald, A.1. Matthew)

Thomas Turk III (Ann, C.6. Robert, B.3. Archibald, A.1. Matthew)

Margaret Turk Robertson (Ann, C.6. Robert, B.3. Archibald, A.1. Matthew)

Sally Turk (Ann, C.6. Robert, B.3. Archibald, A.1. Matthew)

Elizabeth Turk (Ann, C.6. Robert, B.3. Archibald, A.1. Matthew)

Archibald Rhea Turk (Ann, C.6. Robert, B.3. Archibald, A.1. Matthew)

William Turk (Ann, C.6. Robert, B.3. Archibald, A.1. Matthew)

Hiram Kerr Turk (Ann, C.6. Robert, B.3. Archibald, A.1. Matthew)

ROBERT RHEA, JR. (C.6. Robert, B.3. Archibald, A.1. Matthew) (1763-1850)

Known children of **ROBERT RHEA, JR.** and Mary Stephens are:

Jehu Stephens Rhea (Robert, Jr., C.6. Robert, B.3. Archibald, A.1. Matthew)

Louis L. Rhea Halloway (Robert, Jr., C.6. Robert, B.3. Archibald, A.1. Matthew)

Dillian Rhea (Robert, Jr., C.6. Robert, B.3. Archibald, A.1. Matthew)

Mary Rhea (Robert, Jr., C.6. Robert, B.3. Archibald, A.1. Matthew)

Elizabeth Rhea (Robert, Jr., C.6. Robert, B.3. Archibald, A.1. Matthew)

ELIZABETH RHEA COYNER (C.6. Robert, B.3. Archibald, A.1. Matthew) (1765-1841)

Known children of **ELIZABETH RHEA COYNER** and Martin Luther Coyner are:

John Coyner (Elizabeth, C.6. Robert, B.3. Archibald, A.1. Matthew)

Robert Crawford Coyner (Elizabeth, C.6. Robert, B.3. Archibald, A.1. Matthew)

Archibald Rhea Coyner (Elizabeth, C.6. Robert, B.3. Archibald, A.1. Matthew)

Margaret Diller Coyner (Elizabeth, C.6. Robert, B.3. Archibald, A.1. Matthew)

James Burgess Coyner (Elizabeth, C.6. Robert, B.3. Archibald, A.1. Matthew)

Sarah Bingham Coyner Bell (Elizabeth, C.6. Robert, B.3. Archibald, A.1. Matthew)

Martin Luther Coyner (Elizabeth, C.6. Robert, B.3. Archibald, A.1. Matthew)

Rev. David H. Coyner (Elizabeth, C.6. Robert, B.3. Archibald, A.1. Matthew)

Addison Hyde Coyner (Elizabeth, C.6. Robert, B.3. Archibald, A.1. Matthew)

C.7. ARCHIBALD RHEA (B.3. Archibald, A.1. Matthew) (abt. 1725 – 1804)

Thought to be children of **ARCHIBALD RHEA** and Jean McCausland and another possible unknown wife:

JOHN S. RHEA (C.7. Archibald, B.3. Archibald, A.1. Matthew)

ROBERT RHEA (C.7. Archibald, B.3. Archibald, A.1. Matthew)

ANDREW RHEA (C.7. Archibald, B.3. Archibald, A.1. Matthew)

ISABELLA RHEA (C.7. Archibald, B.3. Archibald, A.1. Matthew)

ANN RHEA (C.7. Archibald, B.3. Archibald, A.1. Matthew)

JEAN RHEA (C.7. Archibald, B.3. Archibald, A.1. Matthew)

MARTHA RHEA (C.7. Archibald, B.3. Archibald, A.1. Matthew)

REBECKEA RHEA (C.7. Archibald, B.3. Archibald, A.1. Matthew)

ARCHIBALD RHEA (C.7. Archibald, B.3. Archibald, A.1. Matthew)

WILLIAM RHEA (C.7. Archibald, B.3. Archibald, A.1. Matthew)

MARY RHEA (C.7. Archibald, B.3. Archibald, A.1. Matthew)

C.8. MARGARET RHEA LOONEY RENTFRO (B.4. Matthew. A.1. Matthew) (abt. 1722-1803)

Children of **MARGARET RHEA** and Robert Looney, Jr.:

JOHN (RHEA) LOONEY (C.8. Margaret, B.4. Matthew, A.1. Matthew) (abt. 1744 -abt. 1819)

MOSES LOONEY (C.8. Margaret, B.4. Matthew, A.1. Matthew) (abt. 1745/1748 - 1824)

BENJAMIN RHEA LOONEY (C.8. Margaret, B.4. Matthew, A.1. Matthew) (abt. 1748-1783)

SAMUEL RHEA LOONEY (C.8. Margaret, B.4. Matthew, A.1. Matthew) (abt. 1751/1754 - May 1779)

MARY LOONEY GRIMES: (C.8. Margaret, B.4. Matthew, A.1. Matthew) (Born 1756)

D.8. JOHN S. RHEA (C.5. William, B.3. Archibald, A.1. Matthew) (b. abt. 1752) **(DIRECT ANCESTOR TO PALMER RHEA, SR.)**

Known children of **JOHN RHEA** and Margaret Turk were:

ELIZABETH RHEA WRIGHT (D.8. John, C.5. William, B.3. Archibald, A.1. Matthew)

WILLIAM RHEA (D.8. John, C.5. William, B.3. Archibald, A.1. Matthew)

JOHN RHEA (D.8. John, C.5. William, B.3. Archibald, A.1. Matthew)

MARGARET RHEA WRIGHT (D.8. John, C.5. William, B.3. Archibald, A.1. Matthew)

THOMAS TURK RHEA (SEE E.9.) (D.8. John, C.5. William, B.3. Archibald, A.1. Matthew) (Abt. 1785 – 1842) **(DIRECT ANCESTOR TO PALMER RHEA, SR**

ANN RHEA (D.8. John, C.5. William, B.3. Archibald, A.1. Matthew)

JAMES RHEA (D.8. John, C.5. William, B.3. Archibald, A.1. Matthew)

JANE RHEA (D.8. John, C.5. William, B.3. Archibald, A.1. Matthew)

POLLY RHEA (D.8. John, C.5. William, B.3. Archibald, A.1. Matthew)

Known children of **JOHN RHEA** and Magdalena Dill:

NANCY P. RHEA (D.8. John, C.5. William, B.3. Archibald, A.1. Matthew)

HIRAM RHEA (D.8. John, C.5. William, B.3. Archibald, A.1. Matthew)

SARAH H. RHEA BRASHERS (D.8. John, C.5. William, B.3. Archibald, A.1. Matthew)

HENRY DILL RHEA (D.8. John, C.5. William, B.3. Archibald, A.1. Matthew)

ESTHER J. RHEA (D.8. John, C.5. William, B.3. Archibald, A.1. Matthew)

MARY RHEA (D.8. John, C.5. William, B.3. Archibald, A.1. Matthew)

(According to The Bicentennial History of Bath County, Virginia and *The Descendants of Matthew "The Rebel" Rhea of Scotland and Ireland* by Edward F. Foley)

E.9. THOMAS TURK RHEA (D.8. John, C.5. William, B.3. Archibald, A.1. Matthew) (Abt. 1785 – 1842) **(DIRECT ANCESTOR TO PALMER RHEA, SR)**

Known children of **THOMAS TURK** and Sarah Lynch:

JOHN SHAW RHEA (E.9. Thomas Turk, D.8. John, C.5. William, B.3. Archibald, A.1. Matthew)

Known children of **JOHN SHAW RHEA** and Sarah (Sally) Lyle Rhea:

Sarah Jane Rhea Ratliff (John, E.9. Thomas Turk, D.8. John, C.5. William, B.3. Archibald, A.1. Matthew) (born about 1830)

Thomas Turk Rhea (John, E.9. Thomas Turk, D.8. John, C.5. William, B.3. Archibald, A.1. Matthew) (abt. 1835/1838 – September 13, 1861))

John Shaw Rhea, Jr. ((John, E.9. Thomas Turk, D.8. John, C.5. William, B.3. Archibald, A.1. Matthew) (Born abt. 1836)

Angeline (Angelina) E. Rhea Ayers Smith ((John, E.9. Thomas Turk, D.8. John, C.5. William, B.3. Archibald, A.1. Matthew) (September 28, 1839 – December 8, 1912)

Lucy E. Rhea Miller (John, E.9. Thomas Turk, D.8. John, C.5. William, B.3. Archibald, A.1. Matthew) (May 20, 1840/1845 – March 28, 1926)

James K.P. Rhea (John, E.9. Thomas Turk, D.8. John, C.5. William, B.3. Archibald, A.1. Matthew) (b. abt. 1842)

Charles Andrew Rhea (John, E.9. Thomas Turk, D.8. John, C.5. William, B.3. Archibald, A.1. Matthew) (abt. 1844/1847 – 1907)

SUSANNA LUCY RHEA CORLEY (CAULEY) (E.9. Thomas Turk, D.8. John, C.5. William, B.3. Archibald, A.1. Matthew)

Known children of **SUSANNA LUCY RHEA CORLEY (CAULEY)** and Thomas Corley:

John Molen Corley (Susanna, E.9. Thomas Turk, D.8. John, C.5. William, B.3. Archibald, A.1. Matthew) (1832–1912)

James Thomas Corley (Susanna, E.9. Thomas Turk, D.8. John, C.5. William, B.3. Archibald, A.1. Matthew) (1835–1921)

Elizabeth "Jane" M. Corley Coffman (Susanna, E.9. Thomas Turk, D.8. John, C.5. William, B.3. Archibald, A.1. Matthew) (1837-1910)

Nancy Corley (Susanna, E.9. Thomas Turk, D.8. John, C.5. William, B.3. Archibald, A.1. Matthew) (1839/1841-1856)

Jesse Lee Corley (Susanna, E.9. Thomas Turk, D.8. John, C.5. William, B.3. Archibald, A.1. Matthew) (abt. 1843-abt. 1874)

Malinda Corley (Susanna, E.9. Thomas Turk, D.8. John, C.5. William, B.3. Archibald, A.1. Matthew) (1844-1859).

Allen (Ellen) Corley (Susanna, E.9. Thomas Turk, D.8. John, C.5. William, B.3. Archibald, A.1. Matthew) (b. 1845)

Melvina Corley Goddin (Susanna, E.9. Thomas Turk, D.8. John, C.5. William, B.3. Archibald, A.1. Matthew) (1848-1923)

MARGARET TURK RHEA KINCAID (E.9. Thomas Turk, D.8. John, C.5. William, B.3. Archibald, A.1. Matthew) (1813-1888)

Known children of **MARGARET TURK RHEA KINCAID** and Willis Kincaid.

James N. Kincaid (Margaret, E.9. Thomas Turk, D.8. John, C.5. William, B.3. Archibald, A.1. Matthew) (1830-1911)

Floyd Kincaid (Margaret, E.9. Thomas Turk, D.8. John, C.5. William, B.3. Archibald, A.1. Matthew) (1833-1914)

Charles Kincaid (Margaret, E.9. Thomas Turk, D.8. John, C.5. William, B.3. Archibald, A.1. Matthew) (Born abt. 1837)

Martha Kincaid Dill (Margaret, E.9. Thomas Turk, D.8. John, C.5. William, B.3. Archibald, A.1. Matthew) (1838-1903)

Joseph B. Kincaid (Margaret, E.9. Thomas Turk, D.8. John, C.5. William, B.3. Archibald, A.1. Matthew) (1840-1887)

Elizabeth H. Kincaid Cleek (Margaret, E.9. Thomas Turk, D.8. John, C.5. William, B.3. Archibald, A.1. Matthew) (1842-1890)

Margaret Ellen Kincaid Guinn (Margaret, E.9. Thomas Turk, D.8. John, C.5. William, B.3. Archibald, A.1. Matthew) (Abt. 1845 - 1931)

John Willis Kincaid (Margaret, E.9. Thomas Turk, D.8. John, C.5. William, B.3. Archibald, A.1. Matthew) (1849-1925).

Rachel Virginia Kincaid Campbell (Margaret, E.9. Thomas Turk, D.8. John, C.5. William, B.3. Archibald, A.1. Matthew) (1858-1937)

EVALINE (EVELINE/EVELENE) RHEA CARTER (E.9. Thomas Turk, D.8. John, C.5. William, B.3. Archibald, A.1. Matthew) (1821-1856)

Known children of **EVALINA RHEA CARTER** and William M. Carter:

Thomas H. Carter (Evaline, E.9. Thomas Turk, D.8. John, C.5. William, B.3. Archibald, A.1. Matthew) (1840-1872).

Margaret "Maggie" Angeline Carter Thomas (Evaline, E.9. Thomas Turk, D.8. John, C.5. William, B.3. Archibald, A.1. Matthew) (1848 -1919).

Marcus Carter (Evaline, E.9. Thomas Turk, D.8. John, C.5. William, B.3. Archibald, A.1. Matthew)

Wilson Carter (Evaline, E.9. Thomas Turk, D.8. John, C.5. William, B.3. Archibald, A.1. Matthew) (1852-1933)

Harriet Anne Carter Newcomer (Evaline, E.9. Thomas Turk, D.8. John, C.5. William, B.3. Archibald, A.1. Matthew) (1855-1929).

NANCY RHEA GARVEN (E.9. Thomas Turk, D.8. John, C.5. William, B.3. Archibald, A.1. Matthew)

JAMES THOMAS RHEA (SEE F.10.) (E.9. Thomas Turk, D.8. John, C.5. William, B.3. Archibald, A.1. Matthew) (abt. 1823-1890) **(DIRECT ANCESTOR TO PALMER RHEA, SR)**

REBECCA H. RHEA LOAN (LOWEN) (E.9. Thomas Turk, D.8. John, C.5. William, B.3. Archibald, A.1. Matthew) (b. abt. 1825/1828)

Known children of **REBECCA H. RHEA LOAN** and John Lewis Loan:

> **Elizabeth Loan** (Rebecca, E.9. Thomas Turk, D.8. John, C.5. William, B.3. Archibald, A.1. Matthew)
>
> **Sarah S. Loan Gillispie** (Rebecca, E.9. Thomas Turk, D.8. John, C.5. William, B.3. Archibald, A.1. Matthew) (abt. 1840 – unknown)
>
> **Rachel Loan Carter** (Rebecca, E.9. Thomas Turk, D.8. John, C.5. William, B.3. Archibald, A.1. Matthew) (abt. 1848-1893).
>
> **Nancy Jane Loan Ray** ((Rebecca, E.9. Thomas Turk, D.8. John, C.5. William, B.3. Archibald, A.1. Matthew) (b. abt. 1850/1851 – unknown).
>
> **William L. Loan** (Rebecca, E.9. Thomas Turk, D.8. John, C.5. William, B.3. Archibald, A.1. Matthew) (b. abt. 1850/1852 – unknown)
>
> **John Samuel Loan (Lowen)** (Rebecca, E.9. Thomas Turk, D.8. John, C.5. William, B.3. Archibald, A.1. Matthew) (1853-1923)
>
> **Porter Loan** (Rebecca, E.9. Thomas Turk, D.8. John, C.5. William, B.3. Archibald, A.1. Matthew) (b. 1856)
>
> **Charles Loan** (Rebecca, E.9. Thomas Turk, D.8. John, C.5. William, B.3. Archibald, A.1. Matthew) (b. 1859)
>
> **Joseph Loan** (Rebecca, E.9. Thomas Turk, D.8. John, C.5. William, B.3. Archibald, A.1. Matthew) (abt. 1860/1861-1881).

ELIZABETH "BETSY" ANN RHEA LOAN (E.9. Thomas Turk, D.8. John, C.5. William, B.3. Archibald, A.1. Matthew) (abt. 1829/1930-1879)

Known children of **ELIZABETH ANN RHEA LOAN** and Samuel Loan:

John William Loan (Lowen) (Elizabeth, E.9. Thomas Turk, D.8. John, C.5. William, B.3. Archibald, A.1. Matthew) (1845-1935)

James Lewis Loan (Elizabeth, E.9. Thomas Turk, D.8. John, C.5. William, B.3. Archibald, A.1. Matthew) (1848-1917).

Frances (Fannie) Loan (Elizabeth, E.9. Thomas Turk, D.8. John, C.5. William, B.3. Archibald, A.1. Matthew) (abt. 1852 - unknown)

Floyd Samuel Loan (Elizabeth, E.9. Thomas Turk, D.8. John, C.5. William, B.3. Archibald, A.1. Matthew), (b. 1854)

Rebecca S. Loan McMullin (Elizabeth, E.9. Thomas Turk, D.8. John, C.5. William, B.3. Archibald, A.1. Matthew), (abt. 1858 – unknown)

Andrew W. Loan (Elizabeth, E.9. Thomas Turk, D.8. John, C.5. William, B.3. Archibald, A.1. Matthew) (abt. 1862 - unknown)

Charles Joyce Loan (Elizabeth, E.9. Thomas Turk, D.8. John, C.5. William, B.3. Archibald, A.1. Matthew) (1865-1933)

Mary V. Loan Phillips (Elizabeth, E.9. Thomas Turk, D.8. John, C.5. William, B.3. Archibald, A.1. Matthew) (b. abt. 1867)

F.10. JAMES THOMAS RHEA (E.9. Thomas Turk, D.8. John, C.5. William, B.3. Archibald, A.1. Matthew) (abt. 1823-1890) **(DIRECT ANCESTOR TO PALMER RHEA, SR)**
Known children of **JAMES THOMAS RHEA**.

THOMAS "PAP" HENRY RHEA (G.11.) (F.10. James, E.9. Thomas Turk, D.8. John, C.5. William, B.3. Archibald, A.1. Matthew) (1853-1938) **FATHER TO PALMER RHEA, SR. SEE G.11.)**

NANCY (NANNIE) ENORA RHEA WADE BRINKLEY (F.10. James, E.9. Thomas Turk, D.8. John, C.5. William, B.3.

Archibald, A.1. Matthew) (1853/1854-1938) Nancy had ten children.

MARTHA A. RHEA WOOD (F.10. James, E.9. Thomas Turk, D.8. John, C.5. William, B.3. Archibald, A.1. Matthew) (1857-1883)

Known child of **MARTHA RHEA WOOD** and John Wood:

> **Harry Gratton Wood** (Martha, F.10. James, E.9. Thomas Turk, D.8. John, C.5. William, B.3. Archibald, A.1. Matthew) (1880-1926)

JOHN A. W. (WILSON) RHEA (F.10. James, E.9. Thomas Turk, D.8. John, C.5. William, B.3. Archibald, A.1. Matthew) (1863-1952)

Known children of **JOHN A.W. RHEA** and Mary Elizabeth Brooks Rhea:

> **Earnest E. Rhea** (John, F.10. James, E.9. Thomas Turk, D.8. John, C.5. William, B.3. Archibald, A.1. Matthew) (1887-1913)
>
> **Ella Houston Rhea Zimbro** (John, F.10. James, E.9. Thomas Turk, D.8. John, C.5. William, B.3. Archibald, A.1. Matthew) (1889-1979)
>
> **Zora Lee Rhea Rowe** ((John, F.10. James, E.9. Thomas Turk, D.8. John, C.5. William, B.3. Archibald, A.1. Matthew) (1891-1982)
>
> **Okley Rhea Shinault** (John, F.10. James, E.9. Thomas Turk, D.8. John, C.5. William, B.3. Archibald, A.1. Matthew) (1892-1980)
>
> **Forrest Kincaid Rhea** (John, F.10. James, E.9. Thomas Turk, D.8. John, C.5. William, B.3. Archibald, A.1. Matthew) (1894-1979)

JAMES WILLIAM RHEA (F.10. James, E.9. Thomas Turk, D.8. John, C.5. William, B.3. Archibald, A.1. Matthew) (1866-1957)

Known children of **JAMES WILLIAM RHEA** and Emma Lee Shanks Rhea:

> **Mazie Brown Rhea Loan** (James, F.10. James, E.9. Thomas Turk, D.8. John, C.5. William, B.3. Archibald, A.1. Matthew) (1892-1966)

Known children of **MAZIE BROWN RHEA LOAN**:

Earl Leslie Loan (Mazie, James, F.10. James, E.9. Thomas Turk, D.8. John, C.5. William, B.3. Archibald, A.1. Matthew) (1914-1973)

Anna Lee Loan Fultz (Mazie, James, F.10. James, E.9. Thomas Turk, D.8. John, C.5. William, B.3. Archibald, A.1. Matthew) (1915-2003)

Claude Mitchell Loan (Mazie, James, F.10. James, E.9. Thomas Turk, D.8. John, C.5. William, B.3. Archibald, A.1. Matthew) (1918 -2009)

Homer Rhea Loan, Sr. (Mazie, James, F.10. James, E.9. Thomas Turk, D.8. John, C.5. William, B.3. Archibald, A.1. Matthew) (1920-1985).

Ernest Hollis Loan, Sr. (Mazie, James, F.10. James, E.9. Thomas Turk, D.8. John, C.5. William, B.3. Archibald, A.1. Matthew) (1923-1988)

James Delemo (Delenio) "Doots" Loan, Sr. (Mazie, James, F.10. James, E.9. Thomas Turk, D.8. John, C.5. William, B.3. Archibald, A.1. Matthew) (1925-1997)

Leola Argenbright Rhea Roach (James, F.10. James, E.9. Thomas Turk, D.8. John, C.5. William, B.3. Archibald, A.1. Matthew) (1894-1947)

Known children of **LEOLA ARGENBRIGHT RHEA ROACH**:

James Beverly Roach (Leola, James, F.10. James, E.9. Thomas Turk, D.8. John, C.5. William, B.3. Archibald, A.1. Matthew) (1918-1986)

Allie Mae Rhea (James, F.10. James, E.9. Thomas Turk, D.8. John, C.5. William, B.3. Archibald, A.1. Matthew) (1895-1981)

Octave Thannet Rhea Hinton (James, F.10. James, E.9. Thomas Turk, D.8. John, C.5. William, B.3. Archibald, A.1. Matthew) (1897-1982)

Known children of **OCTAVE THANNET RHEA HINTON**:

Charles James Hinton, III, (Octave, James, F.10. James, E.9. Thomas Turk, D.8. John, C.5. William, B.3. Archibald, A.1. Matthew)

Ruth Thanet Hinton Cupp. (Octave, James, F.10. James, E.9. Thomas Turk, D.8. John, C.5. William, B.3. Archibald, A.1. Matthew), (1930-1980)

Christine Lee Hinton St. Claire (Octave, James, F.10. James, E.9. Thomas Turk, D.8. John, C.5. William, B.3. Archibald, A.1. Matthew) (1933-1960)

Boyd Edmond Rhea (James, F.10. James, E.9. Thomas Turk, D.8. John, C.5. William, B.3. Archibald, A.1. Matthew) (1900-1948)

James Floyd Rhea (James, F.10. James, E.9. Thomas Turk, D.8. John, C.5. William, B.3. Archibald, A.1. Matthew) (1902/1903-1918)

David Franklin Rhea (James, F.10. James, E.9. Thomas Turk, D.8. John, C.5. William, B.3. Archibald, A.1. Matthew) (1906-1973)

Known children of **DAVID FRANKLIN RHEA**:

James Franklin Rhea (David, James, F.10. James, E.9. Thomas Turk, D.8. John, C.5. William, B.3. Archibald, A.1. Matthew) (1959–1974)

Others: Private

SHAW ALEXANDER RHEA (F.10. James, E.9. Thomas Turk, D.8. John, C.5. William, B.3. Archibald, A.1. Matthew) (1868-1944)

Known children of **SHAW ALEXANDER RHEA**:

Henry A. Rhea (Shaw, F.10. James, E.9. Thomas Turk, D.8. John, C.5. William, B.3. Archibald, A.1. Matthew) (1907-1984)

Garnett Roosevelt Rhea (Shaw, F.10. James, E.9. Thomas Turk, D.8. John, C.5. William, B.3. Archibald, A.1. Matthew) (1910-1993)

Percy Coleman Rhea (Shaw, F.10. James, E.9. Thomas Turk, D.8. John, C.5. William, B.3. Archibald, A.1. Matthew) (1912-1979)

(Virginia) Pattie Rhea Curry (Shaw, F.10. James, E.9. Thomas Turk, D.8. John, C.5. William, B.3. Archibald, A.1. Matthew) (1914-2015)

Lillian "Jo" Elizabeth Rhea Michael (Shaw, F.10. James, E.9. Thomas Turk, D.8. John, C.5. William, B.3. Archibald, A.1. Matthew) (1917-1997)

Luther Martin Rhea (Shaw, F.10. James, E.9. Thomas Turk, D.8. John, C.5. William, B.3. Archibald, A.1. Matthew) (1919-1979)

GEORGE BEATY RHEA (F.10. James, E.9. Thomas Turk, D.8. John, C.5. William, B.3. Archibald, A.1. Matthew) (1875-1939)

Known children of **GEORGE BEATY RHEA**:

Theresa Marie "Tessie" Rhea Lawhorne (George, F.10. James, E.9. Thomas Turk, D.8. John, C.5. William, B.3. Archibald, A.1. Matthew) (1900/1901-1966)

Elizabeth Ruth Lawhorne Turner Hatchell (Theresa, George, F.10. James, E.9. Thomas Turk, D.8. John, C.5. William, B.3. Archibald, A.1. Matthew) (1923–2006)

Margrite Irene Lawhorne Merkey (Theresa, George, F.10. James, E.9. Thomas Turk, D.8. John, C.5. William, B.3. Archibald, A.1. Matthew) (1926-1987)

Eleanor Mae "Peggy" Lawhorne Johnson (Theresa, George, F.10. James, E.9. Thomas Turk, D.8. John, C.5. William, B.3. Archibald, A.1. Matthew) (1930 – 2015)

Elmo Thurston Lawhorne, Jr. (Theresa, George, F.10. James, E.9. Thomas Turk, D.8. John, C.5. William, B.3. Archibald, A.1. Matthew) (1933-2008)

Georgie Naomi Rhea Davis (George, F.10. James, E.9. Thomas Turk, D.8. John, C.5. William, B.3. Archibald, A.1. Matthew) (1901-1984)

Lonnie Burnette Rhea, Sr. (George, F.10. James, E.9. Thomas Turk, D.8. John, C.5. William, B.3. Archibald, A.1. Matthew) (1904-1966)

Known children of **LONNIE BURNETTE RHEA, SR.**

> **Lonnie Burnette Rhea, Jr.** (Lonnie, George, F.10. James, E.9. Thomas Turk, D.8. John, C.5. William, B.3. Archibald, A.1. Matthew), (1923-1923).

> **Ruth Rhea Neas** (Lonnie, George, F.10. James, E.9. Thomas Turk, D.8. John, C.5. William, B.3. Archibald, A.1. Matthew) (1924-2006)

> **Myrle Rhea Wood** (Lonnie, George, F.10. James, E.9. Thomas Turk, D.8. John, C.5. William, B.3. Archibald, A.1. Matthew) (1926-2012)

Mable L. Rhea Burley (George, F.10. James, E.9. Thomas Turk, D.8. John, C.5. William, B.3. Archibald, A.1. Matthew) (1909-1950)

Helen Hunt Rhea Edgemon Keyser (George, F.10. James, E.9. Thomas Turk, D.8. John, C.5. William, B.3. Archibald, A.1. Matthew) (1913-1976)

G.11. THOMAS "PAP" HENRY RHEA (F.10 James, E.9. Thomas Turk, D.8. John, C.5. William, B.3. Archibald, A.1. Matthew) (1853-1938) **(FATHER TO PALMER RHEA, SR.)**

Children of **THOMAS HENRY RHEA** and Elizabeth Vest:

JOHN WILSON RHEA (G.11. Thomas, F.10. James, E.9. Thomas Turk, D.8. John, C.5. William, B.3. Archibald, A.1. Matthew) (1878-1909)

Known children of **JOHN WILSON RHEA**:

> **Bernard M. Rhea** (John Wilson, G.11. Thomas, F.10. James, E.9. Thomas Turk, D.8. John, C.5. William, B.3. Archibald, A.1. Matthew) (1908-1927).

NELLIE RHEA HYSONG (G.11. Thomas, F.10. James, E.9. Thomas Turk, D.8. John, C.5. William, B.3. Archibald, A.1. Matthew) (1882-1940)

Known children of **NELLIE RHEA HYSONG**:

Thomas Martin Hysong (Nellie, G.11. Thomas, F.10. James, E.9. Thomas Turk, D.8. John, C.5. William, B.3. Archibald, A.1. Matthew) (1914-1972)

Jerry Edgar Hysong (Nellie, G.11. Thomas, F.10. James, E.9. Thomas Turk, D.8. John, C.5. William, B.3. Archibald, A.1. Matthew) (1917-1969)

GARNETT SUTTON RHEA (G.11. Thomas, F.10. James, E.9. Thomas Turk, D.8. John, C.5. William, B.3. Archibald, A.1. Matthew) (1884-1956)

MOLLIE MAE RHEA PERKINSON LYON (G.11. Thomas, F.10. James, E.9. Thomas Turk, D.8. John, C.5. William, B.3. Archibald, A.1. Matthew) (1886/1887-1965)

Known children of **MOLLIE MAE RHEA PERKINSON LYON**:

Mabel Esther Perkinson Conner (Mollie, (G.11. Thomas, F.10. James, E.9. Thomas Turk, D.8. John, C.5. William, B.3. Archibald, A.1. Matthew) (1904-1978)

HARRY TUCKER RHEA (G.11. Thomas, F.10. James, E.9. Thomas Turk, D.8. John, C.5. William, B.3. Archibald, A.1. Matthew) (1888/1889-1946)

JAMES TALLY RHEA (G.11. Thomas, F.10. James, E.9. Thomas Turk, D.8. John, C.5. William, B.3. Archibald, A.1. Matthew) (1892-1970)

Known children of **JAMES TALLY RHEA**:

James Wilson Rhea. (James Talley, (G.11. Thomas, F.10. James, E.9. Thomas Turk, D.8. John, C.5. William, B.3. Archibald, A.1. Matthew) (1921-2001)

William Gratton "Bill" Rhea. (James Talley, G.11. Thomas, F.10. James, E.9. Thomas Turk, D.8. John, C.5. William, B.3. Archibald, A.1. Matthew) (1924-1996)

Known children of **WILLIAM GRATTON "BILL" RHEA**:

Karen Lucille Rhea Capley (William, James Talley, (G.11. Thomas, F.10. James, E.9. Thomas Turk, D.8. John, C.5. William, B.3. Archibald, A.1. Matthew)

Mollie Marie Rhea Clark. (James Talley, G.11. Thomas, F.10. James, E.9. Thomas Turk, D.8. John, C.5. William, B.3. Archibald, A.1. Matthew)

Known child of **MOLLIE MARIE RHEA CLARK**:

Brenda Marie Clark Fowler. (Mollie, James Talley, (G.11. Thomas, F.10. James, E.9. Thomas Turk, D.8. John, C.5. William, B.3. Archibald, A.1. Matthew) (1957-2001) Daughter to **MOLLIE MARIE RHEA CLARK. Other Private**

Mary Ann Rhea Salter. (James Talley, (G.11. Thomas, F.10. James, E.9. Thomas Turk, D.8. John, C.5. William, B.3. Archibald, A.1. Matthew)

MATTIE MYRTLE RHEA COLEMAN (G.11. Thomas, F.10. James, E.9. Thomas Turk, D.8. John, C.5. William, B.3. Archibald, A.1. Matthew) (abt. 1900-1974)

HENRY MCKINLEY RHEA (G.11. Thomas, F.10. James, E.9. Thomas Turk, D.8. John, C.5. William, B.3. Archibald, A.1. Matthew) (1900/1902-1929)

Known child of **HENRY MCKINLEY RHEA**:

Nolen Elwood Rhea. (Henry, G.11. Thomas, F.10. James, E.9. Thomas Turk, D.8. John, C.5. William, B.3. Archibald, A.1. Matthew) (1927 – unknown)

ALICE BEATTY RHEA BROWN RUSSELL (G.11. Thomas, F.10. James, E.9. Thomas Turk, D.8. John, C.5. William, B.3. Archibald, A.1. Matthew)

Children of **THOMAS HENRY RHEA** and Mamie Gear:

ECHOLS RHEA (STONEY ECKLE RHEA) (G.11. Thomas, F.10. James, E.9. Thomas Turk, D.8. John, C.5. William, B.3. Archibald, A.1. Matthew) (abt. 1909-1932)

COURTNEY RUSSELL RHEA (G.11. Thomas, F.10. James, E.9. Thomas Turk, D.8. John, C.5. William, B.3. Archibald, A.1. Matthew) (1911-1990)

PALMER B. RHEA (See H.12.) (G.11. Thomas, F.10. James, E.9. Thomas Turk, D.8. John, C.5. William, B.3. Archibald, A.1. Matthew) (1913-1989)

HELEN VIRGINIA RHEA CAMPBELL (G.11. Thomas, F.10. James, E.9. Thomas Turk, D.8. John, C.5. William, B.3. Archibald, A.1. Matthew) (1915-1970)

Known children of **HELEN VIRGINIA RHEA CAMPBELL**:

    Betty Jean Campbell Hague (Helen, G.11. Thomas, F.10. James, E.9. Thomas Turk, D.8. John, C.5. William, B.3. Archibald, A.1. Matthew) (1948-2016)

    Clarence Bransford Campbell, Jr. (Helen, G.11. Thomas, F.10. James, E.9. Thomas Turk, D.8. John, C.5. William, B.3. Archibald, A.1. Matthew) (1950-2012)

    Other information private.

CLARENCE RHEA (G.11. Thomas, F.10. James, E.9. Thomas Turk, D.8. John, C.5. William, B.3. Archibald, A.1. Matthew) (1917-unknown)

BABY RHEA (Died at birth) (G.11. Thomas, F.10. James, E.9. Thomas Turk, D.8. John, C.5. William, B.3. Archibald, A.1. Matthew) (1919-1919)

H.12. PALMER B. RHEA (G.11. Thomas, F.10. James, E.9. Thomas Turk, D.8. John, C.5. William, B.3. Archibald, A.1. Matthew) (1913-1989)

Children of **PALMER B. RHEA, SR**. and Mary Margaret Clark:

    PALMER RHEA, JR. (H.12. Palmer, G.11. Thomas, F.10. James, E.9. Thomas Turk, D.8. John, C.5. William, B.3. Archibald, A.1. Matthew)

    JOANN RHEA (H.12. Palmer, G.11. Thomas, F.10. James, E.9. Thomas Turk, D.8. John, C.5. William, B.3. Archibald, A.1. Matthew)

Children of Mary Margaret Clark and Guy Jackson Nicely:

    MITCHELL EUGENE NICELY

    BARBARA ELLEN NICELY

    GENEVIEE MURIE NICELY

    RANDOLPH JACKSON NICELY

    ROXIE LOU NICELY

MARGARET CHRISTINE NICELY
EDITH PAULINE NICELY
Grandchildren and dates omitted for privacy.

NOTE: SOME NAMES AND DATES OF DESCENDANTS WERE INTENTIONALLY OMITTED FOR PRIVACY. Every effort was made for accuracy. At times birth certificates, death certificates, and burial records differ. Please excuse any errors that may have occurred.

CEMETERIES

ALABAMA

Bellefonte Cemetery, Bellefonte, Jackson County, Alabama (buried):
JAMES TURK (Ann, C.6. Robert, B.3. Archibald, A.1. Matthew) (b. abt. 1780-1835) Son to **ANN RHEA TURK**.

FLORIDA

Glen Haven Memorial Park and Mausoleum, Winter Park, Orange County, Florida (buried):
JESSIE PROSSER RHEA (1924-2007) Wife to **LUTHER MARTIN RHEA** (Shaw, F.10. James, E.9. Thomas Turk, D.8. John, C.5. William, B.3. Archibald, A.1. Matthew)
LUTHER MARTIN RHEA (Shaw, F.10. James, E.9. Thomas Turk, D.8. John, C.5. William, B.3. Archibald, A.1. Matthew) (1919-1979) Son to **SHAW ALEXANDER RHEA**.

ILLINOIS

Rosewood Cemetery, Bloomington, McLean County, Illinois (buried):
ADDISON HYDE COYNER (Elizabeth, C.6. Robert, B.3. Archibald, A.1. Matthew) (1809-1856) Son to **ELIZABETH RHEA COYNER**.

INDIANA

Crown Hill Cemetery, Indianapolis, Marion Cunty, Indiana (buried):
MARTIN LUTHER COYNER (Elizabeth, C.6. Robert, B.3. Archibald, A.1. Matthew) (1805-1880) Son to **ELIZABETH RHEA COYNER**.

IOWA

Prather Cemetery (also known as Martin Cemetery), Melrose, Monroe County, Iowa (buried):
THOMAS H. CARTER (Evaline, E.9. Thomas Turk, D.8. John, C.5. William, B.3. Archibald, A.1. Matthew) (1840-1872) Son to **EVALINE RHEA CARTER**.

KANSAS

Fairview Cemetery, Cherryvale, Montgomery County, Kansas (buried):
ARCHIBALD RHEA COYNER (Elizabeth, C.6. Robert, B.3. Archibald, A.1. Matthew) (1797-unknown) Son to **ELIZABETH RHEA COYNER**.

KENTUCKY

East Hickman Cemetery, East Hickman Road Nicholasville, Jessamine County, Kentucky (buried):
JOHN COYNER (COINER) (Elizabeth, C.6. Robert, B.3. Archibald, A.1. Matthew) (1792-1852) Son to **ELIZABETH RHEA COYNER**.

MARYLAND

Cedar Hill Cemetery (also known as Forest Lake Cemetery), 4111 Pennsylvania Avenue, Suitland, Prince George's County, Maryland (buried):

GARNETT SUTTON RHEA (G.11. Thomas, F.10. James, E.9. Thomas Turk, D.8. John, C.5. William, B.3. Archibald, A.1. Matthew) (1884-1956)

Fort Lincoln Cemetery, 3401 Bladensburg Road, Brentwood, Prince George's County, Maryland (buried):

JERRY EDGAR HYSONG (Nellie, G.11. Thomas, F.10. James, E.9. Thomas Turk, D.8. John, C.5. William, B.3. Archibald, A.1. Matthew) (1917-1969) Son to **NELLIE RHEA HYSONG.**

MARTIN WELLINGTON HYSONG (1880-1959) Husband to **NELLIE RHEA HYSONG** (G.11. Thomas, F.10. James, E.9. Thomas Turk, D.8. John, C.5. William, B.3. Archibald, A.1. Matthew)

MATTIE MYRTLE RHEA COLEMAN (G.11. Thomas, F.10. James, E.9. Thomas Turk, D.8. John, C.5. William, B.3. Archibald, A.1. Matthew) (1900-1974) (Death certificate lists Mattie as being buried at this cemetery, but we were unable to locate her cemetery memorial so unsure if this is correct.)

THOMAS MARTIN HYSONG (Nellie, G.11. Thomas, F.10. James, E.9. Thomas Turk, D.8. John, C.5. William, B.3. Archibald, A.1. Matthew) (1914-1972) Son to **NELLIE RHEA HYSONG.**

Loudon Park Cemetery, 3801 Frederick Avenue, Baltimore, Maryland (buried):

JOHN WILLIS KINCAID (Margaret, E.9. Thomas Turk, D.8. John, C.5. William, B.3. Archibald, A.1. Matthew) (1849-1925) Son to **MARGARET TURK RHEA KINCAID.**

Piney Creek Reformed Presbyterian Church Cemetery, 4472 Harney Road, Taneytown, Maryland (buried):
REV. JOSEPH RHEA (B.4. Matthew, A.1. Matthew) (1715-1777)

MISSOURI

Mount Moriah Cemetery, Azen, Scotland County, Missouri (buried):
JAMES THOMAS CORLEY (Susanna, E.9. Thomas Turk, D.8. John, C.5. William, B.3. Archibald, A.1. Matthew) (1835-1921) Son to SUSANNA LUCY RHEA CORLEY.

OHIO

Givens Chapel Cemetery, Givens, Pike County, Ohio (buried):
ELIZABETH BOILER RHEA (1780-1863) Wife to WILLIAM RHEA (Robert, C.5. William, B.3. Archibald, A.1. Matthew)
WILLIAM RHEA (Robert, C.5. William, B.3. Archibald, A.1. Matthew) (1782-1855)
(Other members of the Rhea Family are buried in this cemetery.) Son to ROBERT RHEA.

Green Mound Cemetery, Kilbourne, Delaware County, Ohio (buried):
REV. DAVID H. COYNER (Elizabeth, C.6. Robert, B.3. Archibald, A.1. Matthew) (1807-1892) Son to ELIZABETH RHEA COYNER.

South Salem Cemetery, Church Street, South Salem, Ross County, Ohio (buried):
ROBERT CRAWFORD COYNER, SR. (Elizabeth, C.6. Robert, B.3. Archibald, A.1. Matthew) (1794-1874) Son to ELIZABETH RHEA COYNER.

PENNSYLVANIA

Church of the Redeemer Cemetery, 230 Pennswood Road, Bryn Mawr, Montgomery County, Pennsylvania (buried):
> MARY MILLER BLACK REA (1856-1933) Wife to SAMUEL REA (James D., John, Samuel, B.4. Matthew, A.1. Matthew)
> SAMUEL REA (James D., John, Samuel, B.4. Matthew, A.1. Matthew) (1855-1929)

Rocky Spring Churchyard, Chambersburg, Franklin County, Pennsylvania (buried):
> JOHN REA (Samuel, B.4. Matthew, A.1. Matthew) (1755-1829) U.S. Congressman, Pennsylvania. Son to SAMUEL REA (B.4. Matthew. A.1. Matthew)
> SAMUEL REA (B.4. Matthew. A.1. Matthew) (1725– 1811)

SOUTH CAROLINA

Carolina Memorial Park, 7113 Rivers Avenue, North Charleston, South Carolina (buried):
> GARNETT ROOSEVELT RHEA (Shaw, F.10. James, E.9. Thomas Turk, D.8. John, C.5. William, B.3. Archibald, A.1. Matthew) (1910-1993) Son to SHAW ALEXANDER RHEA.
> HENRY A. RHEA (Shaw, F.10. James, E.9. Thomas Turk, D.8. John, C.5. William, B.3. Archibald, A.1. Matthew) (1907-1984). Son to SHAW ALEXANDER RHEA.
> LILLIAN "JO" ELIZABETH RHEA MICHAEL (Shaw, F.10. James, E.9. Thomas Turk, D.8. John, C.5. William, B.3. Archibald, A.1. Matthew) (1917-1997) Daughter to SHAW ALEXANDER RHEA.
> MARY LOUISE LOWEN RHEA (1912-1987) Wife to HENRY A. RHEA (Shaw, F.10. James, E.9. Thomas Turk, D.8. John, C.5. William, B.3. Archibald, A.1. Matthew)

PAULINE ELIZABETH BAZEMORE RHEA (1920-1957) Wife to **GARNETT ROOSEVELT RHEA** (Shaw, F.10. James, E.9. Thomas Turk, D.8. John, C.5. William, B.3. Archibald, A.1. Matthew)

TENNESSEE

Blountville Cemetery, Blountville, Sullivan County, Tennessee (buried):

JOHN ANGUS RHEA (Joseph, B.4. Matthew. A.1. Matthew) (1753-1832) U.S. Congressman, Tennessee. Son to **REV. JOSEPH RHEA**.

NANCY BREDEN RHEA (1776-1856) Wife to **SAMUEL RHEA** (Joseph, B.4. Matthew. A.1. Matthew)

SAMUEL RHEA (Joseph, B.4. Matthew. A.1. Matthew) (1769-1848) Son to **REV. JOSEPH RHEA**.

(Many other members of the Rhea Family are buried in this cemetery.)

Chilhowee Primative Baptist Church Cemetery (also known as Red Top Primative Baptist Church), 7200 Happy Valley Road, Happy Valley, Blount County, Tennessee (buried):

ROBERT RHEA, JR. (C.6. Robert, B.3. Archibald, A.1. Matthew) (1763-1850)

Lebanon-in-the Fork Cemetery, Knoxville, Tennessee (Three Rivers Cemetery) (buried):

ARCHIBALD RHEA (C.6. Robert, B.3. Archibald, A.1. Matthew) (1756-1793)

Lones Cemetery, Arrowhead Drive, Knox County, Tennessee (Western side of Sequoyah Hills. Cemetery is fenced and locked) (buried):

MOSES LOONEY (C.8. Margaret, B.4. Matthew, A.1. Matthew) (1745-1817 and alternate death date 1824)

New Providence Presbyterian Church Cemetery, Maryville, Blount County, Tennessee (buried):

ANN RHEA TURK (C.6. Robert, B.3. Archibald, A.1. Matthew) (1759-1836)

CAPT. THOMAS TURK, JR. (1755-1833) Husband to ANN RHEA TURK (C.6. Robert, B.3. Archibald, A.1. Matthew)

Weaver Cemetery, Weaver Union Church, 132 Peoples Road, Bristol, Sullivan County, Tennessee (buried):

ELIZABETH MCLLWAINE RHEA (1732-1793) Wife to REV. JOSEPH RHEA (B.4. Matthew II, A.1. Matthew) and monument for husband REV. JOSEPH RHEA (1715-1777) is also erected here.

ELIZABETH RHEA RHEA (Joseph, B.4. Matthew. A.1. Matthew) (1767-1821) Daughter to REV. JOSEPH RHEA.

FRANCES BREDEN RHEA (1764-1850) Wife to JOSEPH C. RHEA (Joseph, B.4. Matthew. A.1. Matthew)

JANE PRESTON RHEA (1758-1800) Wife to MATTHEW RHEA (Joseph, B.4. Matthew. A.1. Matthew)

JOSEPH C. RHEA (Joseph, B.4. Matthew. A.1. Matthew) (1762-1825) Son to REV. JOSEPH RHEA.

MATTHEW RHEA (Joseph, B.4. Matthew. A.1. Matthew) (1755-1816) Son to REV. JOSEPH RHEA.

MAJ. ROBERT RHEA (William, B.4. Matthew. A.1. Matthew) (1776-1841) Son to WILLIAM RHEA.

(Other members of the Rhea Family are buried in this cemetery.)

VIRGINIA

Alleghany Memorial Park, Low Moore, Alleghany County, Virginia (buried):

CLAUDE MITCHELL LOAN (Mazie, James, F.10. James, E.9. Thomas Turk, D.8. John, C.5. William, B.3. Archibald, A.1. Matthew) (1918-2009) Son to MAZIE BROWN RHEA LOAN.

HOMER RHEA LOAN, SR. (Mazie, James, F.10. James, E.9. Thomas Turk, D.8. John, C.5. William, B.3. Archibald, A.1. Matthew) (1920-1985) (Buried at Garden of Reformation, Section H) Son to **MAZIE BROWN RHEA LOAN.**

HOWARD MITCHELL LOAN (1885-1963) Husband to **MAZIE BROWN RHEA LOAN** (James, F.10. James, E.9. Thomas Turk, D.8. John, C.5. William, B.3. Archibald, A.1. Matthew)

MAZIE BROWN RHEA LOAN (James, F.10. James, E.9. Thomas Turk, D.8. John, C.5. William, B.3. Archibald, A.1. Matthew) (1892-1966) (Buried at Garden of the Cross, Section IV) Daughter to **JAMES WILLIAM RHEA.**

Amherst Cemetery, 513 Grandview Drive (Rt. 1108), Amherst, Virginia (buried):

ELEANOR MAE "PEGGY" LAWHORNE JOHNSON (Theresa, George, F.10. James, E.9. Thomas Turk, D.8. John, C.5. William, B.3. Archibald, A.1. Matthew) (1930 – 2015) Daughter to **THERESA MARIE "TESSIE" RHEA LAWHORNE.**

ELIZABETH RUTH LAWHORNE TURNER HATCHELL (Theresa, George, F.10. James, E.9. Thomas Turk, D.8. John, C.5. William, B.3. Archibald, A.1. Matthew) (1923–2006) Daughter to **THERESA MARIE "TESSIE" RHEA LAWHORNE.**

GEORGE BEATY RHEA (F.10. James, E.9. Thomas Turk, D.8. John, C.5. William, B.3. Archibald, A.1. Matthew) (1875-1939)

GEORGIE NAOMI RHEA DAVIS (George, F.10. James, E.9. Thomas Turk, D.8. John, C.5. William, B.3. Archibald, A.1. Matthew) (1901-1984) Daughter to **GEORGE BEATY RHEA.**

HELEN HUNT RHEA EDGEMON KEYSER (George, F.10. James, E.9. Thomas Turk, D.8. John, C.5. William, B.3. Archibald, A.1. Matthew) (1913-1976) Daughter to **GEORGE BEATY RHEA.**

MABLE L. RHEA BURLEY (George, F.10. James, E.9. Thomas Turk, D.8. John, C.5. William, B.3. Archibald, A.1. Matthew) (1909-1950) Daughter to **GEORGE BEATY RHEA.**

MARGRITE IRENE LAWHORNE MERKEY (Theresa, George, F.10. James, E.9. Thomas Turk, D.8. John, C.5. William,

B.3. Archibald, A.1. Matthew) (1926-1987) Daughter to **THERESA MARIE "TESSIE" RHEA LAWHORNE.**

MYRLE JAMES RHEA WOOD (Lonnie, George, F.10. James, E.9. Thomas Turk, D.8. John, C.5. William, B.3. Archibald, A.1. Matthew) (1926-2012) Daughter to **LONNIE BURNETTE RHEA, SR.**

RUTH NAOMI RUCKER RHEA (1879-1918) Wife to **GEORGE BEATY RHEA** (F.10. James, E.9. Thomas Turk, D.8. John, C.5. William, B.3. Archibald, A.1. Matthew)

RUTH RHEA NEAS (Lonnie, George, F.10. James, E.9. Thomas Turk, D.8. John, C.5. William, B.3. Archibald, A.1. Matthew) (1924-2006) Daughter to **LONNIE BURNETTE RHEA, SR.**

THERESA MARIE "TESSIE" RHEA LAWHORNE (George, F.10. James, E.9. Thomas Turk, D.8. John, C.5. William, B.3. Archibald, A.1. Matthew) (1900-1966) Daughter to **GEORGE BEATY RHEA.**

Briarwood Memorial Gardens, 1823 S. Amherst Highway (Rt. 29 Bus.), Amherst, Virginia (buried):
    ELMO THURSTON LAWHORNE, JR. (Theresa, George, F.10. James, E.9. Thomas Turk, D.8. John, C.5. William, B.3. Archibald, A.1. Matthew) (1933-2008) Son to **THERESA MARIE "TESSIE" RHEA LAWHORNE.**

Broad Creek ARP Church Cemetery, Broad Creek Church Road, Rockbridge County, Virginia (buried):
    WILSON CARTER (Evaline, E.9. Thomas Turk, D.8. John, C.5. William, B.3. Archibald, A.1. Matthew) (1852-1933) Son to **EVALINE RHEA CARTER.**

Calvary Baptist Church Cemetery, 429 Crooked Spur Road (Rt. 633), Millboro Springs, Virginia (buried):
    BRENDA MARIE CLARK FOWLER (Mollie, James Talley, (G.11. Thomas, F.10. James, E.9. Thomas Turk, D.8. John, C.5.

William, B.3. Archibald, A.1. Matthew) (1957-2001) Daughter to **MOLLIE MARIE RHEA CLARK.**

EARL LESLIE LOAN (Mazie, James, F.10. James, E.9. Thomas Turk, D.8. John, C.5. William, B.3. Archibald, A.1. Matthew) (1914-1973) Son to **MAZIE BROWN RHEA LOAN.**

Cedar Hill Cemetery, 1521 S. Carpenter Drive, Covington, Virginia (buried):

PVT. JOHN WILLIAM LOAN (LOWEN) (Elizabeth, E.9. Thomas Turk, D.8. John, C.5. William, B.3. Archibald, A.1. Matthew) (1845-1935) Son to **ELIZABETH ANN RHEA LOAN.**

Central Advent Christian Church Cemetery, 3515 Longdale Furnace Road (Rt. 269), Clifton Forge, Alleghany County, Virginia (buried):

BETTY JEAN CAMPBELL HAGUE (Helen, G.11. Thomas, F.10. James, E.9. Thomas Turk, D.8. John, C.5. William, B.3. Archibald, A.1. Matthew) (1948-2016) Daughter to **HELEN VIRGINIA RHEA CAMPBELL.**

BRENDA MARIE CLARK FOWLER (Mollie, James Talley, (G.11. Thomas, F.10. James, E.9. Thomas Turk, D.8. John, C.5. William, B.3. Archibald, A.1. Matthew) (1957-2001) Daughter to **MOLLIE MARIE RHEA CLARK.**

CLARENCE BRANSFORD CAMPBELL, JR. (Helen, G.11. Thomas, F.10. James, E.9. Thomas Turk, D.8. John, C.5. William, B.3. Archibald, A.1. Matthew) (1950-2012) Son to **HELEN VIRGINIA RHEA CAMPBELL.**

HELEN VIRGINIA RHEA CAMPBELL (G.11. Thomas, F.10. James, E.9. Thomas Turk, D.8. John, C.5. William, B.3. Archibald, A.1. Matthew) (1915-1970)

MARY MARGARET CLARK RHEA (1916-1998) Wife to **PALMER B. RHEA, SR.** (G.11. Thomas, F.10. James, E.9. Thomas Turk, D.8. John, C.5. William, B.3. Archibald, A.1. Matthew)

PALMER B. RHEA, SR. (G.11. Thomas, F.10. James, E.9. Thomas Turk, D.8. John, C.5. William, B.3. Archibald, A.1. Matthew) (1913-1989)

Clover Hill United Methodist Church Cemetery, 3457 Fulton School Road, Dayton, Rockingham County, Virginia (buried):
ERNEST HOLLIS LOAN, SR. (Mazie, James, F.10. James, E.9. Thomas Turk, D.8. John, C.5. William, B.3. Archibald, A.1. Matthew) (1923-1988) Son to **MAZIE BROWN RHEA LOAN**.

Crown Hill Cemetery, Clifton Forge, Alleghany County, Virginia (buried):
HARRY GRATTON WOOD (Martha, F.10. James, E.9. Thomas Turk, D.8. John, C.5. William, B.3. Archibald, A.1. Matthew) (1880-1926) Son to **MARTHA A. RHEA WOOD**.

Goshen Baptist Church Cemetery (also known as Riverview Cemetery) in Goshen, Rockbridge County, Virginia (buried):
MARGARET ELLEN KINCAID GUINN (Margaret, E.9. Thomas Turk, D.8. John, C.5. William, B.3. Archibald, A.1. Matthew) (1845-1931) Daughter to **MARGARET TURK RHEA KINCAID**.

Green Hill Cemetery, Fairfax Street, Stephens City, Frederick County, Virginia (buried):
FORREST KINCAID ("POP POP") RHEA (John, F.10. James, E.9. Thomas Turk, D.8. John, C.5. William, B.3. Archibald, A.1. Matthew) (1894-1979). Son to **JOHN A.W. (WILSON) RHEA**.
IDA MAE "NANNY" MYERS RHEA (1898-1984) Wife to **FORREST KINCAID RHEA** (John, F.10. James, E.9. Thomas Turk, D.8. John, C.5. William, B.3. Archibald, A.1. Matthew).

Horeb Baptist Church Cemetery, 5742 Cowpasture River Highway (Rt. 42), Millboro, Bath County, Virginia (buried):

CATHEREN ANN MATHENEY RHEA (1903-1991) Wife to **JAMES TALLEY RHEA** (G.11. Thomas, F.10. James, E.9. Thomas Turk, D.8. John, C.5. William, B.3. Archibald, A.1. Matthew)

FRANCES ARLENE "SASSY JO" MINES RHEA (1934-2013) Wife to **DAVID FRANKLIN RHEA** (James, F.10. James, E.9. Thomas Turk, D.8. John, C.5. William, B.3. Archibald, A.1. Matthew)

JAMES DELEMO (DELENIO) "DOOTS" LOAN, SR. (Mazie, James, F.10. James, E.9. Thomas Turk, D.8. John, C.5. William, B.3. Archibald, A.1. Matthew) (1925-1997) Son to **MAZIE BROWN RHEA LOAN.**

JOHN SAMUEL LOAN (LOWEN) (Rebecca, E.9. Thomas Turk, D.8. John, C.5. William, B.3. Archibald, A.1. Matthew). Son to **REBECCA H. RHEA LOAN (LOWEN).**

Lyle Chapel Cemetery, Bath County, Virginia (buried):

JAMES LEWIS LOAN (Elizabeth, E.9. Thomas Turk, D.8. John, C.5. William, B.3. Archibald, A.1. Matthew) (1848-1917) Son to **ELIZABETH ANN RHEA LOAN.**

Mossy Creek Presbyterian Church Cemetery, 372 Kyles Mill Road, Mount Salon, Augusta County, Virginia (buried):

ELIZABETH RHEA COYNER (C.6. Robert, B.3. Archibald, A.1. Matthew) (1765-1841)

MARTIN LUTHER COYNER (1771-1842) Husband to **ELIZABETH RHEA COYNER** (C.6. Robert, B.3. Archibald, A.1. Matthew).

Mount Comfort Cemetery, 6600 S. Kings Highway, Fairfax County, Virginia (buried):

EVELYN MAE JOHNSON RHEA (1911-1973) Wife to **LONNIE BURNETTE RHEA, SR.** (George, F.10. James, E.9. Thomas Turk, D.8. John, C.5. William, B.3. Archibald, A.1. Matthew).

LONNIE BURNETTE RHEA, SR. (George, F.10. James, E.9. Thomas Turk, D.8. John, C.5. William, B.3. Archibald, A.1. Matthew) (1904 -1966) Son to **GEORGE BEATY RHEA**.

Mount Crawford Cemetery, Mount Crawford, Rockingham County, Virginia (buried):
KATHLEEN AUGUSTA RHEA FUNKHOUSER (1910-1998) Wife to **HENRY MCKINLEY RHEA** (G.11. Thomas, F.10. James, E.9. Thomas Turk, D.8. John, C.5. William, B.3. Archibald, A.1. Matthew)
NOLEN ELWOOD RHEA (Henry, G.11. Thomas, F.10. James, E.9. Thomas Turk, D.8. John, C.5. William, B.3. Archibald, A.1. Matthew) (1927 – unknown). Son to **HENRY MCKINLEY RHEA**.

Oak Lawn Mausoleum and Memory Gardens, 1921 Shutterlee Mill Road, Staunton, Virginia (buried):
WESLEY ROMER ROWE (1897-1984) Husband to **ZORA LEE RHEA ROWE** (John, F.10. James, E.9. Thomas Turk, D.8. John, C.5. William, B.3. Archibald, A.1. Matthew).
ZORA LEE RHEA ROWE ((John, F.10. James, E.9. Thomas Turk, D.8. John, C.5. William, B.3. Archibald, A.1. Matthew) (1891-1982) Daughter to **JOHN A.W. (WILSON) RHEA**.

Pleasant View Lutheran Church Cemetery, 2733 Spring Hill Road (Rt. 613), Verona, Augusta County, Virginia (buried):
RUTH THANET HINTON CUPP (Octave, James, F.10. James, E.9. Thomas Turk, D.8. John, C.5. William, B.3. Archibald, A.1. Matthew), (1930-1980). Daughter to **OCTAVE THANNET RHEA HINTON**.

Revercomb Family Cemetery (formerly Cloverdale Chapel Cemetery), Deerfield Valley Road, Millboro Springs, Bath County, Virginia (buried):
MARGARET "MAGGIE" ANGELINE CARTER THOMAS (Evaline, E.9. Thomas Turk, D.8. John, C.5. William, B.3.

Archibald, A.1. Matthew) (1848-1919) Daughter to **EVALINE RHEA CARTER.**

Rehobeth Community Church Cemetery, 3785 Pig Run Road, Millboro, Bath County, Virginia (buried):
ALLIE MAE RHEA (James, F.10. James, E.9. Thomas Turk, D.8. John, C.5. William, B.3. Archibald, A.1. Matthew) (1895-1981) Daughter to **JAMES WILLIAM RHEA.**
BABY RHEA (G.11. Thomas, F.10. James, E.9. Thomas Turk, D.8. John, C.5. William, B.3. Archibald, A.1. Matthew) (1919-1919)
BOYD EDMOND RHEA (James, F.10. James, E.9. Thomas Turk, D.8. John, C.5. William, B.3. Archibald, A.1. Matthew) (1900-1948) Son to **JAMES WILLIAM RHEA.**
CHRISTINE LEE HINTON ST. CLAIRE (Octave, James, F.10. James, E.9. Thomas Turk, D.8. John, C.5. William, B.3. Archibald, A.1. Matthew) (1933-1960) Daughter to **OCTAVE THANNET RHEA HINTON.**
COURTNEY RUSSELL RHEA (G.11. Thomas, F.10. James, E.9. Thomas Turk, D.8. John, C.5. William, B.3. Archibald, A.1. Matthew) (1911-1990)
DAVID FRANKLIN RHEA (James, F.10. James, E.9. Thomas Turk, D.8. John, C.5. William, B.3. Archibald, A.1. Matthew) (1906-1973) Son to **JAMES WILLIAM RHEA.**
ECHOLS RHEA (STONEY ECKLE RHEA) (G.11. Thomas, F.10. James, E.9. Thomas Turk, D.8. John, C.5. William, B.3. Archibald, A.1. Matthew) (1909-1932)
ELIZABETH VEST (VESS) RHEA (1860-1905) Wife to **THOMAS HENRY "PAP" RHEA (G.11.)** (F.10. James, E.9. Thomas Turk, D.8. John, C.5. William, B.3. Archibald, A.1. Matthew)
EMMA LEE SHANKS RHEA (1870-1953) Wife to **JAMES WILLIAM RHEA** (F.10. James, E.9. Thomas Turk, D.8. John, C.5. William, B.3. Archibald, A.1. Matthew).

HARRY TUCKER RHEA (G.11. Thomas, F.10. James, E.9. Thomas Turk, D.8. John, C.5. William, B.3. Archibald, A.1. Matthew) (1888/1889-1946)

HENRY MCKINLEY RHEA (G.11. Thomas, F.10. James, E.9. Thomas Turk, D.8. John, C.5. William, B.3. Archibald, A.1. Matthew) (1900/1902 -1929)

JAMES FLOYD RHEA (James, F.10. James, E.9. Thomas Turk, D.8. John, C.5. William, B.3. Archibald, A.1. Matthew) (1902/1903-1918) Son to **JAMES WILLIAM RHEA.**

JAMES FRANKLIN "JIMBO" RHEA (David, James, F.10. James, E.9. Thomas Turk, D.8. John, C.5. William, B.3. Archibald, A.1. Matthew) (1959-1974) Son to **DAVID FRANKLIN RHEA.**

JAMES TALLEY RHEA (G.11. Thomas, F.10. James, E.9. Thomas Turk, D.8. John, C.5. William, B.3. Archibald, A.1. Matthew) (1892-1970)

JAMES WILLIAM RHEA (F.10. James, E.9. Thomas Turk, D.8. John, C.5. William, B.3. Archibald, A.1. Matthew) (1866-1957)

JOHN WILSON RHEA (G.11. Thomas, F.10. James, E.9. Thomas Turk, D.8. John, C.5. William, B.3. Archibald, A.1. Matthew) (1878-1909)

LEOLA ARGENBRIGHT RHEA ROACH (James, F.10. James, E.9. Thomas Turk, D.8. John, C.5. William, B.3. Archibald, A.1. Matthew) (death records indicate 1894 and grave indicates 1896 - 1947) Daughter to **JAMES WILLIAM RHEA.**

MABEL ESTHER PERKINSON CONNER (Mollie, G.11. Thomas, F.10. James, E.9. Thomas Turk, D.8. John, C.5. William, B.3. Archibald, A.1. Matthew) (1904-1978) Daughter to **MOLLIE MAE RHEA PERKINSON LYON.**

MALINDA ANN SMITH RHEA (abt. 1836-1911) Wife to **JAMES THOMAS RHEA.** (E.9. Thomas Turk, D.8. John, C.5. William, B.3. Archibald, A.1. Matthew)

MAMIE GEAR RHEA (1891/1892-1919). Second wife to **THOMAS HENRY "PAP" RHEA** (F.10. James, E.9. Thomas Turk, D.8. John, C.5. William, B.3. Archibald, A.1. Matthew)

MOLLIE MAE RHEA PERKINSON LYON (G.11. Thomas, F.10. James, E.9. Thomas Turk, D.8. John, C.5. William, B.3. Archibald, A.1. Matthew) (1886/1887-1965)

OCTAVE THANNET RHEA HINTON (James, F.10. James, E.9. Thomas Turk, D.8. John, C.5. William, B.3. Archibald, A.1. Matthew) (1897 -1982) Daughter to **JAMES WILLIAM RHEA.**

THOMAS HENRY "PAP" RHEA (G.11.) (F.10. James, E.9. Thomas Turk, D.8. John, C.5. William, B.3. Archibald, A.1. Matthew) (1853-1938)

(Many other members of the Rhea Family are buried in this cemetery.)

Rocky Spring Presbyterian Church Cemetery, 567 Marble Valley Road (Rt. 600), Deerfield, Augusta County, Virginia (buried):

EARNEST E. RHEA (John, F.10. James, E.9. Thomas Turk, D.8. John, C.5. William, B.3. Archibald, A.1. Matthew) (1887-1913) Son to **JOHN A.W. (WILSON) RHEA.**

ELLA HOUSTON RHEA ZIMBRO (John, F.10. James, E.9. Thomas Turk, D.8. John, C.5. William, B.3. Archibald, A.1. Matthew) (1889-1979) Daughter to **JOHN A.W. (WILSON) RHEA.**

JAMES N. KINCAID (Margaret, E.9. Thomas Turk, D.8. John, C.5. William, B.3. Archibald, A.1. Matthew) (1830-1911) Son to **MARGARET TURK RHEA KINCAID.**

JOHN A.W. (WILSON) RHEA (F.10. James, E.9. Thomas Turk, D.8. John, C.5. William, B.3. Archibald, A.1. Matthew) (1863-1952)

LILBURN T. ZIMBRO (1889-1975) Husband to **ELLA HOUSTON RHEA ZIMBRO** (John, F.10. James, E.9. Thomas Turk, D.8. John, C.5. William, B.3. Archibald, A.1. Matthew).

MARY ELIZABETH (ELIZA BETH) (LIZZIE) BROOKS RHEA (1855-1927) Wife to **JOHN A.W. (WILSON) RHEA** (F.10. James, E.9. Thomas Turk, D.8. John, C.5. William, B.3. Archibald, A.1. Matthew).

Signal Hill Memorial Park, 12360 Hanover Courthouse Road, Hanover, Virginia (buried):

JAMES BEVERLY ROACH, JR. (Leola, James, F.10. James, E.9. Thomas Turk, D.8. John, C.5. William, B.3. Archibald, A.1. Matthew) (1918 -1986) Son to **LEOLA ARGENBRIGHT RHEA ROACH**.

Thornrose Cemetery, 1041 West Beverley Street, Staunton, Virginia (buried):

BERNARD M. RHEA (John Wilson, G.11. Thomas, F.10. James, E.9. Thomas Turk, D.8. John, C.5. William, B.3. Archibald, A.1. Matthew) (1908-1927) Son to **JOHN WILSON RHEA**.
BESSIE (BETTIE) J. LEWIS RHEA (1889-1957) Wife to **JOHN WILSON RHEA** (G.11. Thomas, F.10. James, E.9. Thomas Turk, D.8. John, C.5. William, B.3. Archibald, A.1. Matthew)

University of Virginia Confederate Cemetery, Charlottesville, Virginia (buried):

THOMAS JEFFERSON CORLEY (CAULEY) (1802-1862) Husband to **SUSANNA LUCY RHEA CORLEY**. (E.9. Thomas Turk, D.8. John, C.5. William, B.3. Archibald, A.1. Matthew)

Walnut Grove Cemetery, 3012 Lee Highway (Rts. 11 &19), Bristol City, Virginia (buried):

MARGARET RHEA PRESTON (Joseph, B.4. Matthew. A.1. Matthew) (1757-1822) Daughter to **REV. JOSEPH RHEA**.
ROBERT PRESTON (1750-1833) Husband to **MARGARET RHEA PRESTON**. (Joseph, B.4. Matthew. A.1. Matthew)
(Other members of the Rhea Family are buried in this cemetery.)

Windy Cove Presbyterian Church Cemetery, Millboro Springs, Bath County, Virginia (buried):

JOSEPH LOAN (Rebecca, E.9. Thomas Turk, D.8. John, C.5. William, B.3. Archibald, A.1. Matthew) (b. abt. 1860/1861-1881) Son to **REBECCA RHEA LOAN**.

WILLIAM L. LOAN (Rebecca, E.9. Thomas Turk, D.8. John, C.5. William, B.3. Archibald, A.1. Matthew) (b. abt. 1850/1852) Son to **REBECCA RHEA LOAN**.

Windy Cove Cemetery, Millboro Springs, Bath County, Virginia (buried):

FANNIE LILLIAN BABER RHEA (1889-1965) Wife to **SHAW ALEXANDER RHEA** (F.10. James, E.9. Thomas Turk, D.8. John, C.5. William, B.3. Archibald, A.1. Matthew)

OKLEY RHEA SHINAULT (John, F.10. James, E.9. Thomas Turk, D.8. John, C.5. William, B.3. Archibald, A.1. Matthew) (1892-1980). Daughter to **JOHN A.W. (WILSON) RHEA**.

PERCY COLEMAN RHEA (Shaw, F.10. James, E.9. Thomas Turk, D.8. John, C.5. William, B.3. Archibald, A.1. Matthew) (1912-1979). Son to **SHAW ALEXANDER RHEA**.

SHAW ALEXANDER RHEA (F.10. James, E.9. Thomas Turk, D.8. John, C.5. William, B.3. Archibald, A.1. Matthew) (1868-1944)

(VIRGINIA) PATTIE RHEA CURRY (Shaw, F.10. James, E.9. Thomas Turk, D.8. John, C.5. William, B.3. Archibald, A.1. Matthew) (1914-2015) Daughter to **SHAW ALEXANDER RHEA**.

WALTER R. SHINAULT (1890-1946) Husband to **OKLEY RHEA SHINAULT** (John, F.10. James, E.9. Thomas Turk, D.8. John, C.5. William, B.3. Archibald, A.1. Matthew).

Woodland Union Church, 347 McClung Drive (Rt. 629), Millboro, Bath County, Virginia (buried):

CHARLES FRANCISCO BRINKLEY (1850-1922) Husband to **NANCY (NANNIE) ELNORA RHEA WADE BRINKLEY** (F.10. James, E.9. Thomas Turk, D.8. John, C.5. William, B.3. Archibald, A.1. Matthew) (1850-1922).

CHARLES JOYCE LOAN (Elizabeth, E.9. Thomas Turk, D.8. John, C.5. William, B.3. Archibald, A.1. Matthew) (1865-1933) Son to **ELIZABETH ANN RHEA LOAN**.

CLARA LUCILLE PLECKER RHEA (1926-2017) Wife to **WILLIAM GRATTON "BILL" RHEA** (James Talley, G.11.

Thomas, F.10. James, E.9. Thomas Turk, D.8. John, C.5. William, B.3. Archibald, A.1. Matthew)

ELIZABETH H. KINCAID CLEEK (Margaret, E.9. Thomas Turk, D.8. John, C.5. William, B.3. Archibald, A.1. Matthew) (1842-1890) Daughter to **MARGARET TURK RHEA KINCAID**.

FLOYD KINCAID (Margaret, E.9. Thomas Turk, D.8. John, C.5. William, B.3. Archibald, A.1. Matthew) (1833-1914) Son to **MARGARET TURK RHEA KINCAID**.

JOSEPH B. KINCAID (Margaret, E.9. Thomas Turk, D.8. John, C.5. William, B.3. Archibald, A.1. Matthew) (1840-1887) Son to **MARGARET TURK RHEA KINCAID**.

MARGARET TURK RHEA KINCAID (E.9. Thomas Turk, D.8. John, C.5. William, B.3. Archibald, A.1. Matthew) (1813-1888)

MARTHA KINCAID DILL (Margaret, E.9. Thomas Turk, D.8. John, C.5. William, B.3. Archibald, A.1. Matthew) (1838-1903) Daughter to **MARGARET TURK RHEA KINCAID**.

NANCY (NANNIE) ELNORA RHEA WADE BRINKLEY (F.10. James, E.9. Thomas Turk, D.8. John, C.5. William, B.3. Archibald, A.1. Matthew) (abt. 1853-1938)

WILLIAM GRATTON "BILL" RHEA (James Talley, G.11. Thomas, F.10. James, E.9. Thomas Turk, D.8. John, C.5. William, B.3. Archibald, A.1. Matthew) (1924-1996) Son to **JAMES TALLEY RHEA**.

WILLIS KINCAID (1811-1887) Husband to **MARGARET TURK RHEA KINCAID** (E.9. Thomas Turk, D.8. John, C.5. William, B.3. Archibald, A.1. Matthew).

WEST VIRGINIA

Chenoweth Cemetery (also known as Daniels Graveyard), Elkins, Randolph County, West Virginia (buried):

MELVINA CORLEY GODDIN (Susanna, E.9. Thomas Turk, D.8. John, C.5. William, B.3. Archibald, A.1. Matthew) (1848-1923) Daughter to **SUSANNA LUCY RHEA CORLEY**.

Coffman Chapel Cemetery, Elkins, Randolph County, West Virginia (buried):

ELIZABETH "JANE" M. CORLEY COFFMAN (Susanna, E.9. Thomas Turk, D.8. John, C.5. William, B.3. Archibald, A.1. Matthew) (1837-1910) Daughter to **SUSANNA LUCY RHEA CORLEY.**

Hillyard-Corley Cemetery, Junior, Barbour County, West Virginia (buried):

JOHN MOLEN CORLEY (Susanna, E.9. Thomas Turk, D.8. John, C.5. William, B.3. Archibald, A.1. Matthew) (1832-1912) Son to **SUSANNA LUCY RHEA CORLEY.**

Mingo Cemetery, Mingo, Randolph County, West Virginia (buried):

ANGELINE (ANGELINA) RHEA AYERS SMITH ((John, E.9. Thomas Turk, D.8. John, C.5. William, B.3. Archibald, A.1. Matthew) (1839-1912). Daughter to **JOHN SHAW RHEA.**

CHARLES ANDREW RHEA (John, E.9. Thomas Turk, D.8. John, C.5. William, B.3. Archibald, A.1. Matthew) (abt. 1844/1847-1907). Son to **JOHN SHAW RHEA.**

JOHN N. MILLER (1835-1915) Husband to **LUCY E. RHEA MILLER.** (John, E.9. Thomas Turk, D.8. John, C.5. William, B.3. Archibald, A.1. Matthew)

LUCY E. RHEA MILLER (John, E.9. Thomas Turk, D.8. John, C.5. William, B.3. Archibald, A.1. Matthew) (1840-1926). Daughter to **JOHN SHAW RHEA.**

(Other members of the Rhea Family are buried in this cemetery.)

(NOTE: There may be other Rhea family members laid to rest at cemeteries listed above that have not been included.)

DIRECT ANCESTORS OF PALMER B. RHEA

A.1. MATTHEW CAMPBELL RHEA (abt. 1665 – unknown) **(THOUGHT TO BE DIRECT ANCESTOR TO PALMER RHEA, SR. ACCORDING TO RESEARCHERS UNLESS OTHER INFORMATION BECOMES AVAILABLE.)**

B.3. ARCHIBALD RHEA (A.1. Matthew): (b. abt. 1688) **(THOUGHT TO BE DIRECT ANCESTOR TO PALMER RHEA, SR. ACCORDING TO RESEARCHERS UNLESS OTHER INFORMATION BECOMES AVAILABLE.)**

C.5. WILLIAM RHEA, SR. (B.3. Archibald, A.1. Matthew) (1718-1802) **(DIRECT ANCESTOR TO PALMER RHEA, SR.)**

D.8. JOHN S. RHEA (C.5. William, B.3. Archibald, A.1. Matthew) (b. abt. 1752) **(DIRECT ANCESTOR TO PALMER RHEA, SR.)**

E.9. THOMAS TURK RHEA (D.8. John, C.5. William, B.3. Archibald, A.1. Matthew) (Abt. 1785 – 1842) **(DIRECT ANCESTOR TO PALMER RHEA, SR.)**

F.10. JAMES THOMAS RHEA (E.9. Thomas Turk, D.8. John, C.5. William, B.3. Archibald, A.1. Matthew) (abt. 1823-1890) **(GRANDFATHER TO PALMER RHEA, SR)** (abt. 1823-1890)

G.11. THOMAS "PAP" HENRY RHEA (F.10. James, E.9. Thomas Turk, D.8. John, C.5. William, B.3. Archibald, A.1. Matthew) (1853-1938) **(FATHER TO PALMER RHEA, SR.)**

H.12. PALMER B. RHEA (G.11. Thomas, F.10. James, E.9. Thomas Turk, D.8. John, C.5. William, B.3. Archibald, A.1. Matthew)

Lillian "Sissy Crone" Frazer and Palmer Rhea, 2019

Printed in the United States
By Bookmasters